M195

MAURY ISLAND UFO:
The Crisman Conspiracy

Cover painting by Kevin Belford

Other books by Kenn Thomas:

Flying Saucers Over Los Angeles
Mind Control, Oswald and JFK
NASA, Nazis and JFK
The Octopus: Secret Government and the Death of Danny Casolaro
Popular Alienation: A Steamshovel Press Reader

The magazine *Steamshovel Press* is available from:

P.O. Box 23715
St. Louis, MO 63121

Single issue: $6
Four issue subscription: $23

MAURY ISLAND UFO:
The Crisman Conspiracy

KENN THOMAS

Library of Congress Cataloging in Publication Data

Thomas, Kenn, 1958--
    Maury Island UFO : the Crisman conspiracy / Kenn Thomas.
          p.   cm.
    ISBN: 1-881532-19-4
    1.   Unidentified flying objects
    2.   Sightings and encounters
    3.   Washington (State)--Maury Island   I. Title.
TL789.6.W2T49   1999
001.942--dc21   99-29419

IllumiNet Press
P.O. Box 2808
Lilburn, GA 30048

Printed in the United States of America

Dedicated to:

Russell Kenneth Thomas
January 27, 1927 - November 20, 1977
Decorated Veteran of World War II and Korea

"I never thought much of a lie, because nobody believes a lie if he has a chance to find out the truth."
—Harry S. Truman
Tacoma, Washington
June 10, 1948

"The experts disagree. And in the final analysis this country...on its space effort and all the rest where we will find the most intense disagreement among those who know the most—in the final analysis the people themselves have to make a judgement..."
—John F. Kennedy
Cheney Stadium, Tacoma, Washington

ACKNOWLEDGEMENTS

Many researchers have distinguished themselves in uncovering information about this earliest event in the modern UFO lore. Foremost among them in the experience of the author is Ron Halbritter, who has collected and collated information on Maury Island for many years. Halbritter has demonstrated a unique and on-going tenacity in pursuing the story, as well as a remarkable willingness to share his research. He is accompanied in this distinction by fellow researchers Vaughn Greene and Jim Pobst. Pobst's unpublished manuscript, *What Happened in Room 502?*, weaves a great deal of period detail around the story of Kenneth Arnold's investigation, some of it speculative but all of it offering a true flavor of the time.

Researchers that the author has never met, such as Thomas R. Adams, Lucius Farish, Larry Haapanen, Kalani and Katiuska Hanohano, the Rev. Bob LeRoy, Floyd Murray, Mike Sylwester and others too numerous to list, also deserve acknowledgement and gratitude. Researchers the author has met, exchanged information with and thanks profusely include Martin Cannon, David Hatcher Childress, Jim DiEugenio, Steven Gaal, Alex Horvat, John Judge, Jim Keith, Jim Martin, Adam Parfrey, Michael Riconosciuto, Duncan Roads, Bill Siebert, William Turner, Peter Whitmey, Gordon Winslow and also too many others.

Cryptozoologist Loren Coleman also deserves great credit for providing the author of this volume much information and many documents, as does the book's publisher, Ron Bonds.

Friends of forbearance during the production of this manuscript include Greg Bishop of the *Excluded Middle*; Robert Sterling of the Konformist (HYPERLINK http://www.konformist.com); and Acharya S.

Of course, Harold Dahl, Charles Dahl, their unnamed shipmates, Fred Crisman, Kenneth Arnold, Captain William Davidson, Lieutenant Frank Brown, Ray Palmer, Richard Shaver and the others involved with Maury Island, including the flying saucer occupants, of course, all deserve various degrees of credit and infamy.

CONTENTS

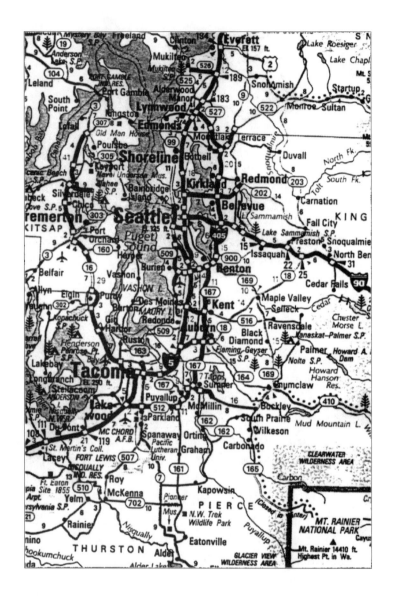

Map of the vicinity around Maury Island, showing Tacoma, Mt. Rainier, McChord Air Force Base, Puyallup and Puget Sound.

INTRODUCTION

This story has never been easy to follow. In fact, it has been interpreted, reinterpreted and misinterpreted for 50 years.

The totally uninitiated reader should know that the Maury Island incident involved the sighting of a group of flying saucers in 1947 that preceded the Roswell affair by over a month. It even happened before pilot Kenneth Arnold's sightings on Mount Rainier, which helped trigger the post-war obsession with UFOs. Arnold, in fact, became the first person to investigate the Maury Island affair.

The Maury Island story contains elements that have become recurrent themes in the UFO literature, lore and reality. It includes the recovery of UFO crash debris; a secret investigation by the Air Force that turned deadly; a visit by one of the notorious Men In Black; missing time; figures who would later become associated with the Kennedy assassination; and links to present day conspiracy scandals. The Maury Island event itself has been dismissed as nothing but a hoax by many researchers, but those who have looked at it closely know that it at least contains some elements of truth that remain important to understanding the UFO experience and conspiracy culture. Others would challenge the "nothing but" notion of whatever part of the Maury Island story was hoaxed.

Readers unfamiliar with the basic story of the Maury Island UFO will find it here, based on the earliest first-hand and press accounts. Veteran ufologists will find that some flesh has been added to the all-too-familiar bare bones of the basic story. Much of what this book offers those readers can be found in the extensive footnotes. Maury Island UFO draws from a detailed look at the accumulated available record. It relies as much as possible on primary and early sources and direct interviews with Maury Island scholars and people connected to the incident itself.

1

WHAT HAPPENED AT MAURY ISLAND?

Harold Dahl, a tall, broad-shouldered and burly seaman,[1] squinted at the sky on June 21, 1947, at approximately 2:00 p.m., looking up from the wheel of his small tug boat. He had taken his son Charles, the pet dog and two crewmen, whose names remain all but lost to history, on the patrol boat to recover resaleable logs along the shore of a bay surrounding Maury Island, in Puget Sound, near the lumber town of Tacoma, Washington. As he focused, he realized that six large flying saucers hovered and spun above him at about 2,000 feet.

Dahl didn't exactly know the objects as "flying saucers," since popular use of that term resided yet in the not-too-distant future. Science-fiction pulp magazines had already coined the term, but nothing suggests that Dahl read such things or had an interest in UFOs.[2]

He saw aircraft shaped like doughnuts. Five of them slowly circled a wavering sixth. They had no visible signs of propulsion and measured about 100 feet in diameter, with doughnut "holes" in the middle about 25 feet in diameter. Dahl later described their color as "shell-like gold" and silver, shining in a variety of ways, "like a Buick dashboard."

Portholes five to six feet in diameter surrounded their exterior, one dark circle of a window spun around the interior and on the bottom. They "appeared completely round, but seemed a little squashed on the top and bottom as if you placed a large board on an inner tube and squashed it slightly."[3]

The central craft continued to topple and lost altitude. It looked to Dahl and to his shipmates—who also stood mesmerized by the silent saucers—as if it would crash into the bay. The team had been headed to shore; now they picked up the pace, beached the boat and pulled out a camera. Dahl snapped three or four photographs of the aerial display. As the central saucer dropped, its five companions remained about 200 feet above it. The center saucer stopped its wobbling descent at about 500 feet above the bay.

The eerie scene froze for a little over five minutes. Then one of the circling craft broke ranks and moved closer to its troubled and now still companion. It touched the lower vehicle and became still itself. According to Dahl, it was "as if it were giving some kind of assistance for about three or four minutes."

Then, a dull thud. An enormous amount of thin, white, newspaper-like metal material began to fall from the center saucer's middle, mostly floating down to the water in the bay. A second black substance started coming down on Dahl and his companions. It was darker and resembled the lava rock. These fragments seemed hot and caused steam to rise from the bay as they hit. Dahl later estimated that twenty tons of it must have fallen. His crew ran for cover, but one piece struck and burned his son Charles' arm. Another struck and killed the dog. The center saucer then lifted and led the other six craft out over the open sea.

Dahl does not report on how long he and the others stared at the departing saucers and the sky into which they vanished. They regained composure soon enough that scraps of the two mysterious substances still burned when they loaded them onto the boat. The boat had sustained some damage to the enclosed area on the deck housing the steering wheel. At some point, Dahl and company tossed the dog's carcass into the waters and became preoccupied with talking about their experience. As the boat made its way back to Tacoma, Dahl attempted to make radio contact but was foiled by great static. In Tacoma, Dahl took his son for medical treatment.

Then he went to explain the boat damage and missing dog to Fred Lee Crisman.

Notes:
1. Physical description of Dahl taken from Jim Pobst's unpublished manuscript, *What Happened in Room 502?* and Kenneth Arnold's and Ray Palmer's *The Coming of the Saucers*, Amherst, WI: Palmer, 1952.
2. Jim Pobst notes that the Tacoma Public Library at the time contained over 150,000 volumes but none about flying saucers. Pobst, Jim, *What Happened in Room 502?*, unpublished manuscript.
3. Harold Dahl's firsthand account of his experiences at Maury Island, as related by pilot Kenneth Arnold, appears originally in *The Shaver Mystery Magazine*, Volume II, No. 1, 1948. Arnold reiterated the story in *The Coming of the Saucers*.

2
ENTER CRISMAN

Time and semantics have made obscure the exact nature of the relationship between Harold Dahl and Fred Crisman. Kenneth Arnold and other observers reported that the two worked officially as harbor patrolmen, but it is more likely that they simply patrolled the harbor to salvage logs. Dahl nevertheless referred to Crisman as his "superior" and felt obligated to report his UFO experience to him, despite the fact that the boat was registered in Dahl's name.[1]

Crisman did not believe Dahl for the obvious reasons. He thought the men might have been drunk. When Dahl produced his camera with the film containing images of the saucers and the debris he had collected, Crisman decided to check out the shore area where it all supposedly happened. This he did on June 23, 1947, an overcast day.

Crisman indeed did see what he estimated to be about 20 tons of the bizarre white and black material Dahl claimed had spewed from the UFOs. As he looked it over, he got to see much more: one of the doughnut-shaped craft appeared and circled in the sky above the bay.

It rose up and entered the center of a thundercloud. Crisman saw the portholes, the inner-tube like structure and the spinning observation window. It appeared gold and silver to him, with intense reflected light as Dahl described, but it had no "squashed" effect.

UNITED STATES TREASURY DEPARTMENT
BUREAU OF CUSTOMS

MERCHANT VESSELS

OF THE

UNITED STATES

1947

(Including Yachts and Certain Government Vessels)

⚓

January 1, 1947

UNITED STATES
GOVERNMENT PRINTING OFFICE
WASHINGTON : 1948

For sale by the Superintendent of Documents, U. S. Government Printing Office
Washington 25, D. C. - Price $6.00 (Buckram)

Seattle, Wash.
   232047 Lively.
Dahl, Carl O., Bayfield, Wis.
   228678 Egersund.
Dahl, Haldor, 1801 N. Union Ave.,
  Tacoma, Wash.
   249586 North Queen.
Dahl, Martin B., Box 539, Seattle,
  Wash.
   116387 Robert Eugene.
Dahl, Roy O., Petersburg, Alaska.
   223542 Curlew.

Ship registration for the North Queen, the boat from which the Maury Island saucers were sighted. The ship was registered to Harold Dahl of Tacoma.

Crisman's experience was even more brief than it had been for Dahl and his companions. When the saucer took off, so did Crisman, after collecting some samples of the weird debris for himself.

That remains the basic story of the Maury Island observation. If it can be believed at all, it can only be seen through the embellishments, reinterpretations, misinterpretations, misreportings, exaggerations and debunkings that have happened many times over the past fifty years. Its elasticity is due in no small part to its attachment to the life and times of Fred Crisman, who carried the tale with him through a long and often disreputable career. Indeed, even champions of the reality of the Maury Island UFO event have reasons to believe that Crisman at least exaggerated his involvement.

For Crisman and Dahl both, however, the flying saucer encounter was only the beginning.

Notes:
1   To underscore: Harold Dahl owned the boat. Researcher Ron Halbritter traced the registration of the vessel, called the North Queen, in Merchant Vessels of the United States, 1947. Dahl was listed as sole owner; no boats were registered to Fred Crisman. The 1942 fishing boat had been commissioned as a mine sweeper during World War II under the name USS Affray. It measured 83 feet in length, 24 feet width, 10.4 feet draft, 300 horsepower oil screw. It was re-outfitted as a fishing vessel again after the war to accommodate a ten person crew. Halbritter notes, then, that the boat was relatively young, large and newly rehabilitated, contrary to description of it as "decrepit" by author Paris Flammonde (*UFO Exist!*, New York: Ballantine Books, 1976) and "beat-up" by Edward Ruppelt (*The Report on Unidentified Flying Objects*, New York: Ace Books, 1956.) By 1948, the North Queen had changed registration to an A. K. Anderson of Tacoma.

3

MAN IN BLACK

Dahl thought the man might have been someone looking to buy salvage lumber, since such buyers often approached him in the wee hours of the morning. The man wore a black suit, however, and drove a black 1947 Buick sedan when he arrived the day after Dahl's encounter with the flying doughnuts. After he accepted the strange man's invitation to breakfast, Dahl drove himself to a small cafe in downtown Tacoma followed by the black-suited man in the black Buick.

The conversation was not about lumber, however. Rather, the Man in Black made it explicit that he knew a great deal about Dahl. He presented some not so veiled threats to Dahl's continued happiness and the future well-being of his family and success of his business. As Dahl took umbrage at what he heard, the mysterious figure described in detail the flying saucer events of the day before. He knew the shape of the craft, their maneuvers, the discharged debris, the reactions of the crew members—the whole story, in detail. "I did think it was rather fantastic how this gentleman happened to know what I had seen," Dahl later told Kenneth Arnold, "and I was quite sure that he hadn't talked to any of my crew, and I know he hadn't talked to me before. In fact, I had never seen him before."[1]

Having made his point, the dark man left the breakfast meeting. Thus an early and consistent corollary experience to many UFO encounters entered into the lore: the Men in Black. The history of these strange operatives has been documented extensively in UFO litera-

ture and lampooned regularly in movies and other popular treatments of the phenomenon.[2] Darkly dressed, tight-
lipped operatives of some sort show up on the scene
after a UFO encounter and either try to threaten witnesses into silence or get involved in some absurd be-
havior.

Not privy to what has now become 50 years of such
surreal chicanery, Dahl apparently had the wherewithal
to disregard the appearance of the Man In Black in his
affairs. He returned to his boat that day and resumed
business as usual, talking openly about the airborne doughnuts and the spewing newspaper metal to his fellow sailors and harbor workers. How could he keep quiet about
such unusual events? He just disregarded his visit from
the MIB.

Later, when he could not find logs he had previously
salvaged from the bay, he attributed it to the tide having
swept them away.

Then his son disappeared. The fifteen-year-old
Charles Dahl, whose arm had been burned by the falling
saucer debris, failed to show up at breakfast one morning. His father called the local sheriff's office, which
tracked and located the boy. In the absurd tradition of
Men In Black aftermath, the historic record is unclear as
to whether they found Charles Dahl in a town called
Lust, Montana[3] or another called Lusk, Wyoming.[4] Either way, the young Dahl was bussing tables at a restaurant, with no idea how got there. If he had run away
from home, he couldn't remember it. Amnesia made it
all missing time to him.[5]

Suddenly, things were starting to turn bad for Harold
Dahl. His wife's poor health had been made worse by
the worry over her son. The executive board of his
lumber company refused to approve sure-fire money
making ideas he had brought forth, and the company

began to lose money. Boats began to stall and fall into disrepair. It took Dahl a week to start taking the Man In Black at his word. He clammed up about the flying saucers.

Notes:
1   "The Mystery of the Flying Discs...A Proof of the Shaver Mystery...". *The Shaver Mystery Magazine*, Volume II, No. 1, 1948., p. 36.
2   Keith, Jim, *Casebook On The Men In Black*, IllumiNet Press, Lilburn, GA, 1997.
3.   This is where Harold Dahl has him in Shaver Mystery, p. 36.
4.   The FBI noted this location in a report on August 27, 1947.
5.   Researchers Kalani and Katiuska Hanohano interviewed Charles Dahl for *UFO Magazine* in 1994 (Vol. 4, #1). He claimed the Maury Island incident was a hoax perpetuated by "smooth-talking con artist" Fred Crisman, but discussed few details of his own disappearance and rediscovery. The medical records of his injury on Maury Island have never emerged despite efforts of researchers.

4

THE COMING OF
KENNETH ARNOLD

It has been repeated many times: aerial phenomena have haunted mankind since the beginning of civilization, but the modern UFO lore begins with Kenneth Arnold's June 24, 1947 sightings in the Cascade Mountains near Mount Rainier, Washington, overlooking Maury Island. (Maury Island, incidentally, was named for a famous meteorologist of the last century, Matthew Fountaine Maury.) A $5,000 reward had been posted for finding the location of the wreckage of a C-47 transport that had crashed the previous December, presumably killing its 32 Marine occupants.[1] Arnold was on the bounty hunt when he got sidetracked by flying saucers. While aloft in his light plane, at an altitude of 9,200 feet, he spied nine UFOs, eight semi-circle shaped and one crescent shaped. They zipped along in the sky at a rate he calculated at 1,200 miles per hour. They skipped along like a rock skimming the surface of a lake, and disappeared heading south over the Mount Adams peak.

East Oregonian reporter Bill Bequette called them "saucer-like" and is often credited for coining the term "flying saucer." One enterprising Ph.D. student of the UFO lore, Herbert Strentz, wrote a thesis, however, pointing out that the term instead probably emerged from several different headline editors for newspapers around the country.[2] The imagery and the term actually had preceded even these editors.[3] The origin of the phrase "flying saucer" has been obscured by these contradictory claims about exactly when it was coined and who

Kenneth Arnold was looking for this wreckage of a Marine Corps C-47 transport, which crashed and killed 32 Marines, when he saw nine crescent shaped objects, beginning the national UFO craze. (*Tacoma Times,* 7/24/47.) This happened on June 24, 1947. The Maury Island sighting happened on June 21.

coined it. A similar problem besets the understanding of Arnold as the "first" modern observer of the phenomenon, since he saw chevrons, not saucers.

Although it began a national obsession, Arnold's sighting was part of a particular, local UFO wave. The *East Oregonian* ran seventeen stories of various sightings in the month that followed its original report on Kenneth

Arnold.[4] Mrs. Morton Elder told of seeing seven "perfectly round, umbrella-like" objects flying in a northeasterly direction over Pendleton, Oregon, on June 30, 1947. The UFOs had no tails, flew in wedge formation and made a buzzing sound similar to that of a toy musical top. Ranch foreman Bill Schuening reported seeing similar objects from the Lester King ranch about 15 miles north of Pendleton.[5] Six to eight flying discs were spotted a few days later by five more Pendleton residents: Mrs. Walter Clark; Mrs. Lena Koeppen; Mrs. Adeline Parks; Mrs. Yarborough and C. E. Douglas.[6] The next day, the entire town of nearby Beatty in Klamath Falls county witnessed two UFOs zipping back and forth across the western sky.[7]

By the fourth of July, the *East Oregonian* was reporting upon hundreds of sightings from around the western states,[8] as were most newspapers in the country, even as the local reports kept coming in. Mrs. C. E. Randall described six discs that she saw in Pendleton at 1:45 p.m. on Saturday, July 5. A friend of hers, Mrs. Jennie Nichols, caught a glimpse of the last one, but a neighbor, James Armstong, saw the same set, only three hours later.[9] The July 4 sightings included two groups of picnickers in Twin Falls, Idaho, both having seen an estimated total of 35 discs. Spokane resident George Astor was part of a group of over 200 people who witnessed one disc circle for a half-hour. A Seattle Coast Guard yeoman named Frank Ryman even photographed one UFO, but it came out only as a pin of light on the photograph negative. No doubt in some areas, it would have been difficult to find someone who had not seen a UFO, or at least reported to have seen one. When Strategic Air Command announced that Spokane would become the main northern Pacific coast base, a B-29

Beauty queen Nan Dawson observes flying pie pans on the front page of the *Tacoma Times,* July 8, 1947, two weeks after the Maury Island incident. The flying saucer social fad developed along with the first post-war UFO wave. Three news stories accompanied this photo, reporting on sightings by police officers in Tacoma, crashed saucers seen by ten people in Idaho, and a wire report from San Francisco on sightings in 38 states.

Superfortress, the *East Oregonian* could not escape the obvious implication and ran the story next to one on the recent UFO sightings.[10]

Once the lingo of the "flying saucer" and Arnold's description helped to give voice to the saucer encounters already happening,[11] it opened the UFO floodgates. Mitigating against the argument that Arnold's original report triggered the wave, however, was the initial *East Oregonian* news story about Arnold's Mount Rainier experience, which gave clear indication that the wave started before Kenneth Arnold. After his sighting, when

Arnold landed in Yakima, Washington and began to tell his story, he found a man from Ukiah who claimed to have seen the same thing the previous day.[12]

Another Yakima woman, Mrs. Ethel Wheelhouse, had a similar sighting the preceding Tuesday. E. H. Sprinkle of Eugene, Oregon, took a photograph of a formation of flying objects on June 18. Reports of sightings from the previous week also came from Mrs. Dennis Howell of Salem, Oregon, Mr. and Mrs. Howard K. Wheeler of Bremerton.[13]

Also mitigating against the idea that Arnold started it all: the Maury Island incident. One pre-Arnold sighting, that of Archie Edes of Wenatchee, seemed eerily similar to what Harold Dahl had witnessed. Near the Moses Lake Highway on the previous Friday, Edes and his family watched a flying object "descending in a long slant. It looked like a long, oval blue-white flame. As we watched, it neared the ground and when it was about 200 feet high, it exploded. There was no blinding flash, but there were great showers of sparks and piles of flame seemed to hurtle to the ground."[14]

Maury Island itself happened three days previous to Arnold's encounter, if one could believe Dahl and Crisman.[15] Could they be believed? As it turned out, Arnold himself would lead the effort to find out.

Details of Kenneth Arnold's biography appear frequently enough in the UFO literature that they hardly need repeating. The Wisconsin born pilot grew up in Scobey, Montana and became something of a sports star at his high school in Minot, North Dakota, even trying out as a "fancy diver" for the 1932 U.S. Olympic trials. He attended the University of Minnesota but soon went to work with a fire-fighting equipment manufacturer called Red Comet. He became a pilot after he started his own similar company, Great Western Fire Control Supply, and needed to fly throughout the west to install the equipment.

Arnold earned his pilot's license in 1943. In January 1947 he bought the three-passenger, single-engine Callair plane he was flying when he saw the nine UFOs over Mt. Rainier.

After the sighting, Arnold became one of the first UFO celebrities. The *East Oregonian* reported upon his evolution from a flying fire equipment salesman to a

Kenneth Arnold, from *The Coming of the Saucers*, 1952.

Kenneth Arnold. "He'll get proof next time, flyer declares." *East Oregonian,* June 27, 1947.

devoted watcher of the skies and popularizer for the veracity of the flying saucer phenomenon. The original news report quotes him as saying, "Impossible! Maybe, But Seein' Is Believin'!"[16] The next day, Arnold is defending his experience against debunkings by the Army and civilian air authorities, and by the following day he has bought a $150 movie camera with a telescopic lens.[17] By July 7, he took the camera and a newsman from Boise over the same air passage between Mt. Ranier and Mt. Adams.[18]

Arnold is also not quick to call the objects extraterrestrial but rather experimental military aircraft. The last contemporary story on Arnold in the *East Oregonian* has him speculating to a crowd in Vert Auditorium that "Any object traveling at that speed would run into a wall of air molecules which would make flight impossible. That wall of atmosphere would have to be destroyed to clear a path for the plane." A cyclotronic device mounted on the nose of a disc, Arnold explained, could destroy the atoms in its path and perhaps use their energy as fuel.

Arnold also mentioned that Army intelligence knew of the disks months before his sighting. Now transformed into a bonafide UFO lecturer, Arnold read extensively to his audience from a writer who chronicled UFO sightings from the 1800s, and expressed confidence that whether the craft were earth-made or extraterrestrial would be known within a year.[19]

That didn't happen, and Arnold went on to several more sightings—one of them while en route to investigating Maury Island—and much notoriety as a lecturer and writer on the topic.

In alliance with publisher Ray Palmer, Arnold produced a classic in UFO literature called *The Coming of the Saucers*, which recorded his involvement with the investigation of Maury Island.[20]

He seemed genuinely to eschew the publicity that grew around his Mount Rainier experience,[21] but it nevertheless became the central fact of his life and ultimately a professional pursuit. While Arnold has been criticized by UFO writers at times for his naiveté, his honesty has often been noted and admired. As one put it, "Arnold, a deputy in his county aerial posse, a well-known salesman and inventor with a small business, was obviously an open and unsophisticated person. He didn't have a career or an inflated social status that could be threatened in order to divert and shut him up."[22]

In contrast, Raymond A. Palmer has been regarded as an exploiter of imaginative UFO fantasy over experiential fact. Like Arnold, his biographical details are well-known, mostly to devotees of science fiction. Palmer appears as a Stephen Hawking-in-reverse-like presence at the center of modern science fiction history. Since his birth in 1911, he suffered from congenital defects and stunted growth, but escaped from the pain through reading and writing for the pulp science fiction novels that flourished in the late 1920s and early 1930s. During the

Depression, Palmer's pro-active life in science fiction fandom earned him a permanent spot in the history of that literary subculture.[23]

In 1938 Ziff-Davis Publishing hired Palmer as an editor for *Amazing Stories*, a pulp magazine founded nine years earlier by publisher Hugo Gernsback that fell

Ray Palmer, from *The Coming of the Saucers.*

victim to a hostile takeover. Palmer transformed the pulp by doubling its size and devoting the extra pages to fiction written by his science fiction fan friends. The strategy helped increase the magazine's circulation ten-fold. In addition to his fannish enthusiasm and the new, unpolished writing talent (stories not written by Palmer under a pseudonym came from the pens of writers with the same demographic profile as *Amazing Stories'* burgeoning readership of adolescent boys), Palmer recruited one writer practically from the trash bin at the Chicago office of Ziff-Davis. In the early 1940s, according to one account, Palmer rescued a manuscript that a co-editor had tossed written by a shipyard worker in Barto, Pennsylvania named Richard Sharpe Shaver.[24] Retitled "I Remember Lemuria," the story ran in the March 1945 issue of *Amazing Stories.*

The readership received it with such enthusiasm that it became the basis of a series by Shaver, one that chronicled the activities of a diminutive race of beings called the deros, a contraction of the words "detrimental" and "robots." The deros lived in underground caves and terrorized mankind with everything from earthquakes to beam weapons.[25]

Shaver, whose physical stature was as large as Palmer's was small, had actually submitted a rant of channeled information about the deros that he regarded as real. He picked up the information from voices in his equipment while welding at a war plant.[26] When Palmer visited Shaver in Pennsylvania, he found the welder/ writer sitting among many, many more pages of similarly channeled rants. He bought it all, rewrote it and parceled it out in *Amazing Stories* with an editorial insistence that it was all real. Readers took to the material enthusiastically and began to write in about their own "real" experiences with the deros. Fred Crisman counted himself among those readers.[27]

After reading about Kenneth Arnold's Mount Rainier encounter, Palmer wrote to him requesting details, and Arnold obliged by sending him a copy of the report he made to the Air Force. Palmer wrote back, this time offering the pilot $200 to investigate the claims of Crisman and Dahl. Clearly, Palmer knew Fred Crisman's name, since he had published two letters by him in *Amazing Stories,* the second including Crisman's name and full address. In response to that second letter, Palmer challenged Crisman to offer details and proof of his encounter with the deros.

Crisman's second letter came in response to an article in *Harper's Magazine* critical of science fiction fans that had quoted his first letter at length. Crisman complained about the armchair philosophizing of the article contrasted with his own real battles with the deros in underground caverns. Crisman had at least two such battles. The first began in Bassein (Puthein) in Myanmar, southeast of India, and culminated in a submachine gun battle in Kashmir, near Jammu and Tibe.

The second encounter happened in Alaska, where Crisman claimed a companion named Dick lost his life. Palmer wrote to *Harper's*

Crisman's angry response in Richard Shaver's *Amazing Stories,* May 1947. The Maury Island incident occurred the following month.

insisting on the reality of the deros, but he responded to Crisman with a demand for some verification of his adventures, which he apparently never received. Nothing indicates that Palmer disclosed any of this previous history with Crisman to Arnold. Perhaps his approach to Arnold was an attempt to finally call Crisman on the carpet for one of his tall tales.

Interestingly, Palmer's letter to Arnold drew the attention of military investigators

Harper's Magazine published an article about post-war science fiction that quoted Maury Island witness Fred Lee Crisman.

who came to talk with him when he returned to Boise, Idaho, three weeks after his Mt. Rainier sighting. By then, July 15, Arnold had accumulated a large file of letters from the curious and others who had experienced things similar to his encounter. One of the investigators wrote down the details of Palmer's address, which Palmer had given as Venture Press in Evanston, IL, ostensibly because of the sizable reward. Few clues have been left about the full contents of the letter, whether it mentioned Crisman by name, for instance, but it did contain reference to the debris Dahl and Crisman had recovered, which would later prove fatefully important to the investigators. The two investigators, Captain William Lee Davidson and First Lieutenant Frank Mercer Brown of the Fourth Air Force A-2 Intelligence, had been dis-

patched by General Carl "Ptooey" Spaatz, an Air Force
commander concerned about the July 4th wave of
sightings.

Under the cover story of a fishing vacation, Spaatz
began an investigation of the Northwestern UFO wave
at McChord Air Base outside of Tacoma.[28] He had previously directed Air Force military intelligence at Hamilton
Field in California to report relevant UFO data to the
Air Technical Intelligence Command at Wright Field in
Ohio, apparently under the command of General Nathan
Twining, and was clearly operating under Twining's
direction also in Tacoma, as were, by extension, the two
young pilots Davidson and Brown.[29] Spaatz provided
them with a B-25 (a pared down A-24 version) and
assigned them the task of interviewing key people who
had reported UFO sightings during the wave.

Although they flew to Boise to interview Arnold, at
the airport they first met and talked with David N.
Johnson, the aviation editor for the *Idaho Statesman*.
Johnson had tried to photograph a flying disk from his
AT-6 at 14,000 feet over Boise's Anderson Dam. Arnold
was surprised to find Johnson at the airport where he
went to meet Davidson and Brown. Johnson had previously contacted Arnold after reading about the Mt. Rainier
sightings, and they became friends. Davidson and Brown
seemed at least as interested in that relationship, and
Johnson's impressions of Arnold, as they were in
Johnson's own experience.

Arnold had already been contacted by one possible
military intelligence source, an acquaintance named Colonel Paul Weiland, who had served as a judge at the
Nuremburg trials. Weiland hired Arnold for a fishing
trip of several days that yielded few fish.[30] During this
trip, Arnold learned that Emil Smith, the captain who
had derided him once but had since had a UFO experience of his own,[31] was meeting press at the International

News Service office. Arnold dropped in for a photo opportunity and then went out for coffee with Smith and his co-pilot before returning to fishing with Weiland.

Perhaps Arnold learned of Smith's proximity from Weiland—he ostensibly picked up the news when he landed his plane at Boeing Field for refueling and had to rush back to Weiland, whom Arnold had left behind and forgotten about[32]—and perhaps they exchanged other information. In their interview with Johnson, Davidson and Brown may have been trying to gauge Arnold's reliability or find out what he had learned from Weiland.

Apparently, the investigators also had an interest in Arnold's speculation that the disks may be secret military craft that used atomic power.[33] Arnold released his speculation about this in a statement to the assistant chief of the Fourth Air Force's A-2 intelligence office on July 12, and it appeared in the press five days later. Davidson and Brown apparently asked Johnson about Arnold's political sympathies and what he expected to gain by casting suspicion on the U.S. military. Johnson talked to them only of Arnold's sincerity and integrity.

Davidson and Brown took Arnold to dinner at the Hotel Owyhee and then returned to his home, where he revealed his correspondence file. Davidson and Brown noted the letters from Palmer but came away convinced of Arnold's basic honesty and told him to report future developments to Hamilton Field. They departed with one last in-bred meeting of the people they came to interview. They then went with Arnold to the Boise airport for a stopover by Emil Smith, where they also met again with Dave Johnson. At that meeting, Johnson advised Arnold to take on the Maury Island investigation and let his newspaper, the *Statesman,* pick up expenses.

Notes:

1. One of the transports left a flying formation traveling between San Diego and Seattle on December 10, 1946, due to the prevailing storm conditions. It lost radio contact over Longmire, WA and disappeared into the tough terrain near Mt. Rainier. Remains of the plane were discovered near Longmire, WA on July 17, 1947, with no survivors. It apparently had crashed into the face of a sheer, 3,000 foot cliff. After seven months, only a fragment from a serviceman's uniform, the weathered remains of one Marine's health record and the small bits of wreckage had been recovered by eight Rainier national park rangers. "Tattered Piece of Uniform, Bits of Wreckage Identify Lost Plane," *East Oregonian,* July 25, 1957, p. 1.

2. "Status Report: Kenneth Arnold and the Birth of the UFO Mystery," *Fortean Times* 100, July 1997, p. 26.

3. Keel, John, "The Man Who Invented Flying Saucers," *The Fringes of Reason*, New York: Harmony Books, 1989, p. 141.

4. Paris Flammonde gave the following analysis of news reports from this period: "...beginning with the Maury Island affair or Arnold's confrontation, the modern era was initiated with what would come to be known as a "flap"—i.e., a time of concerted press coverage of UFO, although not necessarily a period of an unusually large number of reports. The term is often employed in contradistinction to a fairly notable rise in sightings, or a specific concentration of UFO accounts emanating from a particular locale. The majority of sightings were in the American Northwest. Almost three quarters of the accounts were west of the 100 degree longitude line. The National Investigations Committee on Aerial Phenomena (NICAP) analyzed late June and July 1947 some years later. It concluded that, from 125 reports received at that time, almost a third came from Washington with 38. Quantitatively: Colorado with 16, Idaho with 11, Utah with 8, and Oregon, California, New Mexico, Wyoming, and Arizona, with 6, 5, 3, 2 and 2, respectively followed. Farther east, Oklahoma had the most with 9, and several other states had one or two reports. (Flammonde, Paris, *UFO Exist!,* New York: Ballantine, 1976.)

5. "2 Pendleton Area Residents See Mysterious 'Objects'," *East Oregonian*, Monday, June 30, 1947, p. 1.

6. "'Flying Saucers' Observed By Five Pendleton Persons," *East Oregonian*, Wednesday, July 2, 1947, p. 1.

7. "What Is This We See, Klamath Residents Ask," *East Oregonian*, Thursday, July 3, 1947, p. 1.

8. "Hundreds in West See Flying Discs Over July Fourth," *East Oregonian*, Saturday, July 5, 1947, p. 1. This report contains mention of the entire three man crew of a United Air Lines plane—pilot Capt. Emil J. Smith, co-pilot Ralph Stevens, stewardess Marty Morrow—that witnessed five discs "like a pancake standing on end" eight minutes after taking off from Boise, Idaho. Capt. Smith, said, "It's hard to judge size unless you know how far away a thing is." Smith had previously insisted that Arnold's sighting must have been a reflection from his instrument panel. After his sighting, Smith met with Arnold to media fanfare. They traded notes and decided that the UFOs must be experimental U.S. or Russian craft.

9. "Arnold Returns For Second look At 'Discs'," *East Oregonian*, Monday, July 7, 1947, p. 1.

10. "Air Defense In Northwest Stepped Up," *East Oregonian*, Saturday, July 5, 1947, p. 1.

11. The *East Oregonian's* report on the Roswell incident appeared in the July 9 edition, "Captured Disc Proves Balloon," p. 1. Military intelligence interest in Arnold seems to pick up after Roswell.

12. "Impossible! Maybe, but Seein' Is Believin'," Says Flyer," *East Oregonian*, Wednesday, June 25, 1947, p. 1.

13. "Flying Disc Mystery More Involved," *East Oregonian*, June 27, 1947, p. 1.

14. "Arnold Buys Camera, Others See Objects," *East Oregonian*, June 27, 1947, p. 1.

15. In *The Report on Unidentified Flying Objects* (New York: Ace Books, 1956), Edward J. Ruppelt reported that an F-51 pilot flying over Lake Meade, Nevada four days after Arnold's sighting, witnessed a saucer formation similar to the Maury Island sighting. The pilot reported a half-dozen circular objects off the right wing of his plane. The pilot has been identified as a renowned flyer in the state whose name, Dick Rankin, was recognized by Arnold. Ruppelt also discusses a sighting in Redmond, Oregon by a carload of people on July 4, 1947 of four saucers spinning past Mount Jefferson. Two hours later, according to Ruppelt, a Portland city policeman spotted a similar group of saucers. Two other policemen saw a smaller group a bit later, and after that four harbor patrol crew men saw some as well, "shaped like chrome hub caps." (Ruppelt, p. 32). Ruppelt says the first sighting "that really made the Air Force take a deep interest" happened at Edwards Air Force Base (then Muroc AFB) on July 8, 1947, but clearly Davidson and Brown were on Arnold's case, as well as those of Emil Smith and Dick Rankin, just before this. Ruppelt's famous book obsfucates the Maury Island story in many ways. He renames Arnold "Simpson" and calls Crisman and

Dahl "Jackson and Richards," although he retains the correct names of the military officers Davidson and Brown. Paris Flammonde offers a sympathetic critique of Ruppelt in *UFO Exist!*, noting among other things Ruppelt's over-reliance on information from military sources.

16. "Impossible! Maybe, but Seein' Is Believin', Says Flyer," *East Oregonian*, Wednesday, June 25, 1947, p. 1.
17. "Arnold Buys Camera, Others See Objects," *East Oregonian*, June 27, 1947, p. 1.
18. "Arnold Returns For Second Look At Discs," *East Oregonian*, July 7, 1947, p. 1.
19. "Kenneth Arnold Suggests `Flying Discs' May Make Use of Atomic Power," *East Oregonian*, July 17, 1947, p. 1.
20. *The Coming of the Saucers.*
21. "Boise Flyer Who First Reported 'Flying Discs' Would Tell Story Again Despite 'Notoriety'," *East Oregonian*, July 12, 1947.
22. Williams, Fred, *UFOs Are Supernatural*, Cedaredge, Colorado: Freedland, 1991, p. 3.
23. Some science fiction fans might argue that this historical spot is one of infamy. In September 1946, *Harper's Magazine* published a report on post-war science fiction by writer William Baring-Gould that included a description of the contempt in which Palmer was held by science fiction fandom. Baring-Gould quoted one New York fanzine, *Fantasy Commentator,* as saying that Palmer's readers "are not interested in learning anything which would change their beliefs; that they can learn more from their inner consciousness than from without; and some have gone so far as to state that they abhor mathematics and allied modern sciences because they disprove their beliefs...[Palmer's publications] propitiate these crackpots' views in fictional guise." Nevertheless, Ray Palmer remained active in science fiction fandom through the late 1970s, when he contracted to do magazine work for the National Space Institute. The National Space Institute was founded by Paperclip Nazi Werner Von Braun and other professional space industry insiders/science fiction enthusiasts. It later merged with the L5 Society, comprised of rank-and-file science-fiction fans that, as advocates of real-life space colonization, many believed also inflated the reality behind the literary genre. In the 1990s, Ray Palmer's pulp format *Amazing Stories* became a high-budgeted television series produced by filmmaker Steven Spielberg. Baring-Gould's 1946 article quoted an anonymously-penned letter by Fred Crisman, published by Palmer, which served as the catalyst for a second letter by Crisman to Palmer.

24. *Amazing Stories* associate editor Howard Brown told this to pulp
    historian Ron Goulart in *Cheap Thrills: An Informal History of
    the Pulp Magazines* (New Rochelle, NY: Arlington House, 1972),
    pp. 171-173. "I thought it was the sickest crap I had run into,"
    Browne asserted while noting that it doubled the circulation of
    Amazing Stories in four months. Browne is not clear about whether
    the manuscript he refers to became "I Remember Lemuria" or
    the first letter by Shaver printed
    by *Amazing Stories*, published pre-
    vious to the Lemuria article in the
    January 1944 issue. In response to
    the suggestion that Ray Palmer
    wrote some of the articles under
    Shaver's by-line, Shaver com-
    mented in 1973, "It's not true at
    all. There is very little revision
    in any of my work, just cutting
    where it didn't fit. They cut off
    some of the ends sometimes; that's
    all." Shaver died in 1975.

Richard Shaver, 1975.

25. Shaver saw the deros as more than
    just an alien race. He writes, "the
    human whose mind has been under
    the influence of detrimental flows of energy until he has become
    a detrimental robot...I never meant to infer that the dero was
    confined exclusively to the cavern life, but only that the worst of
    earth's deros are to be found among the cavern people...All earth
    people are to some extent deros, and especially considered from
    the viewpoint of all-over result, such as the results we got from
    our last war; all men are deros...But in the caverns this stupid
    following of thought patterns without content of true reason is to
    be found organized, fixed, honored by the observance of centu-
    ries of stupidity; a form of state, a way of life. Up here we have
    not quite that sad a result from deros among us, as yet." (see
    Appendix 1.) In a 1965 interview, Palmer claimed that Shaver
    spent eight years in an insane asylum. "He didn't retreat into an
    imaginary world. Mentally, he entered a very real world...what
    the psychics say is astral." Nevertheless, Shaver strongly denied
    ever having been so incarcerated. Steinberg, Gene, "Remem-
    brances of a UFO pioneer," *UFO Universe #5*, 1998.

26. Shaver described himself as "a simple man, a worker in metal,
    employed in a steel mill in Pennsylvania," while insisting that
    "What I tell you is not fiction!" He wants to convince his audi-
    ence "not because I sound convincing or tell my story in a con-

vincing manner, but because you will see the truth in what I say, and will realize, as you must, that many of the things I tell you are not a matter of present day scientific knowledge and yet are true!...I am no mathematician; I am no scientist. I have studied all the scientific books I can get—only to become more and more convinced that I remember true things. But surely someone can definitely say that I am wrong or that I am right, especially in such things as the true nature of gravity, or matter, of light, of the cause of age and many other things..."

27. Crisman gave a prescient description of a laser-like weapon boring "a hole the size of a dime in [the] right bicep" of a companion's arm. "It was seared inside. How we don't know." No doubt, since lasers had not yet been developed. Crisman gives no indication, however, that he knew or understood Richard Shaver's claims that a Lemurian or Atlantean language had a residual life within the English language. Shaver maintained that he alone could decode Mantong, the deros language, with the help of a recovered memory from a previous incarnation and the information channeled to him through his welding equipment and from a telaug, a device broadcasting mental archives from a long-dead sage named Mutan Mion. (See Appendix One.) Similar rants and channels have come from uncounted sources in New Age milieu to the present day, and the idea of a hidden cant language has been described by Kerry Thornley as a factor in his involvement with the JFK assassination. Ray Palmer published volumes detailing the cosmology and history of the deros entitled *The Hidden World* in the 1960s. Paris Flammonde has a concise summary of the material (*UFO Exist*, pp. 174-183) and notes, "One or two years before the Puget Sound sightings and before the Kenneth Arnold encounter—i.e., a long time before the age of 'flying saucers' began—ufology was confined to the inquisitive minds of occultists and dabblers in the unknown." To this, it should be added that at present the idea of alien beings living and working underground has not faded with time. For many, the idea that diminuitive, deros-like grey aliens work side by side with human workers at Area 51 near Dulce, New Mexico, remains a persistent rumor.

28. In comments to the appropriations committee of the House of Representatives in 1947, Spatz emphasized his fear that an attack on the U.S. could come from long range bombers and guided missiles launched over the arctic, down to the American Northwest. MacKenzie, Dewitt, "If War Comes Again Experts Believe It'll Come Over Top of The World," *East Oregonian*, May 30, 1947, p. 1.

29. An FBI memo from August 6, 1947 reports that in order to ascertain the purpose of the interviews conducted by Brown and Davidson, the reporting agent "contacted Major General Twining of Wright Field, Ohio by phone at Albuquerque, NM, and from him gained the impression that the AAF instituted this investigation to wash out the disc reports."

30. Williams, p. 2.

31. Captain Emil Smith gave the following account of his experience to United Press International:
    "As our flight, No 105 took off from Boise, Idaho, at 8:04 p.m., Pacific time, the tower joshingly told us to be on the lookout for flying saucers. My copilot, Ralph Stevens, also of Seattle, was in control shortly after we got into the air. Suddenly he switched on the landing lights. He said he thought he saw an aircraft, approaching us head-on. I noticed the objects then for the first time. We saw four or five "somethings." One was larger than the rest and, for the most part, kept off the right of the three or four similar, but smaller objects. Since we were flying northwest--roughly into the sunset--we saw whatever they were in at least partial light. We saw them clearly. We saw them in a northwesterly direction for about 45 miles. Then I called the attendant at the Ontario, Ore., radio tower, giving an approximate location and course for the objects. The attendant acknowledged our call, went outside to look, but was unable to see anything like what we described. Finally the objects disappeared in a burst of speed. We were unable to tell whether they outsped us or disintegrated. We were never able to catch them in our DC-3. Our air speed at the time was 185 miles per hour."

32. *Coming of the Saucers*, pp. 16-19.

33. In post-war, pre-UFO times, such speculation was rife. News reports on the development of the nuclear submarine, for instance, included the prediction that "The carrier may give way to speedy interceptor ships bearing pilotless aircraft which can knock down enemy guided missiles..." "Atomic Powered Warships Aim of Special Project," *East Oregonian*, May 7, 1947, p. 1. Davidson and Brown were on a mission to "wash out" discs, of course, not an investigation of Arnold's patriotism. Their early emphasis in this regard may reflect their own skepticism about Arnold's actual sighting.

5

THE SAUCER SPINS

Despite an encounter with nine space saucers and a new-found global celebrity, Kenneth Arnold had not yet experienced weirdness, at least not the depth of the weirdness that his investigation of the Maury Island event ultimately would bring. Next came his second UFO encounter in the Callair single engine. He took off on July 29 at 5:30 in the morning, with a fuel tank only partly full, for a stop to refuel in LeGrande, Oregon. He also had business there, and then he planned to go on to Tacoma to talk to Crisman and Dahl.

Arnold tilted the Callair's wings to acknowledge an Empire Airlines Boeing plane over Baker, Oregon, on his right. As he did so, he witnessed a dozen more saucers flying in a formation like those over Mount Rainier. He grabbed his $150 movie camera with the telescopic lens and got some footage before the speeding objects, only 400 yards away, disappeared. When he had the film developed, however, it showed only small dots. As he watched this new formation, Arnold realized that the smallness of the craft distinguished them from the Mt. Rainier group. These saucers measured no longer than 30 inches in diameter. Their speed and proximity kept Arnold from dismissing them as a flock of ducks or geese.

The size was more significant than Arnold realized. An object measuring 30.5 inches that looked "similar to the cymbals used by a drummer in a band, placed face to face" had been recovered two weeks earlier by Mrs. Fred Easterbrook in Twin Falls, Idaho. Mrs. Easterbrook turned it over to an FBI agent named W. G. Banister. "The gadget is gold-plated on one side and silver, either stainless steel, aluminum or tin on the other," reported the Tacoma paper, which used only Banister as the source.[1] The *East Oregonian* had covered the story of the two-and-half foot saucer and noted that assistant chief of Twin Falls' police E. McCracken said that army intelligence authorities had ordered his department "not to talk" about the mini-saucer. "The object was taken into a back room at the police station and put under lock and key," said McCracken. "We were told to keep our mouths shut, and not describe the object to anyone."[2] All reference to these strong-arm tactics was left out of the next *East Oregonian* report, as were the names of the four

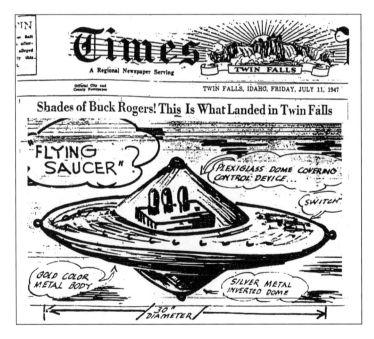

Sketch of disk recovered by Banister, *Twin Falls Times*, July 11, 1947. At this time, Banister knew Jim Garrison, who later investigated him over the JFK murder.

boys that assistant chief McCracken claimed had made the disk from parts of an old phonograph.[3] A clear pattern of cover-up can be seen in the newspaper record of this sighting.

Moreover, the involvement of FBI agent W. G. "Guy" Banister established a distant first link between the Maury Island incident and the assassination of John F. Kennedy. Banister emerged during the investigation of the JFK murder by New Orleans district attorney Jim Garrison, but also previously had been investigated by the Warren Commission. By that time, Banister ran a detective agency in New Orleans, Guy Banister Associates, at 531 Lafayette. The building had a second entrance at 544 Camp Street, which housed an anti-Castro group created by future Watergaters Bernard Barker and E. Howard Hunt, called the Cuban Revolutionary Council.

The Warren Commission determined that Lee Harvey Oswald used the 544 Camp Street as the office address of the ostensibly pro-Castro Fair Play For Cuba Committee, and printed it on his Hands Off Cuba flyers in 1963. After his death, Banister's widow found Fair Play for Cuba literature at Banister's Lafayette street office. Banister also employed as an investigator the albino pilot and Oswald-acquaintance, David Ferrie. Both Banister and Ferrie were gun runners for the Bay of Pigs. Banister's associates included Mafia and right-wing extremist groups like the World Anti-Communist League; he also once worked in the Chicago FBI office with Robert Maheu, a consultant to Howard Hughes who planned murder plots against Castro.[4]

Banister hired men like Ferrie to do grunt investigative work while he pursued intrigue among political groups. Some of his informants supplied him with information on leftist student groups at nearby Tulane and Louisiana State universities, while he published strident anti-communist newsletters like *Louisiana Intelligence*

Digest. Banister also worked as Louisiana coordinator for the Minutemen, an early militia group with a membership that included a pastor whose brother would later claim to have witnessed the Maury Island event.[5] The Warren Commission had looked into an incident involving one of Banister's investigators, Jack Martin, who was beaten by Banister with a .357 Magnum a few hours after JFK was shot. Apparently a drunk Banister was nervous that Martin would expose to authorities the role planned for David Ferrie as pilot for the conspirators' getaway plane.[6]

That Banister enjoyed his double life in law enforcement and criminal conspiracy was made explicit when he testified before the Louisiana Joint Legislative Committee in March 1957 about his decision to move to New Orleans: "I had retired, intending to get out of law enforcement, although I must say I regretted getting out of counter-espionage, counter-sabotage, counter-subversive activity work. It is a fascinating field."[7] He also gave that committee yet another view of the 30-inch disk he was given in July 1947, which the police identified to the newspaper as a children's prank: "Do you remember the Japanese balloon cases that occurred in World War II? Balloons being sent over from Japan? We found the first one on land in Montana [sic; Banister worked for the headquarters of

Guy Banister, who recovered a 30 inch disk in Idaho on July 12, 1947. Banister was later connected to the JFK assassination via Lee Harvey Oswald, whose "Fair Play for Cuba" leaflets were stamped with Banister's 1963 office address in New Orleans.

FBI Drums Up Cymbals-Like 'Disk' in Idaho

BUTTE, Mont., July 11.—Æ—
FBI Agent W. G. Banister said an
object which appeared to be a "flying disk" was found early today at
Twin Falls, Ida., and turned over
to federal authorities there.

Banister, special agent in charge
of the FBI in Montana and Idaho,
said the bureau had reported the
discovery to the army at Fort
Douglas, Utah.

An FBI agent in Twin Falls in-
spected the "saucer" and described
it as similar to the "cymbals used
by a drummer in a band, placed
face to face."

The object measured 30½ inches
in diameter, with a metal dome on
one side and a plastic dome about
14 inches high on the opposite side,
anchored in place by what appeared to be stove bolts. The
gadget is gold plated on one side
and silver (either stainless steel,
aluminum or tin) on the other. It
appeared to have been turned out
by machine, reports from Twin
Falls said.

The FBI agent declined to elaborate further.

News report of Banister's saucer
recovery, *Tacoma News Tribune,* July 12,
1947. Army intelligence ordered local
police not to talk about the mini-saucer
and provided an obvious cover story,
that it had been built as a prank by some
boys.

the Montana-Idaho FBI
division in Butte, Mon-
tana], and I had the job
of finding out where it
came from. It came
through the air, although
a leading balloonist in
this country said no bal-
loon could fly such a
distance. But military ge-
ology—that branch of
military services which
we have—in time began
to chart the exact strata
in Japan they came
from, because they had
sand bags on them, you
remember. And we
found out the reason
why. The winds carry-
ing these balloons origi-
nated in Siberia. We call
them now the jet air
streams. They can ride
one out eastward toward
us. Off the coast they
strike one going much
faster, almost twice as
fast, turning south.
They can ride that until
they cross another go-
ing eastward at about
350 miles per hour. It quite frequently passes over New
Orleans, and they can ride it down. They can be here
quicker than they can get to Chicago."[8]

Interestingly, the Japanese Fugo balloon bomb is one of three balloon theories that have been used to explain the Roswell event, one championed by writer John Keel but challenged by many others.[9]

Certainly the vision of 20-plus small disks that Kenneth Arnold saw as he traveled to meet with Crisman and Dahl was not a formation of Fugo balloons. After he made his refueling stop, Arnold called Dave Johnson, who was happy to get the scoop of the new sighting by Arnold for the *Idaho Statesman*. After the call, Johnson phoned Emil Smith to let him in on Arnold's investigation of the Maury Island incident. A suspicious Smith complained that he had learned that Arnold had attached his name to the July 12 statement connecting the UFOs to atomic energy. His suspicions were assuaged as Johnson reiterated his feelings about Arnold's basic honesty.

Meanwhile, Arnold attempted to find lodging from the Sky Harbor airport where he landed at Chehalis, Washington. Conventions were keeping the hotel "No Vacancy" signs lit, but Arnold surprisingly found a room at the Linnard-Western Winthrop Hotel—reserved already in his name! Because of the scarcity of rooms he had discovered from phone calls, Arnold hopped on the airport's shuttle service to room 502, a double with bath, before he could figure out how it came to be his. He had not made the reservation. By the time he reached the Winthrop, the clerk he had spoken with on the phone was off work and could not be reached. Arnold's attempt to uncover the Maury Island mystery kept sinking him more and more into mystery.

The pilot picked up the phone book and looked up "Dahl." The phone book contained almost forty Dahls. He dialed the "H.A. Dahl" listing, Proctor 7116, an exchange in the city's north, and it turned out to be a good guess. Harold Dahl answered, and, upon realizing he was talking to UFO celebrity Kenneth Arnold, he told him to back-off of the investigation and return home. Dahl was still smarting from his contact with the Man In Black and the subsequent misfortunes of his family and business. He explained that the newspapers refused to listen to his story, that he was not anxious to involve police or military authorities, and that his "superior" Fred Crisman had made the first overtures to Ray Palmer. Arnold's characteristic all-American honesty and sense of urgency about the truth did finally succeed, after about a half-hour of stalling, in getting Dahl to agree to come to the hotel.

Dahl gave Arnold the basics of his UFO experience in the waters around Maury Island. He deferred questions about his employment to Fred Crisman, who he suggested could come by the following day. He again suggested that Arnold forget about it and go home. When Arnold asked him about the son who had sustained an injury after the encounter, Dahl told him about how the boy had disappeared and then gave all the details about his encounter with the Man In Black. After more description of the actual saucers—repeatedly comparing them to Buicks—and more warnings from Dahl that Arnold should drop his investigation and just go, the conversation turned to the slag.

Arnold wanted to see it. Dahl explained that he had only saved what he had picked up from the boat; Crisman picked up more of the stuff from the shore during his visit, and that was in Crisman's possession. Dahl's own pieces were kept in a safe house, away from his own home, at a building where his office work was sometimes conducted. Arnold pushed to see them, and Dahl ultimately relented and agreed to drive him to the storage site.

The house where the slag was stored needed paint, but otherwise it was fairly ordinary, equipped with a piano and assorted ceramic decorations. A 40-year-old widow with children lived and sometimes brought work home there, according to Dahl as he introduced her to Arnold. Dahl left Arnold in the kitchen with the woman and went to retrieve a slag piece from another room. He had been using it as an ashtray. Arnold, who was smoking at that point, checked it out.

Arnold declared that the ashtray was nothing but lava rock. Dahl insisted that it came from the saucer slag discharged upon the boat, but said also that Crisman held onto a box of the white metal. He offered to take Arnold to visit Crisman that night and view the white metal, but Arnold demurred until the next day. Dahl seemed genuinely confused and again suggested to Arnold to abandon his investigation lest he face personal calamities similar to those that happened to Dahl after his encounter with the Man In Black. The pair spent the rest of the night, until midnight, discussing hunting and fishing. Dahl returned the tiring Arnold to the Winthrop hotel and made an arrangement to meet with him in the morning with Fred Crisman in tow.

Arnold ate breakfast and read the paper at the hotel coffee shop the next morning and returned to his room before Dahl and Crisman knocked on the door. Arnold later described Crisman as dark complected, stocky, "happy go lucky," alert and cheerful. He was shorter than Dahl, about 30 years old, less fearful and more animated. Arnold first tried to get clear the exact nature of the relationship between Dahl and Crisman. Crisman clarified that neither worked for the city or the military, but that Dahl regarded Crisman as his "superior" in the log salvaging business. Crisman explained that he thought Dahl had been drinking when he returned that day with the story of the six slag-spewing donuts.

Arnold was surprised to discover that Crisman was not among the original witnesses. He was impressed, however, when Crisman said his judgement about his partner's inebriation began to change as he examined the damage to the boat. The damage had been done to the wheelhouse and upper deck; drinking-impaired navigation would most likely wreck the bottom of the boat as the drunk sailors crashed into rocks. For this reason, Crisman explained to Arnold, he went to check out the story the next day and discovered all the lava rock and white metal debris. As he stood there at Maury Island, looking over tons of the debris stretched along the beach, he had his own sighting. One plump donut, not squashed as in Dahl's description, zoomed out of a cumulus cloud and circled the bay.

Arnold was alternately impressed and suspicious as Crisman continued to talk. Dahl receded into the background, saying very little. Crisman noted that, unlike Dahl, he held a commercial pilot's license. He also mentioned having previously worked with AmVets and the veteran's bureau. He even mentioned the missions he flew over Burma during the war, although he said nothing about his encounters with deros laser rays as he did when reporting about this part of his career in letters to Ray Palmer. His experience with aircraft gave him confidence to describe the saucer he witnessed at Maury Island in more detail. It had portholes five feet in diameter, an observation window, and a golden metal exterior. It shined more brilliantly than one would expect even in the sun.

When Arnold asked about how he came to write to Palmer's magazine, Crisman explained that he had simply picked a copy up on the newstand. He noted that the magazine's title was not *Venture Magazine*, as Palmer had named it on his stationery, but could not recall the actual name. He chose it as the place for his story because its readers believed that many of its pulp fiction tales actually were real. Crisman noted that he had several issues of the magazine at home. The conversation ended with more of Crisman's war stories. He bragged about retrieving a radio stolen from a fellow serviceman that he had tracked to a pawn shop. He also complained about the treatment of veterans. Dahl shuffled and looked askance as Crisman talked.

After ordering coffee from room service, Arnold pushed for going out to Maury Island with the two men. A newsclipping Arnold carried described lava ash particles that had fallen from a formation of flying saucers over Mountain Home, Idaho, on July 12, and this added to his interest in the story that Crisman told. As Crisman and Dahl talked out the scheduling problems of taking Arnold to the island, Arnold came up with another inspiration: why not bring in the United Airlines pilot E. J. Smith? Smith had been skeptical of Arnold's initial report until he too had a close encounter. That skepticism and experience would be useful in making some kind of judgement about Crisman's and Dahl's story, which Arnold also hoped would add credibility to his and Smith's stories.

Arnold then called Smith and made arrangements to pick him up by plane in Seattle at 4:00 that afternoon. Crisman drove Arnold to the airport.[10] Arnold noted that "Big Smithy" no doubt found his single engine aircraft a disappointment after the DC-6s he had been flying, if not a downright danger.

After agreeing to the trip, Smith had phoned Arnold's newspaper ally Dave Johnson at the *Idaho Statesman* and Maurice Roddy, who worked as aviation editor for the *Chicago Tribune*, a friend of Smith's to whom he had agreed to report any interesting developments, despite assuring Arnold that he would keep a tight lid on publicity. Smith met Arnold at an airport coffee shop

Emil Smith, Arnold, and Smith's co-pilot Ralph Stevens, from *The Coming of the Saucers.*

and was brought up to speed on the encounter with Crisman and Doyle. Smith apparently did make some remark about the similarity between the diminutive instrument panel of Arnold's plane, which Arnold took as a reference to Smith's dismissal of the Mt. Rainier sightings as reflections off same. Smith also compared it and Dahl's sighting to the concentric circles on a Buick dashboard.[11]

They discussed Crisman and Dahl some more before landing and having Crisman drive them back to the hotel from the airport. Crisman declared that he would go to pick up Dahl and return. In the hotel lobby, Arnold and Smith were approached by a reporter for the *Tacoma Times* named Paul Lantz. Lantz asked them about what was going on in the hotel room. Both Arnold and Smith had commitments to other papers, and Arnold still had his obligation to Palmer, and so they refused interviews. As they left Lantz behind and entered the elevator, Arnold remarked on the level of interest their situation was sure to cause as time went on. Indeed, Lantz made a few more attempts to contact the men in their room.

Smith continued to express doubts about the entire affair, where Palmer got money to spend on investigating it; where the hotel room came from; why newspapers were sending them instead of reporters. He also confided that Arnold's newspaper patron, Dave Johnson, and the Air Force investigator Lt. Brown were old chums. Dahl and Crisman returned about an hour and a half later, each explaining their story to Smith individually. Smith cross-examined them both thoroughly. Crisman noted that the saucer he saw was not like what Arnold had seen, and not like anything he expected the U.S. military would have, speaking from the perspective of a still active member of the Air Reserve. He also told Smith about a magazine article he had read regarding the possibility that flying saucers came from German technology captured from Nazis.[12] Dahl offered another lava rock specimen.

Smith was intrigued enough by what the pair had to say to cancel his work for the next day and stay to take a trip to the harbor. The meeting broke up when Crisman volunteered to drive Smith back to Seattle for his things and Dahl left for business elsewhere. The meeting resumed again when Smith returned, having had his ear bent with Crisman's war stories to Seattle and back. After dinner, Crisman and Dahl came back. Dahl debriefed Smith on his Man in Black experience and the unfortunate circumstances he fell into after the Maury Island encounter. Smith was intrigued but still very suspicious. Did Crisman have a copy of this *Venture Maga-*

zine? Crisman promised to bring one, and Dahl promised more fragments. It was agreed that they would meet and go to Maury Island in the morning.

Smith stayed in Arnold's room. When he crashed on the hotel room bed, a .32 automatic gun fell out from underneath the pillow. Arnold explained that the gun had been given to him by Paul Weiland, the Nuremberg judge who had hired him for a fishing trip when all this began. The men laughed at the prospect of a gun having any utility in this situation. They talked a bit more before retiring, laughing at their predicament but with some serious concern about the character of Dahl and Crisman. Were those two con men? Were they Soviet agents? Was the hotel room bugged? Arnold would later summarize what he really feared at that point: "It was publicly known that we had been interrogated by Military Intelligence. Russian agents might assume that we had been secretly assured that these craft were of our own manufacture. By watching us or getting us involved in something of this kind, we might privately confide in each other what, supposedly, the military had secretly assured us. Thus a foreign government would have an assured knowledge of what these things were and where they came from in case they were being sighted over their own country.

At this time we didn't even dream of the possibility that they could come from another world. Although Smithy and I did not talk much about it that evening, we both felt safer with a gun in our possession."[13] They also searched the room for surveillance bugs.

The two had not even begun to pass into a paranoid sleep when the phone rang. It was a reporter from United Press International named Ted Morello. Arnold repeated what he had told Paul Lantz[14] in the lobby: no comment. Morello insisted that he had not called to collect information but to give it. An anonymous informant had been calling his office several times in the past day and a half, keeping UPI apprised of Arnold's movements and the goings on at the hotel. Arnold tried again to blow off Morello, but Morello stunned him with precise details about his past day's conversations with Crisman, Dahl and Smith. Smith took the phone and demanded to know Morello's source. Morello repeated that the source was anonymous and explained that he was calling because he would rather get information direct. Smith declined again, suggesting that Morello was being deceptive and manipulative. Morello defended himself well, however, and agreed not to broadcast the fact of their presence at the hotel, and agreed also to contact them if he received any more calls. Arnold and Smith in turn promised him to report anything significant that might come from their investigation. The pair tore up the room some more looking for bugs, whispered the rest of their conversation and retired to an uneasy sleep.

Interestingly, Ted Morello also recently had reported upon a different UFO incident similar to the one described by Crisman and Dahl. On July 7, 1947, a Monday at 2:30 a.m., two police car patrol officers in Tacoma, Stan Johnson and Evan "Skip" Davies, were dispatched to North 33rd and Adams Street in Tacoma to check out a possible burglary. As they sat in their patrol car looking for a burglar, they both spied several saucers over a tree to their left. They stared in silence at first, until Johnson remarked to Davies that he thought he was seeing things. The two men saw one central saucer surrounded by several smaller ones making sorties to the large one and then flying away.

Although the officers could make no accurate measurement, the smaller saucers appeared softball-sized and traveled at an altitude of approximately 10,000 feet. They threw off sparks and attracted them back, "like a mother hen with a brood of chicks." Johnson and Davies chased the objects and watched them change color from red, to purple, to blue-white and back to red. One disk shot up another 5,000 feet "quicker than you could snap your fingers." Johnson even threatened to shoot one of the things down with his prowl car shotgun, but was dissuaded by his partner, who argued "It might blow up Tacoma!" The two police officers described the sighting in progress to their radio dispatcher, D. F. Erickson. Morello reported this as the first flying saucer sighting at night. He personally had interviewed both of the officers.[15]

Crisman and Dahl woke up Arnold and Smith the next morning, Dahl with some more fragment rocks and this time also with a piece of the white metal he said had spewed from the saucer.

They traveled to the bay by car, Crisman leading, where they all had a hot breakfast and met several other harbor sailor associates of Crisman and Dahl. Arnold brought his movie camera and filmed these events, although the footage does not survive.[16] Crisman made a call from a phone booth and discovered that the Maury Island dry-dock was closed. The men reluctantly returned to the hotel, where they had locked up Dahl's debris offerings.

The smooth, curved rock-like fragments fit together such that Arnold could imagine them as a tube lining with a six foot diameter. His clear impression of the white, thin metal fragment was that it was no more out of the ordinary than aluminum, but that it had unusual rivets. He knew Crisman would recognize the stuff, as would any pilot, and wondered what gain could come from trying to pass it off as coming from a spacecraft. Smith asked about the medical records of Dahl's son, supposedly injured by the falling debris, and Dahl replied that he had them somewhere. Crisman basically said the same thing about the photos Dahl took of the

Maury Island saucers before turning his camera over to him. He had them, but could not find them before he left in the morning. He promised to bring them in the afternoon. The compilation of fishy circumstances and excuses gave Arnold the idea to call the Air Force investigators who previously had spoken with him, Smith and Arnold's newsman ally Dave Johnson. Crisman seemed excited by the idea, but Hal Dahl, no doubt still burning from his experience with the Man In Black, refused to talk to anyone in military intelligence.

Brown in Italy, 1944.

Things started getting weirder still when Arnold called Brown. Brown refused to accept the call on the military line but rather called Arnold back on a pay phone. Arnold described the Maury Island story as having "real credence" but gave few other details. Brown explained that he and Davidson were busy making preparations for the upcoming Air Force Day festivities. This was the official day that separated the Air Force from the Army. Brown related, though, that he and Davidson had just interviewed Portland pilot and recent UFO witness Dick Rankin, a name known by Arnold, and that they also recently came into possession of a photograph from Arizona of a crescent-shape saucer similar to what Arnold had described to them[17] from his own sighting. Brown said that if he did not call Arnold back in an hour, he and Davidson would be there at the Hotel Winthrop.

Between that call and the time Brown and Davidson arrived, Arnold, Smith and the others had two more encounters with the local press. Ted Morello called again, clearly having gotten wind of the pending visit by the military investigators, only moments after Arnold hung up with Brown. Morello claimed that his informant had called again, from a pay phone like Brown. No sooner had Morello been brushed off when the *Tacoma Times* reporter Paul Lantz called from the lobby and a few minutes later showed up at the hotel door. Emil Smith shook him down and sent him on his way. Dahl decided to split, too, saying that Crisman could explain everything to the Air Force intelligence people, but leaving behind his phone number. According to Arnold, Smith took Crisman down to the lobby at that point.[18]

So Arnold met Brown and Davidson alone at the hotel when they arrived at 4:30, July 31, but Smith and Crisman returned shortly thereafter. Smith and Arnold explained about the phone calls they had been receiving and Crisman went on about the pieces of debris still strewn around the hotel room. He gave the military investigators the full story as he had previously told it to Arnold and Smith. Brown and Davidson asked him to pinpoint the location on a map and asked also if they could take some of the debris back with them to Hamilton Field. They did not produce the photograph from Arizona, but rather a sketch of it. It was a crescent-shaped craft, like the main saucer Arnold had seen on Mount Rainier but never had included in any of his statements to the press.

Crisman went on for over two hours explaining what he knew of Dahl's experience. After that, the A-2 men got more details from Arnold and Smith. The meeting went on past dinner and through to midnight. In the end, Crisman agreed to hand over about thirty pieces of UFO debris. He would pick them up immediately so that the two investigators could fly back to Hamilton Field right away. Arnold and Smith offered to have the pair stay in the hotel room that night, but both were required to get back to base for Air Force Day preparations.

The pair's lack of enthusiasm at that late time convinced Arnold that the two A-2 agents already had concluded that Crisman and Dahl were hoaxers, although they seemed certain that "you two," Arnold and Smith, were above suspicion. Neither had a strong concern about the possibility that Room 502 had been bugged; neither showed any great excitement over the Kellogg's Corn Flakes box Crisman gave them with samples of the saucer residue. Crisman had retrieved the box from his home shortly before the midnight end of the meeting. Arnold noted that the fragments it contained were thicker than what they had in the room. When Davidson and Brown finally departed for their B-25 at McChord Field in an army command sedan, Arnold and Smith were left with a slight sense of embarrassment. Arnold had decided not to show them a letter Dahl had given him from an anonymous writer claiming that UFOs were piloted by beings "less dense" than humans who were under attack by another race of aliens.

Crisman, Arnold and Smith had coffee after saying their good-byes to Davidson and Brown. Crisman then left, and the other two returned to the room to crash. Instead, they got a call from Ted Morello repeating to them everything that had happened in the meeting, explaining that he was once again in contact with his mysterious informant. Smith hung up on Morello, and the two men in the room looked further for bugs and speculated about the informant's identity. Crisman? Dahl?

Despite their impression that Davidson and Brown did not take the Maury Island UFO story seriously, neither seemed to suspect that the A-2 men would try to turn it into the *Tacoma Times'* next derogatory flying saucer story by playing the role of secret informant. In any event, Arnold and Smith laughed the whole thing off with some sense of relief and went to sleep. They had done their civic duty. The case was now in the hands of military investigators.

They planned to finally make that trip to Maury Island with Crisman in the morning before leaving this whole strange experience behind them. When they awoke, Arnold took a few more photographs and began

Lieutenant Frank M. Brown, who died along with Captain William Lee Davidson, in the crash of a B-25 while investigating the Maury Island incident.

to ruminate over what he would tell Ray Palmer, the man who paid for this trip. Smith got into the bathtub when Arnold received a call from Crisman, at about 9:20 a.m., August 1. Crisman reported that the B-25 Davidson and Brown had left in had crashed and exploded at 1:30 that morning, killing both men.

Notes:

1. "FBI Drums Up Cymbals-Like 'Disk' in Idaho," *Tacoma News Tribune*, July 12, 1947.
2. "Idaho Found Disc Gets Hush-Hush," *East Oregonian*, July 11, 1947, p. 1. In the previous day's paper, the *East Oregonian* reported on a "metal saucer, 30 inches in diameter" that was found in a geranium bed at the North Hollywood, California home of construction engineer Russell Long. The FBI in this case also intervened and turned the disc over to the military. Long had first called the fire department, however, and fire battalion chief Wallace Newcombe exhibited it to the press. A reporter gave this description of that disk: "A radio tube on top was set down into the saucer which was about 5 inches thick at the middle and tapered to a thin perimeter. there were wires leading to a plug embedded in the center of the lower half. There was a rudder type wing on the top." ("LA Resident Finds Saucer In Flower Bed," *East Oregonian*, July 10, 1947, p. 1.)
3. "Boy-Made Discs Puzzled FBI," *East Oregonian*, July 12, 1947, p. 1. This article said that the device was put together by the boys in two days "from parts of an old phonograph, burned out radio tubes and other discarded electrical parts. It had a plexiglass dome, radio tubes, burned wires and glistening gold and silver sides."
4. Fensterwald, Bernard, *Coincidence or Conspiracy?*, New York: Kensington, 1977, pp. 225-227.
5. LeRoy, Rev. Robert, *Alarming Cry Newspaper* and various tracts, published in Langley, Washington, 1992-1998.
6. DiEugenio, James, *Destiny Betrayed: JFK, Cuba and the Garrison Case*, New York: Sheridan Square Press, 1992, p. 38-39.
7. "Subversion in Racial Unrest," Hearings of Louisiana Joint Legislative Committee, 10:00 a.m., Court of Appeals, Fourth Floor, Louisiana State Capitol Building, Baton Rouge, Louisiana, March 7, 1957, p. 5.

8.   "Subversion in Racial Unrest," Hearings of Louisiana Joint Leg-
      islative Committee, 10:00 a.m., Court of Appeals, Fourth Floor,
      Louisiana State Capitol Building, Baton Rouge, Louisiana, March
      7, 1957, p. 10.
          Banister also gave to the committee more of a view of the
      kinds of problems he faced while working in the Pacific North-
      west: "I recall one outbreak of 'hoof and mouth disease' which
      occurred in dairy herds in Canada. Legally, it was not possible
      to establish that it was done—planted there. But an intelligence
      officer is never quite satisfied with a legal definition. And I have
      talked to many men. You can't be certain. We can't be certain
      that the man who was supposed to have taken it there was the one
      who actually did. Someone else could have put it there. We have
      the example of the 'wheat stem rust' which hit Durham wheat in
      Eastern Montana and Western Dakota— the kind of wheat where
      we get our macaroni. That was an upflare. In that case I talked to
      the nation's leading plant pathologists in that field. We don't
      know where those spores came from. They trapped them at 15,000
      feet in the air. Maybe it's a test run. We don't know. Maybe it's
      natural. But we must be suspicious now. We can't afford to pass
      it off as natural, as an example."
          Banister also had a role in the FBI investigation of Kenneth
      Arnold. His name has been redacted from the relevant Freedom
      of Information documents. Ron Halbritter notes that the names
      of Special Agents in Charge (SACs) of Seattle and Portland,
      while redacted, were nevertheless recovered by diligent research-
      ers from mentions missed by the FBI. The agency did not miss
      any references to Banister, however, and Banister's link went
      untold until the emergence of the 30 inch disk news item.
          A sketch of Banister's UFO appeared on the front page of
      the July 11, 1947 edition *Twin Falls Times*, a newspaper in Twin
      Falls, Idaho. Of the sketch, researcher Steve Gaal writes "Please
      note the hooked areas. [The circles on either end of the craft.]
      This is a Mogul Project (1947 Mogul, not later Mogul), not mini-
      electrogravitics. Mogul 1947 version may have delivered biolo-
      gies to incite Uncle Joe for Cold War." Correspondence with
      author, 1997.
9.   Sofian, Terry, "UFOs and Fugos," in *Popular Alienation: A
      Steamshovel Press Reader*, Lilburn, GA: IllumiNet Press, 1995,
      p. 131. Sofian points out that the Fugo balloon project was halted
      in March 1945 and that "the mechanics of the balloon…would
      have made it impossible to remain aloft for two years." Still, the
      acknowledged casualties of an exploded Fugo balloon bomb, a
      woman and five children, happened in Lakeview, Oregon in May

1945. Compare the 1947 news descriptions of the 30 inch disks to Sofian's description of the Fugos: "The aerostatic platform consisted of a gas bag or envelope...a small mechanical device linked paired ballast bags with a gas release valve...rubbered silk balloons carried radio equipment to help determine the effectiveness of the weapons. They could be tracked to their targets by long range radio receivers."

10. According to Arnold's earliest recollection, he first called Lieutenant Frank M. Brown. Also according to that story, when Smith and Arnold returned to Hotel Winthrop, Smith and Crisman took off together somewhere and Arnold was alone in room 502 when Lt. Brown called back. "The Mystery of the Flying Discs...A Proof of the Shaver Mystery..." *The Shaver Mystery Magazine*, Volume II, No. 1, 1948., p. 38.

11. *What Happened in Room 502?*, p. 19-20.

12. *What Happened in Room 502?*, p. 22

13. *Coming of the Saucers*, pp. 44-45.

14. Arnold spelled the name "Lance."

15. The *Tacoma Times*, July 7, 1947, p. 1; "'Saucers Seen In Tacoma,'" *The Tacoma News-Tribune*, July 8, 1947, p. 1.

The *Tacoma News Tribune* reported that another witness in South Tacoma had called in excitedly that same night to report he had witnessed the same UFO show.

Caught up in that summer's UFO flap, the *Tacoma News Tribune* did what it could to calm its hyped-up readership. Even before the reports became more localized, it filled its columns with debunking mythology. The paper ran the explanation of an unnamed source at California Institute of Technology that the discs had something to do with "the transmutation of atomic energy" ("Air Discs Baffle Nation," July 6, 1947). Dr. Harold Urey responded to this by noting, "You can transmute metals, not energy."

Two days later, the *News Tribune* reported the theory that the UFOs were "clouds of flying gases discharged from airplane exhausts," which the paper attributed to former public works commissioner J. W. Silver ("Tacomans Give Answer, Advice On Flying Disk," July 8, 1947.) That story included also a letter from reader Birtley A. Ball anticipating that a saucer or debris would soon be recovered. "If some substance were available which could continue to expand and push against the air (for motive power), I could make a concave disk of plastic and magnesium foil and mount the power substance in capsules with jets pointed tangentially and slightly downward: the disk would have several radial slits, bent to climb when rotated."

Over the next several days, the *News Tribune* published a satirical column about the saucer flap ("Zounds! Hal Boyle Kidnapped by Crew of Mars' *Flying Saucer*," July 9, 1947; "Hal Boyle Gets Down To Earth; Sabotages Mars 'Flying Saucer'," July 10, 1947.) It also included news stories intended to make the topic look ridiculous ("Juggler Accounts For 'Saucers': He Misjuggled Some," July 9, 1947, p. 4; "Saucer Silly Folks Fail To Bother G-Men," July 10, 1947, p. 1; "Disk Calls Mount, Reporters Disk-Happy," July 10, 1947, p. 20; "Down To Earth People Think Little of Disks," July 13, 1947), helping create a circus atmosphere around Arnold's investigation. It reported the Guy Banister connection to the 30 inch disk in Butte ("FBI Drums Up Cymbals-Like 'Disk' in Idaho," July 11, 1947), but in the follow- up cover story noted that the four boys who supposedly made the small disk were "laughing up their sleeves" ("Idaho's Disk Is Brain Child of Four Lads," July 13, 1947, p. 3.) The story followed more satire by writer Hal Boyle.

The *News Tribune* reassuringly reported the Roswell weather balloon cover story, the first of what became three "official" explanations from the US Air Force over time. However, that report also included rancher W. W. Brazel's cryptic remark (after a brow-beating from the military, according to lore) that "If I find anything else short of a bomb it's going to be hard to get me to talk." ("Found Disk Just Balloon," July 10, 1947).

The *News Tribune* also ran two reports about the airport into which Kenneth Arnold had flown ("Oswald Flying Service Is Well Equipped," July 13, 1947; "Tacoma Flying Service Long Established," July 27, 1947.)

16. The proceedings of the First International UFO Congress in Chicago in 1977 quote Arnold as saying, "I no longer have motion-picture equipment. Someone broke into my hangar and stole it, but I've still got all my films." (p. 370) Nevertheless, the films have never emerged.

17. Pobst, p. 33.

18. *Coming of the Saucers*, p. 51

6

...AND SPINS...

The Air Force had suffered its first UFO casualties on the very day it gained recognition as an independent branch of U.S. military service. Davidson and Brown had died trying to return to McChord Field for Air Force celebrations, a Kellogg's Cornflakes box or something similar, filled with saucer slag, in tow.[1] As the details began to emerge in the press, the new Air Force surely understood that it also had a serious public relations problem.

"Sabotage Hinted In Crash of Army Bomber!" blared the headline of the *Tacoma Times* story on the B-25 crash.[2] Paul Lantz, who had approached Arnold and Smith at the hotel, wrote the story. It included reference to Major George Sander, who had previously done public relations work for General Carl Spaatz, and who had pumped Davidson and Brown for information after their meetings

IDENTIFY TWO AIR VICTIMS

McCHORD FIELD, Aug. 2.—*P*— The pilot and co-pilot of an air force B-25 bomber based at Hamilton field, Calif., were killed in a fiery crash yesterday and two other occupants of the aircraft were saved when they parachuted to earth.

Coroner Gordon Quarnstrom of Cowlitz county reported the dead were Capt. William L. Davidson, pilot, and Lt. Frank M. Brown, co-pilot.

News report of the B-25 crash.

with Arnold, Smith, Dahl and Crisman and again before the fatal flight. Sander told the reporter that Davidson and Brown left in the B-25, flight #1316, with classified material. Lantz took this to mean the UFO slag.

Davidson and Brown were joined on flight 1316 by a hitchhiker, a young sergeant from Texas named Elmer T. Taff. Taff survived the crash to tell the tale of how the B-25's left engine ignited into flame over the Columbia River, near Kelso-Longview. Crew chief Woodrow Matthews helped both Taff and Davidson put on parachutes as an attempt was made to land in a nearby field. Eyewitnesses on the ground described the engine fire as "flares going off."[3] Taff recalled being pushed out of the plane at 10,000 feet, a memory verified by Matthews but contradicted by official investigators because of how far the pair landed from the B-25. Matthews also reported that just before the crash Davidson insisted on staying aboard longer for the sake of his classified mission, and Brown's escape had been blocked by one of the wings, which had broken off. Taff described a footlocker of material being put aboard before take-off, not a Cornflakes box.

Brown's body was found in the wreckage and Davidson's was found thirty feet away, respectively, by a team of nine people including a photographer. The survivors had made it to distances of a half-mile and fifty yards, and wound up at the farm of Fred Renner. George Sander was among the people who questioned the pair when they were brought back to McChord Air Force Base.

It took a day to find the bodies of the two A2 men amidst the wreckage. The footlocker and/or Cornflakes box was never recovered, although a Counterintelligence Corps team was dispatched to the scene. Following the incident, the Air Force set policy to report the movement or disappearance of similar classified material to the office of Foreign Technology.[4] Interestingly, in 1997 retired army colonel Philip Corso identified the Foreign Technology desk as the office that parceled out alien technology back-engineered from the Roswell spaceship crash.[5] Davidson's remains were buried in San Francisco and Brown's were sent to Long Beach.

Kenneth Arnold and Emil Smith worked the phones for information on the Davidson and Brown crash as they waited for Fred Crisman to show up for their prearranged Maury Island sojourn. Smith called McChord Field to verify what Crisman had reported, then made another call to Ted Morello for details. He made arrangements to exchange info with Morello after they were debriefed by the Air Force.

Arnold called Ray Palmer and talked to him for the first time on the phone, distraught that his involvement of the two A2 officers led to their deaths, concerned over his own safety and that of his family, and generally put out by all the rest of the high strangeness he had encountered. These deaths were the final straw in this investigation for Arnold; he had called Palmer to tell him that he was off the case, and would send the $200 back to him. As Palmer tried to calm him, Fred Crisman came into the room. Palmer convinced Arnold to hold onto the money and asked to talk to Crisman.

According to Arnold, "Later Raymond Palmer told me that he recognized Crisman's voice. He was positive that it was the same voice that had called him long distance on other occasions from various parts of the country. Brother, what a mess."[6] Emil Smith took the phone briefly to express his angst to Palmer. When he returned it, Palmer agreed with Arnold that the investigation should end, but that Arnold should keep the money. It happened to be Palmer's birthday, and the conversation ended with well wishes from Arnold to him. Arnold remained a nice guy despite his edginess.

Morello failed to talk Smith into coming to his office to await debriefing by the Air Force. Instead, the men continued to make calls from the room and readied themselves for the trip to Maury Island, still on despite Palmer's advice. Emil Smith made contact with a friend at the *Chicago Tribune*, Maurice Roddy, to tell of the link between the Davidson and Brown crash and the investigation of Crisman and Dahl, but the newspaper declined pending Air Force confirmation. (When Roddy called back the following day, he explained that the *Tribune* was working on the story, particularly emphasizing Ray Palmer and his *Venture Press*. The paper was still waiting for a quote from "Ptooey" Spaatz.) Smith's contact at McChord called back to make sure Smith and Arnold would be around for questioning about it all later.

The three men were joined for lunch by Harold Dahl. Dahl was as guilt-ridden and befuddled as the others over Davidson and Brown, but he reassured Arnold and Smith that they had nothing to worry about. Davidson and Brown had said the same thing, but now the stakes were higher in terms of possible criminal charges stemming from the deaths of the two airmen.

The group spent the next several hours reviewing the circumstance of their acquaintance. A break came when they received a note under the hotel room door that service personnel at the Winthrop were about to go on strike. The strike bothered Arnold because it threatened phone service, and they were all doing little other than waiting for calls. He got an assurance from the front desk that any important calls would still be patched through. By then, the men had given up idea of going to Maury Island. Crisman and Dahl left.

When Morello called again that evening, he asked once more if Smith and Arnold might come over, perhaps the following day. This time, he told them his anonymous informant now claimed that Davidson and Brown's B-25 had been blown out of the air by a 20mm cannon, and that the same cannon had aimed at, and missed flights by both Smith in Montana and Arnold in Oregon. According to the informant, similar sabotage was involved in the downing of a passenger transport that killed singer Grace Moore in Copenhagen, and another one the previous May at LaGuardia airport. Additionally, the informant said that military intelligence would call in Smith to Wright-Patterson for interrogation on August 5. Recall that the same informant had a remarkably accurate track record in keeping Morello posted about the goings on in the hotel room.

This time, however, the informant was dead wrong, as Arnold determined later: "This is what I later found out about the above predictions. Captain Smith told me that he was not called to Wright-Patterson nor was he interrogated by Military Intelligence. If either of our planes were shot at in the air it was something of which we were unaware. The official military explanation of the B-25 bomber was that it was simply an accident caused by the loss of an exhaust collector ring on the left engine...Regarding the prediction that Captain Smith's airliner had been shot at over Montana, that was wrong as he did not fly over Montana. Concerning the airline crash on take-off at LaGuardia Field, about a month after this it was determined by the Civil Aeronautics Administration and their investigators that the gust locks had been left on accidentally. I was unable to find any official explanation of the Copenhagen crash."[7] Still, the details of the predictions were enough to seriously pique the interests of Arnold and Smith at the time.

Morello also claimed mysteriously that he had a recording the two men would like to hear, but he gave no details. The two men agreed to meet with Morello the next day.

Recall also that Morello had been the point man for an earlier flying saucer tale similar in many details to the Maury Island incident, and his relationship with this extremely well-informed informant was never fully understood. Despite genuine mystery that still surrounds his role in the story, Morello, in time, became an early debunker of the Maury Island affair, especially with regard to Kenneth Arnold. Morello came to regard Arnold not as an honest but deluded nice guy, or as a hoaxer, but simply as paranoid. Ironically, if that characterization of Arnold fit at all, it certainly was in part because of Morello's own actions.

Details of Ted Morello's involvement with the Maury Island players and his personal perspective emerged from obscurity with the 1998 publication of a 1950 dissertation by Morello's friend DeWayne Johnson.[8] Johnson quotes Morello himself in discussing an earlier meeting with Arnold and Smith: "During the entire course of the interview Arnold, particularly, was extremely jumpy. He questioned us closely about hidden dictaphones and, not satisfied with our assurance that none was planted, made a personal investigation of the tiny office. However, he did not discover that the intercom had been converted into a microphone…Throughout the interview he (Arnold) sat at the desk on which the intercom rested and drummed the tabletop with a paperweight. Subsequent playing of the records showed the drumming had nearly drowned out many portions of the conversation."[9]

Similarly, when Arnold re-contacted Morello a year later to inquire about the death of reporter Paul Lantz, Morello scoffed at Arnold's legitimate concerns—about Lantz and Morello's own early resignation from UPI—but took $20 from him to provide a written report.[10]

In 1947, however, Arnold and Smith made their rendezvous with Morello the next day as planned. The recording that Morello had for them was of Elmer Taff, the hitchhiking sergeant who had barely escaped the grisly fate of Davidson and Brown. Taff recounted the crash experience, emphasizing how heavy the UFO slag was and how it was packed in a large footlocker. The details mattered less to Smith and Arnold than the artifact of the wire recording presented to them by Morello. How did he get such a high quality recording? He answered that he got it off the phone. He was unable to explain how his phone call got past military security. He also had no explanation as to why he never recorded the mysterious informant who was keeping him apprised of activity at the Winthrop hotel. Finally, Morello had words of admonition for the pair before they left. He said that Davidson and Brown's plane had been under surveillance while they were interviewing Crisman and Dahl, and that all should leave town before the details of their real mission emerged in the press. Arnold and Smith left shaking their heads.

Back at the hotel, Smith wrote some letters and Arnold phoned and cabled family to reassure them that he was all right, but succeeded only in worrying them more. Smith also talked on the phone to Dave Johnson at the *Idaho Statesman* and Maurice Roddy at the *Chicago Tribune*, telling them the story thus far but reporting that they only had six pieces of the UFO slag when the room actually was littered with them. Arnold started pacing, puffing cigarettes and even stepped out to get a copy of Ray Palmer's *Amazing Stories* pulp magazine.

The next day he and Smith tired of waiting to get debriefed by the military. Smith made one last attempt to get in touch with Intelligence at McChord and decided to resume trying to get to Maury Island. Harold Dahl called at about noon and asked them to come out for lunch. They met in a small St. Helen's restaurant, and before too long Crisman showed up. The group hopped in Crisman's car and drove to the pier.

Crisman did not have the photos of the boat he claimed he had, and he had failed to bring the copy of "Venture Magazine"—a non-existent Ray Palmer title—he had promised Arnold. Nevertheless, he fast-talked his way through the trip to the pier and, along with Dahl, took Smith and Arnold on board the North Queen. He pointed out damage to the rail and windows, but nothing that looked like the product of a full scale assault of saucer slag. Arnold filmed the entire scene. Crisman suddenly remembered that his photos were in his mountain cabin and offered to take the pair up there. They declined and had Dahl take them back to the hotel. Their last image of Crisman had him waving goodbye from the dock.

Dahl dropped them off at the hotel and went to a movie serial. Waiting again for some kind of debriefing from the Air Force, the pair received a call from Ted Morello. Morello's anonymous informant had told him that Crisman had been taken to a military prison in Alaska aboard an Air Force transport plane. As unbelievable as it seemed, since they had just waved to Crisman from the Puget Sound dock, Smith verified with McChord that a transport had left for Alaska. He could not get a passenger list, however. Smith worried that Dahl might also turn up missing, and he and Arnold made several unsuccessful calls to various movie houses to locate him. When Dahl finally returned to the hotel room, he did not seem overly concerned about Crisman's fate. Crisman could take care of himself, said Dahl, and the military could talk to the remaining three any time they wanted.

Dahl invited them to lunch the next day. Smith and Arnold were left flabbergasted again. They made one visit to the Sky Harbor to make sure Arnold's plane had not been sabotaged, and then ended another confused day.

Dahl showed up the next day with a letter from Crisman, saying that Crisman had voluntarily disappeared, leaving Dahl to tend to the remaining business about the Maury Island incident. Dahl only reported this to Smith and Arnold; he did not show them the letter. He drove them south, to a favorite restaurant for their latest lunch engagement. Dahl was accompanied by his secretary, the 40 year old widow that Arnold had encountered during their first meeting. The only thing keeping Smith and Arnold from returning to their regularly scheduled lives at this point was the desire to tell authorities everything that happened to them involving the Maury Island incident. At the restaurant, Smith tried to phone an FBI acquaintance named Bobbit to no avail, and then placed a call to Major George Sander, the Carl Spaatz operative who seemed to be keeping close tabs on the story. Sander had been there to question the survivors of the Davidson and Brown crash. He arranged to meet Sander, but only after Dahl had returned them. Dahl drove them back to the hotel after dropping his woman companion off at her home. Smith made his contact and met with Sander without informing Arnold.

Smith finally got to download the information he had been carrying concerning the incident to Sander. He met Sander at a diner determined in the previous phone call, and told him all he knew. Sander suggested that the Cornflakes box of UFO slag had not figured prominently in the crash of Davidson's and Brown's plane. Nevertheless, he wanted to see the fragments left at the hotel.

Smith took Sander back to the Winthrop Hotel. It had been his plan to give his version of the Maury Island story without letting Arnold know and then have Arnold tell his version independently. Arnold, as anxious to unload as Smith, told all he knew, corroborating all that Smith had volunteered. After taking it all in, Sander suggested that Crisman and Dahl might have been perpetuating a hoax but that it would take time to determine that for certain. He collected slag fragments for testing.

He asked for secrecy from the two airmen and promised that a full report would be sent to them by A2
Military Intelligence of the Fourth Air Force. The B-25
crash of Davidson and Brown, Sander reassured them,
was just a tragic accident. "It's too bad that a misleading
story was printed in the newspaper." Arnold was almost
totally relieved: "Right there I looked at Captain Smith.
We knew that the story, if it was misleading, was so
from only one standpoint—that no definite proof had
been established regarding the possible sabotage of the
B-25. We were so blamed happy we let this remark go.
At last we felt free to leave Tacoma and go home."[11]

Sander had one more adventure for them, however.
After insisting on taking every piece of the slag—something that also caught Arnold's suspicion—he told the
men to get in his car. He drove them to a spot on the
peninsula near Maury Island, the site of something called
the Tacoma Smelting Company. Piles of lava-like smelter
slag surrounded the area. The slag looked like the fragments Smith and Arnold had been handling the past several days, but it did not feel the same. "I can't very well
explain or demonstrate the difference in the feel of things
such as this," Arnold later reported in his book. "To
give you an idea as to how I evaluated this in my mind,
close your eyes and have someone hand you a rock, a
piece of brass, a piece of steel, a piece of aluminum, and
a piece of copper. If you try this, as I have many times,
you will notice that each one of these items has a particular feel to your fingers. It is something that your memory
of feelings retains."[12]

Sanders clearly wanted Smith and Arnold to believe
that their slag came from here; Arnold even suggested
that Sanders might have tried to hypnotize them into this
belief.[13] Despite their great desire for closure on the Maury
Island incident, Smith and Arnold could not so easily
dismiss all of the events of the past several days as an

elaborate hoax. They were ready to move on, but Arnold at least regretted that Sander would not let them compare the smelter slag with the UFO slag directly. He was unconvincing when he told Sander that he believed him. Having now been debriefed by a military figure, as they had wanted, albeit unsatisfactorily, Arnold and Smith returned to the Winthrop Hotel and checked out. Smith planned to take Arnold to his plane at the airport and then drive home himself. The two men agreed that they should say goodbye to Harold Dahl first, and so detoured to the house of Dahl's woman companion, where Dahl said he would be working for the rest of the day.

When they arrived, they found a house that "looked completely deserted and as if it had not been lived in for months."[14] A befuddled Arnold observed "there wasn't a stick of furniture inside, just dust, dirt and cobwebs everywhere." Smith became uncharacteristically quiet,[15] with no explanation about the mystery house and the disappearance of Dahl, his "secretary," her children and all of the furniture. The pair was in no mood to open a new avenue of investigation, however.

Smith continued with Arnold on to the Sky Harbor airport. He made one last gesture of shared paranoia by looking over the Callair and making sure it had not been sabotaged. Arnold looked down on Captain Smith as he took off for Boise, Idaho, with a pit stop planned at Pendleton, Oregon, to gas the plane. After refueling at Pendleton, he took off again, only to have his engine go dead at 50 feet. He maneuvered the plane back on the runway but bent its landing gear and broke its left spar in the process. A small crowd gathered as Arnold got out his plane to examine the problem. His fuel valve had been shut off, and the only possible suspect was himself, although he had no recollection of doing it, no reason for it and was not in the habit of shutting the valve. The events at Maury Island had made Arnold a cautious man, however, and he told no one of the cause. "The realization that my thought or mind in some peculiar way was being controlled or dictated to," he later confessed, "or that it could have caused this to happen would seem perfectly preposterous to anyone who had not experienced what I had just experienced."[16]

Notes:

1. Paris Flammonde notes, "The plane crash killing Brown and Davidson was within the UFO gestalt, but there was no testimony that an unknown ever approached the ship in which they went down." (*UFO Exist!*, p. 218.)

    Captain Thomas F. Mantell, Jr. holds distinction as the most widely accepted first fatal UFO encounter victim in the U.S. Air Force. The 25-year-old National Guardsman and two others were ordered to fly their F-51s to investigate an unknown over the skies near Standiford Field, north of Godman Air Force Base in Louisville, Kentucky, on January 7, 1948. The two others turned tail at 15,000 feet, but Mantell continued to pursue. As he approached 20,000 feet (at the same altitude as TWA Flight 800, which crashed under mysterious circumstances, including UFO sightings), he reported "I see something above and ahead of me" and may have also reported "I've sighted the thing. It looks metallic and it's tremendous in size...Oh my God, there are men in it!" His plane crashed shortly thereafter, and Mantell was killed.

2. "Sabotage Hinted In Crash of Army Bomber At Kelso," *Tacoma Times,* August 2, 1947, p. 1.

3. *Room 502,* p. 37

4. *Room 502,* p. 38

5. "In 1961, regardless of the differences in the Roswell story from many different sources who had described it, the top-secret file of Roswell information came into my possession when I took over the Foreign Technology desk at [the U.S. Army's Research and Development department]. My boss, General Trudeau, asked me to use the army's ongoing weapon's development and research program as a way to filter the Roswell technology into the mainstream of industrial development through the military defense program." Corso, Philip with Birnes, William J., *The Day After Roswell,* Toronto: Pocket Books, 1997, p. 4. Corso also discusses the role played by Army Counterintelligence in the Roswell event. He makes no mention of Maury Island, however.

6. *Coming of the Saucers,* p. 59.

7. *Coming of the Saucers*, p. 64.
8. Johnson, DeWayne, *Flying Saucers Over Los Angeles*, with introductory material by Kenn Thomas, Adventures Unlimited Press, 1998. Johnson's dissertation provides a full history of UFO lore from 1947 to 1950. It remained hidden in UCLA files until research on this book led to its rediscovery and publication. Johnson identifies Morello as an "intimate friend...whose integrity is fully respected by the author," despite the fact that he reveals for the first time that Morello surreptitiously recorded a conversation with Arnold and Smith. "The records, never intended for public release, were to be kept in a secure place until the possible significance of the information vanished."
9. This passage demonstrates that Morello was a secret taper, a liar and a braggart about his covert skills. Arnold, on the other hand, shows great skill at interfering with being spied upon, although the effort comes to no avail. Morello acknowledged that "handling of the saucer-plane crash episode had been secretive and often contradictory. For the first few days after the crash, I am convinced, McChord was as much in the dark as we were. Later McChord officials were unable to speak because Fourth Air Force headquarters at Hamilton Field had taken over. Whatever material was gathered by McChord officers was sent to Hamilton for release by officials there.

"General (Ned) Schramm finally admitted the two Air Force officers had been investigating flying disc reports. But 48 hours earlier he had denied flatly that the officers' mission to McChord Field was in any way connected with Smith and Arnold."

The closest that Johnson comes to uncovering the identity of Ted Morello's mysterious informant is in his report that Morello's assistant, Ann Shephard, found that Fred Crisman had been in conference with local prosecutor Patrick M. Seele and the McChord Field public relations officer George Sander. Shepherd, however, says she learned this "through sources" that remain unidentified.
10. FSOLA, p. 87
11. *Coming of the Saucers*, p. 76.
12. *Coming of the Saucers*, p. 78.
13. *Coming of the Saucers* includes this description of Sanders: "Maybe Major Sander was not conscious of what Captain Smith and I mentally said to one another. I thought, 'This Major Sander is a pretty smooth guy, but he's not smooth enough at this point to convince me that these fragments aren't pretty important in some way.' I suddenly felt that no one had played a hoax on anybody! I thought, 'Major Sander is a phony dressed up in a lot of sheer intelligence as to how psychologically to handle men.' (p. 77)

14. *Coming of the Saucers*, p. 80.
15. The FBI memo of August 18, 1947 states that Dahl drove Smith and Arnold to this house to pick up his secretary in the morning for their breakfast meeting. This visit from earlier that same day makes the suddenly empty house all the more mysterious, and Smith's silent and confused manner all the more understandable.
16. *Coming of the Saucers*, p. 84. Steve Gaal asserts that "Kenneth Arnold's second sighting was MK (that is, part of the MKULTRA brainwashing program), as he himself suspected. He turned off his own airplane gas!"

7
LIFE OF CRISMAN

As noted, Kenneth Arnold became a UFO celebrity, but he primarily went back to selling fire control supplies, and for a while in the 1950s became a uranium prospector. He ran unsuccessfully as an Eisenhower Republican for Lieutenant Governor of Idaho in 1962 and for Congress in 1966. He died outside of Seattle in 1984.

Kenneth Arnold with Dwight D. Eisenhower, 1962. Arnold ran for Idaho's Lieutenant Governor's office that year.

Captain Emil Smith resumed his career, eventually working air traffic control at Kennedy Airport in New York before retiring to Florida.

Arnold tried to make phone contact with Harold Dahl again but to no avail. Public record seems to indicate that Dahl did remain in Tacoma, that he sublet a house to the owner of a typewriter rental office, and that he once operated a gun shop with a federal export license. He also sold antique furniture and at one time, and owned a plane, even though he never had a pilot's license. Harold Dahl died in Tacoma in 1980.

F. L. CRISMAN
Subpoened

Tacoma News Tribune, November 1, 1968.

The journalists of the story followed conventional paths. Ted Morello wound up teaching journalism at the University of Washington and then found work in the television industry. The writer Paul Lantz died in January of the following year, not in the following weeks as Arnold later suspected and others repeated, but nevertheless leaving the suspicion that his death might have been connected with his Maury Island reportage. The official cause of Lantz's death was meningitis.

Fred Crisman, however, led a long, complex and very public life after ostensibly vanishing aboard an Army bomber following the Maury Island events, "a flight no civilian could have boarded" as Arnold noted.[1] He would, in fact, leave a biographical trail connecting his earliest-of-all modern UFO experiences at Maury Island (or the manipulation of his fantasy about same), through the most significant political event of contemporary American politics of the 1960s—the JFK assassination—and into the still-current parapolitical landscape.

The public record fills in basic details about Fred Crisman's life, but the line between historic record and Crisman's braggadocio blurs early. His social security records reflect that he was born on July 22, 1919,[2] and an application to the Atomic Energy Commission notes that he attended Vale High School in Vale, Oregon in 1939 and 1940. It also claims that he attended Eastern Oregon College in LaGrande, Oregon, although that has been disputed.[3] Political ads from 1946 claimed that he attended law school at the University of Oregon, which had no law school. In 1941 he married Filomena Veristain and they had a daughter, Chris. That year, He also worked as a fireman on the Union Pacific Railway, although an A2 report says he was an "oil technician" while previous to working with the Criminal Investigation Division in Washington state.

Again according to the 1946 political ads, Crisman enlisted into army service on May 26, 1942 for a four year career. As a captain in the Army Air Corps, he spent nearly two years in China, Burma, India and the Pacific as a second air commando fighter pilot. According to the ads, he flew 211 combat missions, was wounded twice and was shot down twice.

He separated from the Army Air Force on February 19, 1946 and went to work for the State Department of Veteran's Affairs the following month, a job that ended March 31, 1947. In May, 1946 he campaigned unsuccessfully as a Democrat for the office of Pierce County Coroner. After his defeat, he returned to Vale and began teaching at the junior college.

Crisman's letters to *Amazing Stories* began appearing the next month. The first described his submachine gun versus laser ray battle against the deros near Burma. His second letter, responding to the *Harper's Magazine* criticism and describing another deros encounter ending in the death of his companion "Dick," appeared in May 1947.

Three months later he ostensibly disappeared to Alaska (and/or Greenland, according to some accounts) after the events at Maury Island. Yet, he and Harold Dahl gave statements about Maury Island to the FBI on August 8, statements that led the Fourth Air Force headquarters to revoke his Air Force Reserve Commission as "an undesirable and unreliable officer."

Nevertheless, Crisman used the GI Bill to return to college, where he received a Bachelor's Degree from Willamette University in Salem, Oregon, in 1950 and was listed as the president of the Oregon Student Association the previous year.

He made an application through the Atomic Energy Commission on August 21, 1947, but it remains unclear what became of it. The Atomic Energy Commission protected the secrets of atomic power and bombs, and as such, reigned over the processing of plutonium.

It is possible that the Maury Island UFOs—or something else—may have been dumping radioactive waste illegally in the bay at the behest of the AEC. The threats that the Man in Black made against Dahl, therefore, could have been an attempt to cover up the illegal dumping Dahl had witnessed. Dahl's photos had been fogged, as if exposed to radioactivity. His son Charles' burns and the death of the family dog could have been due to radiation as well.

The Hanford nuclear processing plant in Washington state served as an old war-horse for a fledging industry of atomic power and bombs. Its proximity raises interesting possibilities with regard to Maury Island. The Nagasaki bomb was manufactured at Hanford, where weapons-grade nuclear material was produced throughout the 1950s. It eventually had to be closed down due to radioactive contamination.

Writer Paul B. Thompson speculated that Crisman's military and intelligence cover thereafter may have been the beginning of "a lifelong stipend from the U.S. government" awarded to him for his role in preventing disclosure of illegal radioactive waste dumping at Maury Island.[4] The theory contrasts with another developed by researcher Ron Halbritter: that Crisman was rewarded for his cover-up of extra-terrestrial UFOs with life-long work among the spooks.[5]

Crisman next emerged in the letters page of *Fate* magazine in January 1950, responding to an earlier article that made the Maury Island affair out to be a hoax. Crisman makes the salient point that if he and Dahl had pulled such a dangerous and ultimately deadly prank they were inexplicably relieved of any culpability by authorities. "Why," Crisman asks, "if we were such blackguards...and deliberately caused the deaths of two Air Force pilots and the loss of a $150,000 airplane, did not the government or some agency there attempt to seek justice through the courts of the state and federal government?" Why indeed.

Despite the August 14, 1947 recommendation to revoke his flying status and Reserve commission, Crisman was recalled to active duty during the Korean war in 1950. He returned to his military career as a fighter pilot for the next two and a half years, and his family moved to Japan to join him. Anxiety attacks, apparently regarding visions of his own mortality and exacerbated by a growing dependence on barbiturates, caused him to be reassigned to fly transport planes back and forth from Korea and Japan. He left the service a second time on March 30, 1953 and spent the summer of 1953 in Ft. Belvior, Virginia, recovering from war wounds. Crisman eventually returned to teaching, this time at the high school in Elgin, Oregon.

After advancing to a position of school superintendent at a school near Huntington, Oregon, Crisman's fortunes began to take a downward turn. He was arrested for reckless driving under barbiturate intoxication, which led to his dismissal at the school. He lost a second job in the Tacoma school district. Shortly thereafter, his daughter died in a car accident and he divorced his wife. He underwent psychiatric treatment at Fort Stelicom, Washington.

Crisman's life began to normalize in the late 1950s, when he finished an education course at Pacific Lutheran University. His writing output also began to pick up, and he had an article published in *Flying Saucers* magazine in 1958, under the pseudonym "Eldon Everett."[6] He became a teacher again at White River School in Buckley, Washington, but he was forced to resign in June 1960. That same month he went to work for Boeing as a "roving personnel representative."

Much of Crisman's life prior to this public record comes in the form of rumor and secondary speculation. During World War II, for instance, he supposedly belonged to the Office of Strategic Services (OSS), a forerunner of the CIA, which included flying saucer prototypes; and so, if there was anything to the connection, this may have been the origin of Crisman's involvement with Maury Island.[7] More importantly, Crisman's OSS associates[8] may have included Clay Shaw, the New Orleans socialite prosecuted for involvement with the assassination of John Kennedy by that city's district attorney, Jim Garrison.

Shaw also belonged to the board of directors of Permindex, a group described variously as a shadowy, transnational corporate presence and "a CIA front company."[9] Other members of its board included an OSS major named Louis Bloomfield and Ferenc Nagy, the premier of Hungary overthrown by communists in 1947. Shaw's military service apparently did develop around his CIA/OSS involvement dating back to the late 1940s. According to writer, Shaw "had been in business with former Nazis and European fascists involved in several CIA-sponsored covert operations throughout Europe."[10]

Those covert activities included Paperclip, a spoils-of-war operation that

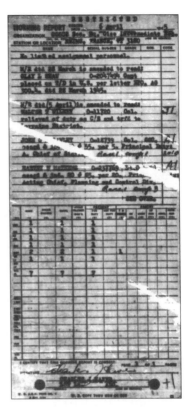

Exculpatory of Shaw? This never before published morning report from the Commanding General/General Staff section, Oise Intermemediate Sector, Communication Zone, European Theater of Operation shows that Shaw was placed on temporary duty in the U.S. as "per letter ETO, AG 300.4. dtd 28 March 1945." The morning report was amended to reflect this change, and no note of his return appears through June. Von Braun surrendered in May, 1945.

successfully transplanted top Nazi aerospace scientists into the American space program, along with scientific equipment and files on the Nazi rocket program rumored to include its occult and extraterrestrial origins. Werner Von Braun and Walter Dornberger were among the top Nazi rocket scientists so incorporated. They directed a team of 118 former Nazis stationed at Redstone Arsenal in Huntsville, Alabama, and became architects of the successful U.S. space program which ultimately landed men on the moon.

While many regarded these geniuses at rocketry as having been exploited by the Nazi state, their enthusiasm for Hitler's cause and their role in developing weapons of mass destruction ultimately stained the history of U.S. successes in space. Von Braun had been a major in Hitler's SS and not only developed the V2 rocket, which terrorized and killed thousands in the UK during World War II, but did it through the use of slave labor at the Nazi Nordhausen, Dora and Mittelwork concentration camps, where slaves were starved and exterminated by the hundreds.[11]

In 1945 Von Braun and the other Paperclip Nazis abandoned their rocket research facility at Peenemunde and surrendered to First Lieutenant Charles L. Stewart near the Austrian border. Among the other U.S. soldiers possibly connected to the event: Major Clay Shaw, who served as an aide to the deputy chief of European operations, General Charles O. Thrasher.[12]

The Crisman-Shaw connection first came to the attention of Jim Garrison—whose unsuccessful case against Shaw became the subject of much study, including a 1992 Hollywood movie, *JFK*, by director Oliver Stone[13]—when he received the following letter in early 1968:

ANNEX C (Cont'd)

On 7 January 1948, a ANG F-51 pilot was lost near Godman AFB, Kentucky. After being directed to lead his flight of four F-51s by the tower, Captain Thomas Mantell pursued a large metallic object alone after two pilots returned to Godman AFB, and finally his wingman was ordered to return to the field. It is believed that Mantell was following a large, structured object not in the flight path of a classified Navy SKYHOOK balloon. Mantell radioed Godman tower that he was at 22,000 feet and still climbing. At one point Mantell said that the object had paced his aircraft for several minutes, then would speed up. His last transmission to the tower was, "It appears to be a metallic object . . . and it is of tremendous size . . . It appears to be a metallic object or possibly the reflection of sun from a metallic object." When Godman personnel arrived at the crash scene, Mantell's F-51 was found in many pieces, not large sections as one would find from a free stick descent. The wreckage contained unusual damage as if Mantell's plane was repeatedly hit by shotgun blasts. Some of the metal had pitted surfaces and unusual scoring. All rubber material had disintegrated in a soft powdery substance. There was no indication of gunfire damage or foul burn. The crash site and debris exhibited an unusually high amount of radiation of undetermined nature. The site was cleared of debris and covered. Mantell's plane was subsequently sent to Wright-Patterson AFB, Ohio for examination. A autopsy was conducted on the body and interned in storage for future study. It is believed by the Air Force investigators that Mantell's plane had been destroyed by a ionization phenomena, possibly from the propulsion wash of the object's exhaust.

From 1949 to late 1950, there have been several crashes of B-36 bombers on routine arctic patrol that bear all the earmarks of the Mantell incident. None of the crews were found. The atomic bombs were not recovered, thus creating a serious problem for the Air Force when nuclear weapons are lost over friendly countries.

The death of two Air Force counterintelligence officers in the crash of their B-25 aircraft enroute to Hamilton AFB, California, after interviewing two auxiliary CG men who reported six UFOs over Maury Island, Washington, in June 1947. CIC agent Crisman had spoken to Kenneth Arnold, who on 26 June 1947, had reported a flight of UFOs over Mt. Rainier, Washington, and filed his report after he had spoken to Captain Davidson and Lieutenant Brown. The material given to Davidson and Brown was believed to come from Maury Island and may be celestial fragments containing metal from a nuclear reactor from a UFO. Fragments were turned over to CIA agent Shaw, and Crisman was ordered to the Alaskan ADC for assignment in Project IVY.

-11-

Dubious document? Art Bell posted this on his website, one among many newly-surfaced pages purportedly originating with the secret government/alien interface group, MJ12. Bell's source for this document, the International Space Sciences Organization of Santa Clara, CA, notes that it "strongly suggest[s] that you focus your energies on tying together the historical events and people described in the documents, rather than exclusively concentrating on the history of the pages themselves." Those historical events include the possibility that Fred Crisman worked for counter-intelligence, and that Clay Shaw received the Maury Island fragments.

Mr. G:

Out on the coast is a man you should talk with. Trace his information out. His name is Fred Lee Crisman, of Tacoma, Washington; he flys to New Orleans steadily. 1964, eleven times, 1965, 17 times, 1966, 32 times, 1967, 24 times. He is the first man that Bechham called also. He was questioned by both CIA and FBI in 1966 but he is able to call Wash. and they laid off of him in a hurry. He is very good friends with the Cubans and specially S.A. in Dallas (he goes there too) and J. R. in New O. [handwritten margin notes: Jorge Rodriguez and Arnesto Rodriguez]

Mr. Crisman is a very odd man. He supplied the money for certain political campaigns and in return is very much protected by both Lou. politicos and Wash. state people. He has a diplomatic passport issued on the word of a senate chairman of a committee. He seems to have no income and certainly spends a large sum of money on air travel. He is friends with F. Gremillion of your state. His private office has an unlisted number (206 Ma7-4790) and it is the meeting place for many odd characters from Cubans to political figures. Ask him take a lie detector test and then ask him where he put the $200,000.00 dollars delivered to him by Beckham in August of '67 (Cuban money). Money that is used to recruit killers to be sent to Cuba to try for Castro. Ask him if it is not true that he has sent 5 different men to S.A. in Dallas for final briefing. Make Crisman talk and you will have the answer to why there has been fighting among certain Cuban factions over the money in certain buried places. You know this is true because some special Cubans have dropped out of sight (Dropped in Torpedo Junction). Crisman is also a pilot. He is the man that through Beckham and S.A. paid off certain people. Is it not odd that he is a friend of Clay's as well as Beckham. Is it not strange that he knew Tippit! Just ask Crisman certain questions under a lie detector and see what the answers are. He is the one that advised Mark Evans to hide out in

Iowa and NOT to go to N.O. to make any statement about money or anything. Have an investigator check out the amount of long distance calls that Beckham (Evans) has made to Crisman in the past year and the wild places Crisman calls. He is leaving for Europe in Jan. Keep digging, Jim, you have some odd fish on the run.
[handwritten: D. White (Army) is listed at same address (Man = Ft. Lewis); Photo of Fred Crisman]

The letter's origin[14] remains obscure, but it did list known participants in the conspiracy that Garrison pursued. "Arnesto" or Ernesto Rodriquez, for instance, was one of Lee Harvey Oswald's contacts at the Cuban embassy in Mexico City,[15] and introduced to him to an anti-Castro exile activist.[16] These Oswald connections, both pro and anti Castro, put Crisman at the heart of the ambiguities faced by Garrison surrounding his pursuit of justice in the assassination case. The letter also mentions a large amount of "Cuban money"—a reference perhaps to money from Fidel Castro[17] but apparently used to recruit possible assassins of the Cuban dictator.

Garrison's interest may have predated the letter, however, and may have reached all the way back to Maury Island. Like Crisman, Garrison had fought in World War II and was reactivated for Korea. In between, he worked for a short time with the FBI in the Pacific northwest,[18] apparently at the time of the Maury Island incident and evidently with Guy Banister, the agent who recovered the 30 inch saucer near that time who also would later be intimately connected with Lee Harvey Oswald. Garrison, in fact, discussed his FBI service in his biography, *On the Trail of the Assassins*:

"Upon my return to civilian life after World War II, I followed my family tradition and went to law school at Tulane, obtaining both Bachelor of Laws and Master of Civil degrees. Shortly thereafter I joined the FBI. As a

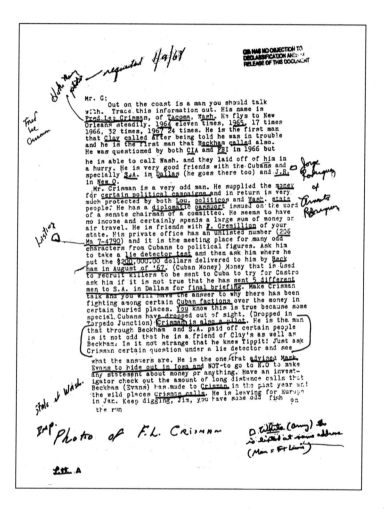

Garrison began investigating Fred Crisman after receiving this letter, noting among other things, a connection between Shaw and Crisman.

special agent in Seattle and Tacoma, I was very impressed with the competence and efficiency of the Bureau. However, I was extremely bored as I rang doorbells to inquire about the loyalty and associations of applicants for employment in a defense plant. So I decided to return to the law profession."[19]

He also discussed his relationship with Banister:

Jim Garrison in Army uniform. When he left the service, he joined the FBI in the Pacific Northwest before obtaining a law degree from Tulane University in New Orleans. Like Crisman, he went back into the military during the Korean War. He became New Orleans District Attorney in 1961. On March 1, 1967 Garrison arrested businessman Clay Shaw for conspiracy to kill JFK, beginning his famous investigation and prosecution of the case.

"I knew Banister fairly well. When he was with the police department, we had lunch together now and then, swapping colorful stories about our earlier careers in the FBI. A ruddy-faced man with blue eyes which stared right at you, he dressed immaculately and always wore a small rosebud in his lapel."[20]

It is difficult to imagine that the stories Banister swapped with Garrison did not include his flying saucer encounter on 1947. Did it also include stories about Maury Island? Fred Crisman? Did Garrison have access to the complete file on Maury Island and its investigation by Kenneth Arnold and Emil Smith? In fact, Garrison quite probably worked for the FBI in Tacoma in 1947.[21]

So the full picture that Jim Garrison had of Fred Crisman when he issued a subpoena for his testimony on Oct 31, 1968 remains obscure. Even the press release that accompanied the subpoena gave generalities rather than details:

"Our information indicates that since the early 1960s (Crisman) has made many trips to the New Orleans and Dallas areas in connection with his undercover work for that part of the warfare industry engaged in the manufacture of what is termed, in military language, 'hardware'—meaning those weapons sold to the U.S. government that are uniquely large and expensive."

A little over a year later, particulars of this broad stroke painting of Fred Crisman as an operative in moving large, military hardware (which could have been anything from submachine guns to UFOs) emerged in the form of a samizdat paper called the Torbitt Document. The Torbitt Document actually had been written by a conservative lawyer in Texas named David Copeland under the pseudonym William Torbitt. Copeland counted among his clients Penn Jones, a well-respected JFK assassination research figure and publisher of the *Midlothian Mirror* in Midlothian, Texas. The Torbitt Document not only outlined the Paperclip Nazi connections of Werner Von Braun and crew, it introduced two police agencies as suspects in the murder of John Kennedy: Division Five of the FBI and Defense Industrial Security Command. According to the Torbitt Document, Crisman had ties to both. The Torbitt also accused Crisman of being at the assassination site on November 22, 1963.

The Torbitt's take on Crisman begins with the contact man for an assassination team allegedly kept by the FBI in Mexico, John Howard Bowen, who used the alias Alexander Osborne. Osborne accompanied Lee Harvey Oswald on his trip to the Cuban embassy in Mexico City. The Torbitt document continues:

> Osborne, alias John Howard Bowen, was discovered to have another person working with him who also used the alias John Howard Bowen. This second person also traveling as Bowen was Fred Lee Chrismon [sic], another agent for the munitions makers police agency Defense Industrial Security Command. Chrismon also posed as a missionary and also used other aliases. Among the cognomens for Chrismon were Fred Lee, Jon Gould and Jon Gold.
>
> Osborne and Chrismon also bore a marked resemblance and appeared to be about the same age. Chrismon was a Syrian immigrant and had been closely associated with Osborne since the 1920s.
>
> Chrismon, Osborne and their riflemen charges in Mexico were based at Clint Murchison's huge ranch when not posing as missionaries in other areas of Mexico.[22]

The Torbitt's last accusation, however, would forever place Fred Crisman at the center of the one of the most hotly debated topics in Kennedy assassination research, namely the identity of the three tramps arrested in the railyard behind the picket fence at Dealey Plaza:

The chain of evidence connecting Albert Osborne, Fred Lee Chrismon, alias John H. Bowen, Permindex, and his co-workers became iron-clad when a Black Star photographer snapped a picture a few minutes after the assassination of Chrismon, alias Bowen, and two of his charges in the process of being arrested by two young Dallas police officers at Dealey Plaza. Fritz later released all three. The Chrismon, alias Bowen, arrest picture received limited public distribution in 1969 when it was published in the *Midlothian Mirror* by Penn Jones, the Texas editor.

The Torbitt Document reproduced this photograph of the three "tramps" arrested at the Dealey Plaza railyard on November 22, 1963. The caption underneath read: "Co-Director of the Mexico based assassins, John H. Bowen, alias Fred Lee Chrismon, alias Jon Gould, alias Jon Gold, and Thomas Beckham, front, and another assassin in the process of being arrested at Dealey Plaza immediately after the assassination."

One of Chrismon's Mexican professionals, Manuel Gonzales, firing from the fence to Kennedy's right side.
Caption: Co-Director of the Mexico-based assassins, John H. Bowen, alias Fred Crisman, alias Fred Lee, alias Jon Gould, alias Jon Gold, and Thomas Beckham, front, and another assassin in the process of being arrested at Dealey Plaza immediately after the assassination.[23]

Did Garrison work from this information? The Torbitt document suggested that he did, concluding its remarks about Crisman by returning to the language of Garrison's subpoena of Crisman:

After two years of intense and extensive investigation, Jim Garrison made a well-recorded public statement showing beyond doubt that he had traced the Nazi rocket scientists, the World Trade Center and Permindex, the Fascist Solidarists, American Council of Christian Churches, Free Cuba Committee, the gambling syndicate and Mafia, and NASA's Security Division into its umbrella controlling organization, the Defense Industrial Security Command of Columbus, Ohio and Hunstville, Alabama.

Garrison had traced DISC into its larger umbrella, Di-

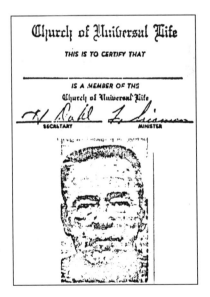

Certification of membership in the Church of Universal Life.

vision Five of the FBI and the Defense Intelligence
Agency supervised by the Joint Chief of Staff in the
Pentagon. Here is how Garrison's statement came
about. On October 31, 1968, Jim Garrison subpoenaed a Tacoma, Washington man for questioning in
his continuing investigation of the John F. Kennedy
assassination. Fred Lee Chrismon, a "bishop" of the
Universal Life Church, was called to appear before
the Orleans Parish Grand Jury on November 21,
1968. Garrison's office said that Chrismon "has been
engaged in undercover activity for a part of the industrial warfare complex for years. His cover is that
of "preacher" and a "person engaged in work to help
the gypsies."
Garrison's statement continued:

> Our information indicates that since the early six-
> ties, Chrismon has made many trips to the New Or-
> leans and Dallas areas in connection with his
> undercover work. He is a "former" employee of
> Lockheed Aircraft Company in Los Angeles. In in-
> telligence terminology, this ordinarily means that the
> connection still exists, but that the 'former employee'
> has moved into an underground operation.
>   Garrison said that evidence had been developed
> indicating a relationship between Chrismon and "per-
> sons involved in the assassination of President John
> F. Kennedy."[24]

Although Copeland acknowledged that Crisman, and
his partner Thomas Beckham, "played only small roles
in the big picture"[25] he nevertheless fit them squarely in
the center of Garrison's effort and the meaning he had
taken from it:

> Garrison further reiterated the general findings
> of his controversial investigation. "President
> Kennedy was murdered by elements of the indus-

trial warfare complex working in concert with individuals in the United States government. At the time of his murder, President Kennedy was working to end the Cold War. The annual income of the defense industry was well over twenty billion dollars a year, and there were forces in that industry and in the U.S. Government which opposed the ending of the Cold War."

As has been pointed out earlier, Fred Lee Chrismon used the alias John Howard Bowen and traveled and worked with the Mexico-based assassins, Albert Osborne, Thomas Beckham and others. Bowen, alias Chrismon, and Beckham are shown in photographs taken November 22, 1963. In the picture they are being taken after arrest by Dallas police across Dealey Plaza immediately after the President's murder.

Fred Lee Chrismon, alias John H. Bowen, alias Dr. Jon Gold, and his partner, Thomas Edward Beckham, and Albert Osborne were all working for the Defense Industrial Security Command through the American Council of Christian Churches.[26]

Copeland was not terribly forthcoming about the sources for his Torbitt Document; their provenance and their veracity remain the subject of great dispute. Clearly much of it emanated from Garrison. But where did Garrison get it? From Crisman? Had Crisman injected himself into Garrison's controversial probe of the Kennedy assassination in his role as a self-promoter, as perhaps he did with Maury Island? He certainly did not write the Torbitt Document. He may have written that initial letter to Garrison, however.[27] He may also have written a detailed report and/or fabrication of his own background that Garrison may have later included in his research materials. Known as the "Easy Papers" (after the EASY 4250ece section of the CIA discussed in the report), this report was released to researcher Thomas Adams in June 1981 and has since circulated among Maury Island researchers, although never previously published.

The following statements and records have been extracted from the Central Intelligence Agency file (current) concerning: Crisman, Fred Lee, file number OSS/CIA 4250ece. The file is located at Control Records Dispatch, Davenport, Iowa.

File Number OSS/CIA 4250ece contains an incomplete record, as some of the material has not been classified low enough to be placed in this Pers. File rank. A great deal of material is left out, and some of the pages of the file simply state "deleted" and give no reason for deletion. The most important information in the file reveals that Crisman has served many years as an active agent for the old OSS and later the CIA. He is rated an "extended agent." He is an information specialist and highly trained in Internal Security. He has worked overseas and has served as a regular USAF and AF officer but his primary training has always been slanted in that direction of disruption work inside the borders of the U.S.

Crisman was an original recruit in the service of the Old Office of Strategic Service in 1942 when he was selected to be trained as a liaison officer with the British Royal Air Force. He was an aviation cadet and completed his training as a pilot. He was assigned to the 1st Air Commando Group and later the 2nd Air Commando Group in the China-Burma-India theatre of war. His mission was to establish liaison with the British V-force then at odds with the OSS 101 Detachment and bring both units into direct liaison and cooperation. His recent training as a special liaison officer with the British was considered valuable and he appears to have accomplished his mission. He was rated by a Col. Arthur Hunak as a top man and his records marked for further training. Most of his service in World War II seems to have been straight military with the provision that he would be further trained at a later date. He was sent to Tokyo, Japan, at the close of the war and was given intensive training in a school that is only referred to as Isece. He was in Saigon, Indo-China in December and January of 1945-46, and his reports from there were marked "excellent." There are no copies of these reports in Central Dispatch as they were removed in 1967 on "draw and study order" by Col. M. Deveraux, of the USAF.

Crisman was returned to the United States in 1946, and, supposedly discharged by the military, he went directly to Washington, D.C. and entered a special Internal Security school of the OSS. He was transferred from OSS to CIA duty and returned to the same school under the CIA to be given more training. He was then officially assigned as an "extended agent" and returned to the state of Washington.

He was appointed a special investigator for the state of Washington and served as such while becoming deeply involved with the politics of the period. He was a valued worker in the campaign of a Paul Olson for mayor of the city of Tacoma, and reports that he sent to the CIA show that Olson was a suspect in a large effort of the communist Party in Washington. Crisman gave the information to Harry P. Cain that assured Olson's defeat at the polls. The information was gathered in Washington and sent to Crisman with direct orders to use it to defeat Olson. The records contain film that indicate that Crisman sent the CIA over a thousand reports on the political situation in Washington and on political leaders of the state. The year 1947 shows that he submitted a request to the CIA Assignment Bureau requesting permission to return to college, and the request was granted with the proviso that he go to either the University of Washington or the University of Oregon. This was changed by the Assignment Bureau to Willamette University in Salem, Oregon.

Crisman studied Political Science and Education, with minors in Psychology and History. His course of study was an odd patchwork of courses that brought him to the attention of the officers of the university and Crisman submitted a report to the Assignment Bureau that was highly critical of the Education and Training Section and requested that he be left alone to finish his directed studies. His reports were used as a basis for re-drawing the complete civil training methods of the [missing word], and Crisman was ordered to report to Ft. Lewis for "summer training" in 1948-49.

The "summer training" courses that Crisman attended were not military, though he reported to a military base each time. He was listed as being trained at the base at Ft. Lewis, Washington, Ft. Benning, Georgia, and Ft. Sill, Oklahoma. Each of these bases were CIA training areas, and they conducted special classes taught by civilian, and military teachers in many courses. The main courses taught to a few selected agents were in that highly classified field known inside the CIA as Isece and coded as Easy Section. The CIA has denied to congressional investigating Committees that Easy Section does not exist. It does exist and is the sub-section of Internal Security known as a disruption planning center. Crisman is a trained Disruption Agent and has worked in several fields.

The file shows that he submitted a series of reports on judges, lawyers, and a long report on civilian law training methods. He was instructed to become a friend to Mark O. Hatfield, a professor at Willamette University, former naval officer and member of the OSS. Hatfield is now the senior senator from Oregon and [missing word] a moderate conservative.

Crisman was a key man in several of Hatfield's campaigns for public office and still maintains a close liaison with him. Hatfield is not a member of the

CIA but serves on a secret committee to review funds for the CIA and is counted as a possible extended agent.

In 1949 the CIA took an odd interest in the National Education Association and sent several agents into that organization. Crisman became president of the Ore. Student Association and attended the national convention. He submitted several reports on a variety of people connected with the Oregon Education Assoc. where he mentioned that those people were not to be trusted as future political material. He also had an office of some nature with the National Student Association but was ordered to resign and he did resign.

It is felt that agents of Crisman's training were given great latitude in some of their work and they sometimes overlapped. This was evident in his becoming a part of the NSA.

In 1950 the regular recall of many pilots for the Korean War caught Crisman as a reserve officer, and the CIA made some effort to stop his recall. It was stopped until he could be graduated from Willamette University, and then he was released by the CIA and Crisman was ordered to Wichita Falls, Texas. He was sent to the Army base at Ft. Sill, Oklahoma, again to take special courses and was then sent to Japan. He was taken from the direct replacement pilot supply depot and was assigned to several reserve and National Guard general officers as an aide-de-camp. He submitted a stream of reports on these generals and on their views on the Korean War.

Crisman was assigned to a photo-reco section used to gather photo information concerning prisoner of war camps, and was wounded in combat. His return to active duty brought him to a special set of interior training classes at the University of Tohuku in Sendai, Honshu. His list of reports from this period has been extracted from the file, and there is no record of further reports from him until 1954. A separate folder states that he was ordered to the USA and went to CIA school at Ft. Belvoir, Virginia during the summer of 1953. He was again placed in Internal Security and he applied for several teaching positions in Oregon. He was still recovering from wounds and was not asked for political reports for a period of sixteen months. He was then contacted by the CIA and asked to find a teaching position in the area of the Idaho-Oregon Snake River Dam complex, then being built by the Idaho Power Company. He wrote a series of reports on the long range effects of these dams on the local economic and cultural levels. These long reports have been extracted from the file and sections of them deleted and then turned over to certain sections of the Agriculture and Commerce Departments.

Crisman was at the time serving as Superintendent of Schools at Huntington, Oregon and he was suddenly ordered to resign and report to the Tacoma - Seattle and general Puget Sound area. He applied for a job in the Tacoma school system and was accepted but was ordered to resign the job and instead find a "cover job" closer to the Seattle area. He applied for and was accepted as an English teacher at a school in Buckley, Washington. He attempted to become active in the state political affairs by joining the Rosellini forces. He was ordered to cease all political activity and he did drop all contacts with all politics.

There are no reports of any type during the years of 1958-59 and in 1960 this agent was sent as an observer to the national convention of the National Education Association. This information is in a separate folder, and it can be presumed that Crisman was organizing certain CIA contacts with that organization. In view of the later problems that were to develop in the CIA with their contacts with the NSA it is understandable that his activity in this field would be removed from the inner files.

Crisman suddenly resigned his contract with the Buckley school system in the same month that he had signed it in 1960 and reported to the Boeing Company in Seattle. He was given a roving assignment as a Personnel Representative, and this allowed him access to any part of the plant complex of that company.

The Security Section of Boeing Company seemed to have been aware that he was a type of government agent, but they were under the impression that he was an Air Force Intelligence agent. His conduct there was not that of an Air Force agent. Boeing was under a great reorganization program, and many departments were in a complete state of confusion as they were being re-organized into an Aero-Space concept. Crisman built an internal network of informants that fed him a steady stream of information on the business and private lives of many of Boeing's top executives. He filed several lengthy reports that demanded Boeing rearrange their hiring process and their security measures. There is no doubt that he was instrumental in the firing of several top executives that had a shadow of private homosexuality in their private lives. None of the men (one woman) had any public record of any problem with sex.

This agent deliberately set person against person until one whole project had to be abandoned due to the vast amounts of ill feelings engendered by his deliberate conduct. It is almost impossible to believe that one man, even a well-trained agent, could cause so much disruption in any one division of a super-corporation as large as Boeing. The Boeing operation alone makes a file 11 inches thick and with nearly 800 microfilm reports. During the last three months of disruption he was aided by another CIA agent and a woman employee. The other agent is not listed by name, the hired woman was Deana Wooley. She was not aware that she was working for the CIA.

Boeing agents finally tracked down the source of the trouble and complained to the Air Force plant representative, Col. J. Walter Green. Col. Green called in the man Crisman and talked to him. He later was called to Washington and upon his return did not deny Crisman as an AF agent. Crisman abruptly resigned from Boeing in November of 1962. He returned to Washington, D.C. until January 1, 1963 and then to Tacoma, Washington.

For the rest of the year of 1963 (until 1963 Sept.) he was a teacher in the Tacoma school system and did not submit many reports aside from a few reports on the tenor of the teaching in Tacoma. He considered it to be very loose and needed a great deal more discipline. His reports on the Tacoma School Supt. were not very good and he definitely stated that he felt that he was communistic in his views. He did file a long report on that Supt. when he was a principal and school administrator in Sunnyside, Washington and seems to have made a trip to Sunnyside to verify his findings.

He was next placed in a position of authority in the Longmire, Washington school system. He was hired as a principal, but did not work at the position as he resigned and took a job directly across the river from Longview in Rainier, Oregon. The next position appears to have had some relation to the disruption of a drive to organize a large Port Authority on the Oregon side of the Columbia. His reports are not in a completed state, and little time was available to study this section of the file; however, there is no doubt that he did enter into the port politics and was very instrumental in bringing the whole idea to a halt. For some reason the Isece did not want the Port Authority formed. It still has not been formed.

Some of the harsh feelings engendered by Crisman between those involved will never be forgotten. He was commended for his work here as the higher authority in the CIA felt that it would take two or three years to bring this matter to a halt, but it was accomplished in one year.

Crisman left the Rainier, Oregon area and spent several months in New Orleans where he appears to have been very friendly with several political figures. He made the city of New Orleans a headquarters for several small disruption areas later taken over by the EASY section of the CIA through a different and separate set of agents. It is odd to note that Crisman became quite friendly with the Perez family at Porta La Hacho, La. He was also known by James Garrison and was later remembered by Garrison, Garrison did not know at this time that Crisman was a CIA agent, or that he was in any way a federal employee.

Crisman returned to Oregon and entered into the employment of the Salem school system, where he started a new information drive on top level state employees. A great many reports on the Federal Aid to Education program were filed by Crisman at his time. Here, at this place in the file is the only copy of a direct disrupt order. He was assigned to prevent the appointment of a man, John Drake, to the Federal Aid Program. Drake was a district superintendent, and as such was a man directly in line with the work that Crisman was doing.

Unfortunately, Drake was a man who did not respond to that series of unfortunate events that seem to befall those are the targets of the Disruption agents. The complete staff, under the leadership of Crisman, rebelled against Drake, and still Drake did not leave the system or make those moves that would place his ability in doubt with the Federal Aid to Education officers of the Department of Health, Education and Welfare of the federal government.

Finally the main building, where all Aid to Education records were kept, burned, and the records were destroyed. The Federal Bureau of Investigation was informed of certain areas of money discrepancy and all this was filed with the school board and the HEW department, Drake was finally discredited as an able person who was to be used in a high federal education position. The long-range reason for the attack on Drake was not listed; only reports that listed the refusal of the man to buckle to pressure.

At the same time that the attack upon John Drake was being pursued, a similar attack was being made upon the local county school superintendent. This man was not hard to discourage, and he soon left his position, which was filled by direct appointment. No attacks or reports on his successor are listed. At this same time Crisman left this area and returned to New Orleans where he worked very hard in two legislative campaigns and elected two city councilmen to the New Orleans city council. Again, he was known to the local district attorney, Jim Garrison, and Garrison attempted to have his record checked out. Senator Russell Long was able to confirm that Crisman was a government agent but assumed that he was an FBI information agent. Garrison was so informed, and Crisman was listed as such in the New Orleans records.

Crisman returned to Tacoma, Washington, and entered into a series of moves that had to do with certain bills in the Washington state legislature. He formed a small research company and entered into a series of quiet lobby moves, mostly behind a man by the name of Wesley Keene. He also put together a series of rapid non-profit organizations that were fronts for some operation later taken over by Thomas E. Beckham, another CIA from the midwest. There are no reports in this file on the purpose of these organizations. It is presumed that he merely organized these as fronts for an operation taken over by another agent. There is a report on a John O'Connell, the attorney general of the state of Washington. These front organizations came to his notice and in turn Crisman requested permission to run a full investigation on John O'Connell. He reported that John O'Connell was to run for governor of the state of Washington, and he did not feel that he should be governor of that state. There is a note attached to a report that shows Crisman's judgement was backed by another agent, and it was allowed to be a project that proceeded with the blessings of the Isece Section of the CIA. There were two more regular CIA agents assigned to this project in 1968. It became a full-fledged project in September of 1968 when Crisman reported that a definite platform of help was needed to defeat John O'Connell.

That help was forthcoming, and it was fast: there were several information men who were to help Crisman. Contact was made with the Conquistador Corp. in Las Vegas, and certain copies of gambling debt checks were flown to Seattle, where they were turned over to Crisman. He sent in a report that he was not satisfied with this method and went to Las Vegas where his CIA contact told him that the Conquistador Corp. would not cooperate further. Crisman evidently went to Washington D.C., and from there to New Orleans. His report states that he was asking to get help in New Orleans, and upon his return to Las Vegas, the Conquistador Corp. cooperated with no objections. The report does not state what pressure was used on the Cosa Nostra, but it is evident that they fear the CIA more than any other branch of any law enforcement agency.

Oblique references in the reports lead one to the conclusion that the Easy section of the CIA would not hesitate to enter into a full-fledged gang war with the underworld to get the cooperation they feel they need. The hoodlums also are well aware that the CIA Easy agents are not interested in crime fighting unless it is a part of one of their control efforts. The Cosa Nostra cooperate and they stay out of the way of all CIA agents. The CIA does not make arrests. They have been known to kill an enemy and they consider all persons in their way as an enemy.

It was later ascertained that it was the effort to block John O'Connell which was responsible for giving Jim Garrison the information that Crisman was an actual CIA agent and a specialized agent of the department. He was informed by Cosa Nostra friends in Las Vegas that Crisman was interested in the complete New Orleans and Washington state operation of both Boeing and the politics involved. This led Garrison to later accuse Crisman of being a government-military CIA complex agent.

Crisman was given orders in 1968 to enter the political field to remove the type of government that is known as Manager-Council government from the city of Tacoma. He has made no effort to keep his name in the background of the political fight and no effort has been made to give him special cover. This may be due to the fact that he claims Tacoma, Washington as his place of birth and rearing. His biggest move to date has been to launch a radio program wherein he has made a steady attack on the Tacoma government for a year.

There is a copy of an order for him to enter this operation, but there is no reason given as to why it is felt by the Easy section of the CIA that this form of government is wrong for this area. Reference is made to Project W-21, but here is no clear reference that will tell what Project W-21 might be. The CIA does not appear to be unduly upset or interfering in other places where there has been a Manager-Council form of government.

Most of Crisman's recent reports have not stated progress reports but have been pleas for help. He asked for money (granted), assistance (granted) and he has asked for interference of the CIA with the FCC in a license matter for station KAYE in Puyallup, Washington (the station he broadcasts over). This help was also granted to him and he has not stated how long he feels the project will take but he has been ordered to Vietnam by November 1969. There is a copy of a late request asking cancellation of the Vietnam order.

Currently his reports state that the situation is well under control and that he might not be needed to remove the Manager form of government from Tacoma but he is not allowing his efforts to slacken. His control of the situation seems to be very complete and he has asked for an investigation into the beginning of regional government in Seattle. The Project has not started as of this date. (9/8/69).

There does not seem to be any short-range purpose in this effort in Tacoma and it appears that Crisman has submitted reports that have not been taken from the current file and placed in the record file. All that is known at the present time is that the EASY 4250ece Section of the CIA is active in Tacoma and that it has assigned one of it's best Disruption Agents to the local job there.

Did Crisman make all of this up? Does it perhaps review, embellish and censor a real career? Although ostensibly a third-person account, the prose reflects the kind of excited detail a reader would ordinarily expect in the first person. The "Easy" papers do repeat known biographical facts about Crisman. The papers do not mention the people or events found in the Torbitt Document, save for the name of Thomas Beckham. The papers make no mention of either Maury Island or the Kennedy assassination, in fact, except for references to Garrison's fledgling investigation. Correspondence released along with the "Easy" papers include a cover letter for them suggesting to a "Mrs. Banfield" that "This man, Crisman, is a man that is dangerous to the future of America" and "that if you do love this nation we cannot have CIA people such as him interfering with local government."[28]

Crisman himself may have been referring to this report when he wrote in his 1969 book, *Murder of a City*: "My own information sources and friends in Washington DC told me that the poor old man had actually sent a copy of some of Chief Zittle's raw files back to the FBI, and included a copy of some silly material that had been circulated 'proving' that I was a member of the Central Intelligence Agency."[29] And what to make of CIA Freedom of Information Act officer John E. Bacon's statement in his letter to researcher Thomas Adams that the papers "were produced by an unknown person for an unknown reason, but apparently were intended to damage Mr. Crisman. Mr. Crisman never had any connection with either the CIA or OSS in any capacity."[30]

Jim Garrison, however, was not only interested in Crisman's intelligence community links, but also in his connection to right-wing and anti-Castro groups and causes.

One particular interest involved a Los Angeles resident named G. Clinton Wheat, an activist in American Nazi Party and rightist Christian movements like the Christian Defense league and the Church of Jesus Christ-Christian. According to one source, after Wheat defied one of Garrison's subpoenas, Garrison tracked him to Crisman's Oregon ranch.[31]

Wheat and Crisman had attended meetings where speakers included Christian Defense League founder William Gale, a former guerilla fighter under Douglas MacArthur who joined the Anti-communist Liaison group started by MacArthur's intelligence chief Charles Willoughby. Gale retired from military service at age 33 to work for Howard Hughes and thereafter hooked up with evangelist Wesley Swift and the Ku Klux Klan.[32] More importantly, however, he also became a founder of the California Rangers, an offshoot of a group called the Minute Men.

The Minute Men were founded by Robert DePugh and had associations as well-known as general Edwin Walker and oil billionaire H. L. Hunt. One of the first federal agents to interview Lee Harvey Oswald, Frank Ellsworth, once remarked that the Minute Men organization was "the right-wing group most likely to have been associated with any effort to assassinate the president."[33]

Many years later, the name of the Minute Men would re-emerge in the Maury Island story. A founder of the national Minute Men group headquartered in Missouri, the Reverend Bob LeRoy claimed in 1996 that his deceased brother, Bernard Ramey LeRoy, was fishing off Piner Point at the island in 1947 when he witnessed the same UFO event as Harold Dahl. "On the evening of June 21st, 1947. Barney came by our home very excited telling us about the strange flying disc that let tin foil flakes out onto the bay near where he was fishing with others...Barney and the other fishermen were about 200 feet or more apart. They always fished that way, to prevent lines from tangling up. Sometimes 3 or 4 lines to a boat going down 150 to 200 feet deep for Lynncod, etc."[34]

Reverend LeRoy was born in Ellensburg, Washington in 1923. He grew up in the Tacoma region and as a young adult became involved with radical right-wing, populist religious and political groups, including those of the Presbyterian radio evangelist Dr. Carl McIntire and Gerald L. K. Smith. LeRoy began military service in 1943, serving as a paratrooper in the South Pacific until 1946. He documented his World War II experiences in a book, *From My Foxhole to Tokyo*, which he published in 1992.

After he returned, LeRoy studied at Pacific Lutheran College in Tacoma and found work as a public school teacher. He was dismissed after complaining to a superintendent that he believed a fellow teacher was a communist. LeRoy also dropped out of his membership in the American Legion and the VFW because he felt those groups were soft on communism. In 1962, he joined a group in Norcross, Missouri called the Minute Men. After losing a teaching job in Nebraska in 1965 because of his political views, LeRoy became the chaplain of the Minute Men and traveled nationally as its speaker. The Warren Commission at one time placed into evidence two exhibits suggesting a link between the assassination and the Minute Men, but later withdrew them. From

1965 to 1968 LeRoy met with members of the FBI and answered questions about possible Minute Men involvement in gun-running operations.[35]

Because of his convictions as a Baptist evangelist, LeRoy eventually split with Minute Men founder Robert DePugh and formed the Christian Sons of Liberty in Liberty, Missouri in 1970. He organized anti-communist protest rallies and became known as the "parachuting preacher" because of his paratrooper background. In 1980 he moved the headquarters of the Christian Sons of Liberty to New Jersey and then to Langeley, Washington in 1981, where he continued to be active in anti-communist and right-wing populist causes.

These rightist church groups were central to Jim Garrison's concerns over Fred Crisman, particularly with regard to Crisman's association with Thomas Beckham. The Torbitt Document lists Beckham only as a member of DISC, and another of the assassins on the railyard. In notes from 1977 about Beckham, however,[36] Garrison did not make this assertion, although he repeated the possibility of Crisman's railyard presence. (In fact, Garrison suggests that Beckham may appear in "film taken immediately following the assassination in front of the Book Depository.") Garrison instead calls Beckham a protégé of Crisman's and a member of "the Banister cell," the private detective office in New Orleans of the former FBI man from the Pacific Northwest. Garrison lists as members of that cell a number of other individuals of some disrepute in the annals of the JFK assassination, including the albino pilot David Ferrie and Kerry Thornley, who had written a novel about Lee Harvey Oswald, *The Idle Warriors,* and later became well known in the conspiracy information underground. In 1992 Thornley claimed that he had been drawn into the Kennedy assassination by E. Howard Hunt, a Watergate burglar who has also been identified as one of the railyard hoboes.[37] Oswald himself belonged to the Banister cell, according to Garrison, as did William Dalzell, Sergio Arcacha, Grady Durham, Luis Babel, Carlos Quiroga, Emilio Santana and others active in the anti-Castro Cuban Revolutionary Front. More importantly, however, Garrison regarded Beckham as a key to understanding "that bizarre cluster of 'Old Church' evangelical sects which we found recurrent in the whole affair and which characterized some of the apparently more radioactive individuals we came across in the course of digging away at the New Orleans sub-structure."

Garrison notes that frequent arrests characterized Beckham's early years. Even in the Army, records indicate that Beckham spent time in stockades at Camp Leroy Johnson and Fort Leonard Wood. These problems abated after 1962[38] as he developed relationships with David Ferrie and later Fred Crisman. Beckham eventually came to describe himself as an ordained priest of the Old Orthodox Catholic Church, a claim also made by David Ferrie, and later as a minister in the Universal Life Church. Garrison notes that Crisman later claimed to be a Universal Life Church bishop. Beckham trotted these church credentials to Omaha, Nebraska, "under the apparently specific sponsorship of Crisman. Garrison also notes an ersatz relationship between Beckham and an Air Force colonel named Lourry and suggests a connection there with Crisman because of Crisman's Air Force background and his work with Boeing. Garrison also mentions that Frank Sturgis, another of the Watergate burglars identified by some researchers also as one of the railyard hoboes,[39] "applied in Florida to found a corresponding obscure sect of his own." He adds, "Nor would I be inclined as accepting as pure coincidence of this consistent, gratuitously present divinity, the fact that the killer of Officer Tippit accomplished this act in the vicinity of a temporarily unoccupied, unnamed (but open)

First tramps photo. The last two tramps have been identified by Alan J. Weberman and Michael Canfield as Watergate burglars E. Howard Hunt and Frank Sturgis (*Coup D'Etat in America,* Quick American Archives, 1992). The "Hunt" tramp conceals himself from the camera. The "Sturgis" tramp, in front, also has been identified as Charles Harrelson, father of actor Woody Harrelson. Candidates for the remaining tramp include CIA operative Don Carswell and career criminal Chauncey Marvin Holt—and Crisman? Dallas police arrest records found recently give John Gedney, Gus Abrams and Harold Doyle as the names of the tramps. Weberman notes that the arrest reports contradict statements by the supervising officer, D. V. Harkness.

evangelical church at 10th and Crawford, in the rear entrance of which—after circling the block—he seems quite literally to have found sanctuary."

Garrison's summary of his suspicions about the right-wing church connection:

> A bizarre situation, to be sure, but its very strangeness—its threadbare irrelevance—makes it all the more safe from possible investigators who are looking for spies wearing trenchcoats and carrying, like so many James Bonds, gold cigarette cases. The churches—like all churches—are virtually free from official inquiry by virtue of the Constitution, not to mention American custom. The 'ministers' and 'bishops' can accumulate money (religious fund raising) without serious inquiry as to the source. They are free from the 9 to 5 routine expected of normal, patriotic Americans, free to operate in relative seclusion from the expected social involvement, free to engage in obscure crusades or missions and free to travel extensively (for unmarked and unobserved periods) as assignments may dictate. And where, as may be the case in some instances, there may actually be a home structure for the particular church.

When Garrison extradited Beckham from Omaha over Beckham's objections, Crisman told a mutual acquaintance named Bob Lavender that he, Crisman, would "kill Beckham if I am subpoenaed as a result of anything he says—not that I know anything about the conspiracy, of course." Lavender told this to Garrison investigator William Hoxley in an interview that also shed light on the connection between the rightist churches and the anti-Castro Cubans. Interestingly, Lavender and his attorney expressed apprehension that Hoxley might ask questions "into matters which they implied were under investigation by Federal authorities," and shortly thereafter members of the Minute Men were arrested by the FBI for conspiring to rob banks in Seattle.

Lavender claimed to have met Beckham in Omaha in February of 1967, but Hoxley established that the two must have known each other at least three years earlier. Lavender also claimed that Beckham had split from the Universal Life Church to start is own church organization and that he met David Ferrie through Guy Banister's aid Jack Martin. According to Lavender, Beckham filed incorporation papers for various people and businesses and made a living with the fees charged. In 1966 Beckham and Crisman incorporated seven businesses in Olympia, Washington.

Most importantly, however, Lavender claimed that Beckham told him he had assisted in establishing a fund raising office for Sergio Arcacha and Louis Rabel, for anti-Castro activity in New Orleans. Crisman, said Lavender, made numerous trips from Olympia to New Orleans and Dallas for meetings, stating almost gratuitously that "Crisman has described himself as being sadistic in sexual practice preferences." Crisman also told him that that Arcacha Smith and Louis Rabel had raised between four and five hundred thousand dollars from the various church fund raising ventures and other private backers. This money had been given to Beckham in a suitcase, and he flew it from city to city across the country as a matter of safe-keeping. The money was intended to be used to assassinate Kennedy. The plotters even had an ancilliary plan to take $30,000 of it to Miami to throw off the FBI and the CIA.[40]

In the broad strokes, these details matched those of the anonymous letter Garrison had received that first put him on Crisman's trail. The body language between Lavender and his attorney, however, had Hoxley conclude that "Lavender was on stage reiterating a story which he

Clay Shaw, one of two defendants Jim Garrison attempted to prosecute for the JFK assassination. California governor Ronald Reagan refused to extradite the other defendant, Edgar Eugene Bradley. The Torbitt document claimed that former Nazi rocket scientist Werner von Braun "first met Clay Shaw in 1945 when he, Walter Dornberger and about 150 other Nazi rocket scientists abandoned Peenemunde and traveled south to join the American forces in Germany close to the French border." Shaw and Crisman ostensibly were connected by membership in the CIA predecessor group OSS, although the CIA has never declassified records that might reflect this. Could Crisman's involvement with the Maury Island UFOs trace back to an OSS project to recover Nazi aerospace and occult technologies?

had been encouraged to tell us.[41] Hoxley suspected that Lavender's story, and perhaps even the letter to Garrison (as well as a second letter from Orlando)[42] were stories that originated with Jack Martin, Banister's assistant. "It's recommended that the facts contained therein be taken with a generous portion of salt. If for no other reason than the fact that I have never met anyone either in the CIA or among right-wing donors to political causes who would (A) entrust a large sum of money to either

Beckham or Lavender or others of their ilk, or (B) permit such funds to be flown around the country in a suitcase."[43]

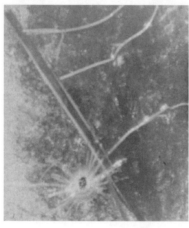

Photographs of bullet hole damage to a car driven by Crisman in October 1968, from *Murder of a City*. Crisman claimed that this was an assassination attempt against him.

Nevertheless, Garrison had accumulated a large exhibits file on Beckham that documented his bogus church activities, including a circular for "Dr. Beckham, Evangelist" decorated with a swastika and one for Beckham's pseudonym, Mark Evans, listing Crisman as his Hollywood agent. An interview with David Lewis affirmed details of Beckham's biography, as did more circular materials, correspondence and affirmation that Beckham joined the Old Catholic Church through the direction of Jack Martin. When these exhibits emerged as part of the House Select Committee of Investigations in 1977, they were accompanied by interrogatories by Garrison written August 25, 1977, with questions that he still had for Beckham.

FEDERAL BUREAU OF INVESTIGATION
WASHINGTON, D.C. 20537

11-18-68   34 LMP

The following FBI record, NUMBER   636 691 G   , is furnished FOR OFFICIAL USE ONLY.
Information shown on this Identification Record represents data furnished FBI by fingerprint contributors. WHERE
FINAL DISPOSITION IS NOT SHOWN OR FURTHER EXPLANATION OF CHARGE IS DESIRED, COMMUNICATE
WITH AGENCY CONTRIBUTING THOSE FINGERPRINTS.

CONTRIBUTOR OF FINGERPRINTS	NAME AND NUMBER	ARRESTED OR RECEIVED	CHARGE	DISPOSITION
Chief of Pol Ontario Oreg	Fred Lee Crisman	5-19-57	drk disorderly resisting arrest pulled gun on officer	$100
PD Tacoma Wash	Fred Lee Crisman #28049	10-31-68	reckless driving no valid operators lic on person & diso (CCW) * Chrg: in contempt lof Ris	

Notations indicated by * are NOT based on fingerprints in FBI files but are listed only as investigative leads as
being possibly identical with subject of this record.

John Edgar Hoover
Director

Crisman's arrest record, October 31, 1968.

The grand jury had already indicted Clay Shaw, now the retired director of the New Orleans International Trade Mart, for conspiracy to commit the murder of JFK. It had also indicted Edgar Eugene Bradley, described in the press as a representative to Dr. Carl McIntire, the radio evangelist who had been an inspira-

Tacoma News Tribune, November 2, 1968.

tion to members of the Minute Men.[45] Crisman accepted
the subpoena to testify in October 31, 1968, understanding that it would keep him from being arrested in New
Orleans for complicity. Press speculation had it that
Crisman had been subpoenaed as a result of Beckham's
testimony, which had come in a wave of testimony that
had included Lawrence Howard and Loren Eugene Hall,
other anti-Castro Cubans living in southern California.
That wave of testimony also was to have included G.

Clinton Wheat, who refused and may have been hiding at Crisman's ranch,[46] a possibility that raises a question about the timing of Crisman's subpoena.

Crisman received a paltry $500 check to fly to New Orleans from Tacoma to give his testimony. He asked for more, having acquired the service of an attorney, Robert Griffith. He wanted Griffith to accompany him, so he appealed to Garrison's office.[47] Garrison's office did agree to reimburse Griffith's expenses, but apparently that never happened. Crisman was accompanied by Griffith during his stay in New Orleans, however. Crisman testified under oath for about an hour. "Most of the time was spent on questions about local politics in Louisiana," he later told the press, "about which I know nothing. Garrison also refused to pay expenses for my attorney." Referring to Beckham, Crisman asserted "I didn't meet anyone in New Orleans until the winter of 1966-67."[48]

His nonchalant approach to the grand jury testimony belied the many problems that beset Crisman's life at that time. For one, as he told it, an assassination attempt had been made against him earlier in the month. On October 4, 1968, someone fired shots into the window of the car he drove on his way home from work at a radio station in Tacoma. He attributed the attack to "the hatred of Far Left groups and individuals" opposed to his work as a controversial radio personality. In fact, according to Crisman it was the second such attack.

When he returned from New Orleans, Crisman's problems moved from the mean streets to the courtroom. In January he was charged with reckless driving, having no valid driver's license and carrying a concealed weapon. The arrest record shows the incident happened on October 31, 1968. (It also notes a previous arrest on May 19, 1957 for drunk and disorderly conduct, resisting arrest by pulling a gun on a police officer.) Another attack?

Crisman entered innocent pleas, was convicted of the drunk driving charge in March, paid fines and entered appeals.[49] Later in January, the radio station KAYE in Puyallup, Washington, where Crisman had been conducting a talk show under his pseudonym Jon Gold, was slapped with a $350,000 lawsuit. Crisman's chum Robert Lavender, who had been interrogated by Garrison's investigators, alledgedly accused a human relations worker named Lynn E. Hodges of being a communist. Crisman, Lavender, their wives and the radio station were named as defendants.[50]

Crisman had started at KAYE on August 1, 1968, under the on-air name of John Gold. According to his 1970 autobiographical book, *Murder of a City,*[51] published under the Gold pseudonym, he had been attracted to the radio station because he felt it was a way to express his concern over the Gypsy minority and that it would be useful in his political cause: the elimination of the city management style of government in Tacoma. The Easy Papers mention that Crisman's zeal in this matter stemmed from orders given him in 1968, "but there is no reason given as to why it is felt by the East section of the CIA that this form of government is wrong for this area." Crisman's reasons, as well as his general philosophy (described by Crisman as "Liberal Democrat"—and he had indeed run for office as a Democrat—but clearly shown as anything but in his writing) and a detailed look at his political and business associations, provided the basis for his book. *Murder of a City* reviews the struggles between Tacoma's city manager, Dave Rowlands, and its mayor, A. L. "Slim" Rasmussen—a struggle that Crisman viewed as having lost.

In March 1969, Crisman helped create a non-profit corporation to pursue this ambition of eliminating city management government in Tacoma.[52] It failed, of course, and by January of the following year Mayor Rasmussen was administering his final session, having lost the previous November election. One of his final acts was to appoint Fred Crisman to Tacoma's library board. The move received criticism for all that Crisman had done in local politics and his infamy as a right-wing radio commentator, but he assured his critics that "I respect the library and use it frequently for my own studies as well as for background...and would not think of attempting to influence [the library director] in his choice of books." [53]

Crisman's change of fortunes continued when the defamation lawsuit against KAYE was dismissed.[54] He got involved with cable-TV franchising to no success, however, and lost his bid for election to the Civil Service Board of Pierce county by 1559 votes[55] in September 1971. Shortly thereafter, charges of mismanagement began to circulate about the library manager, apparently emanating from Crisman, who believed that his opposition to city manager government kept him from being made the board president of the Tacoma Public Library.[56] Petty bickering about library politics continued in the Tacoma press until Crisman resigned in October 1973.[57]

As early as 1967, however, Fred Crisman began to again turn his attention to the events at Maury Island of 1947. On July 22 of that year he lectured on the topic at the annual Northwest UFO Conference in Seattle.[58] He lectured the group about the seriousness of the subject, apparently a bit disgruntled at some of the carnival-like atmosphere that attends UFO gatherings (then as now). He made the claim that he had been the first person to photograph the UFOs and that he still had prints of the Maury Island photographs. He discussed the flying saucer slag and insisted that it was quite different from the discarded product of the local smelter works. He talked at length about the press distortion of the subject and how he hoped the true facts would someday emerge.

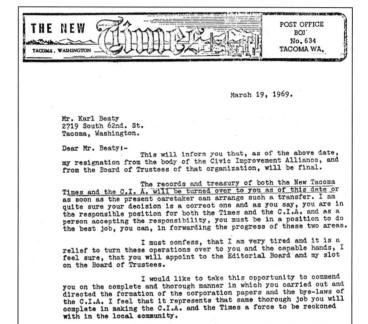

Correspondence on Crisman's resignation from the "Civic Improvement Alliance," or CIA.

If Crisman was making a bid to become a UFO celebrity like Kenneth Arnold, he did little after that to further the cause. When he finished lecturing in Seattle, a young UFO researcher named Gary Leslie approached him anxiously to get copies of the Maury Island photographs. Crisman declined to offer his own address due to his distaste for publicity (a claim contradicted by his soon-to-come career as a shock jock, if not by the lecture itself), but he did provide an address for Harold Dahl. Dahl, after all, had the photographs in his possession. Leslie found Dahl to be an amicable correspondent. He offered to provide copies of the photos and a written statement about his experiences at Maury Island, plus one from his son. He forwarded Leslie's inquiries to Crisman's New Orleans address,[59] and reported that he had photographs of the North Queen boat taken at the time of the incident. Dahl also spoke very glowingly of Crisman, comparing him, in fact, to the character played by Roy Thinnes in the then current TV show *The Invaders*, a character who hunted for his secret knowledge of flying saucers—and explained that nothing could be done without his partner's approval.

A few days later, Leslie received an angry response from Crisman. "I do not want this matter in public print!" he declared and expressed his anger that Dahl was so forthcoming. "He will not correspond with you again."[60] Leslie had the ambition of collecting information from the pair and publishing an unvarnished version of the Maury Island story. He was quite disappointed in Crisman's hostility and tried through several letters to both Dahl and Crisman to ameliorate the controversy, if indeed it was "Dahl." Some researchers suggest that the letters from Harold Dahl, the Easy Papers, and much of the other written documentation of this story may have actually been written by Crisman, even though the address was in Tenino, Washington, not New Orleans.[61]

In any event, "Dahl" caved in to Crisman's concerns immediately, but he kept in contact with Leslie for other purposes. He had an interest in promoting the work of Dr. Frank E. Stranges of Van Nuys, California. "Dahl" sought the help of Leslie's UAPRO group to

Another view of the tramps, with police guards casually lowering their weapons. House Select Committee on Assassinations investigator Gaeton Fonzi reported that the HSCA investigated only the possibility that the "Hunt" tramp was Crisman (*The Last Investigation,* New York: Thunder's Mouth Press, 1993), although he more clearly resembles the first one above (and the "Sturgis" tramp looks more like Crisman's associate Thomas Beckham.) Fonzi's use of the "Chrismon" spelling suggests that HSCA relied on the Torbitt document identification.

organize a showing a film by Stranges. Leslie obliged and continued to pursue the photographs and written statements from "Dahl." In a last letter from Crisman/ Dahl ("I am irrevocably tied to Hal in any questions that arise on the Maury island incident"), he claims that he has only shared his views and research materials on Maury Island with small business and academic groups "that have extra and advanced knowledge" about UFOs. "I travel widely and this allows me to be in areas that do have certain of the extra 'attentions' of the UFOs. It has always been a type of precise 'high-wire' balance act to

STATE OF WASHINGTON
DEPARTMENT OF HEALTH

STATE OF WASHINGTON DEPARTMENT OF SOCIAL AND HEALTH SERVICES
VITAL RECORDS
CERTIFICATE OF DEATH

#31

LOCAL FILE NUMBER

1. NAME - FIRST, MIDDLE, LAST: Harold A. Dahl
3. SEX: M
3. DEATH DATE (MO DAY YR): Jan. 30, 1982
146-8 2 00272
STATE FILE NUMBER

4. RACE (WHITE, BLACK, AM. IND.): White
5. AGE - LAST BIRTH. DAY (YRS): 70
8. BIRTHDATE (MO DAY YR): Aug. 15, 1911
9. COUNTY OF DEATH: Grays Harbor

10. CITY, TOWN OR LOCATION OF DEATH: Mc Cleary
11. PLACE OF DEATH: Mark E. Reed Hospital
12. RECEIVED EMERGENCY CARE: No YES/NO

13. BIRTH STATE: Washington
14. CITIZEN OF WHAT COUNTRY: USA
15. MARRIED, NEVER MARRIED, WIDOWED, DIVORCED: Divorced
16. SPOUSE (IF WIFE GIVE MAIDEN NAME):
17. WAS DECEDENT EVER IN U.S. ARMED FORCES? No YES/NO

18. SOCIAL SECURITY NO.: 536-12-8475
19. USUAL OCCUPATION: Surplus dealer
20. KIND OF BUSINESS OR INDUSTRY: Self employed

21. RESIDENCE - NUMBER AND STREET: 326 W. First
22. CITY/TOWN OR LOCATION: Roy
23. INSIDE CITY LIMITS: Yes
24. COUNTY: Thurston
25. STATE: Washington

26. FATHER - NAME FIRST, MIDDLE, LAST: Theodore Dahl
27. MOTHER - MAIDEN NAME FIRST, MIDDLE, LAST: Anastasia Nork

28. INFORMANT - NAME: Betty L. Preston
29. MAILING ADDRESS STREET OR RFD NO. CITY OR TOWN STATE ZIP: P.O. Box 429 Roy, Washington 98580

30. BURIAL, CREMATION, REMOVAL, OTHER: Burial
31. DATE (MO DAY YR): Feb. 3, 1982
32. CEMETERY/CREMATORY - NAME: Fern Hill Cemetery
33. LOCATION - CITY/TOWN, STATE: Aberdeen, Washington

34. FUNERAL DIRECTOR (SIGNATURE):
35. NAME OF FACILITY: Selene Mortuary 202 E. 9th
36. ADDRESS OF FACILITY: Olympia, Washington 98501

37. TO THE BEST OF MY KNOWLEDGE DEATH OCCURRED AT THE TIME, DATE AND PLACE AND DUE TO THE CAUSE(S) STATED.
41. ON THE BASIS OF EXAMINATION AND/OR INVESTIGATION, IN MY OPINION DEATH OCCURRED AT THE TIME, DATE AND PLACE AND DUE TO THE CAUSE(S) STATED.

SIGNATURE AND TITLE: X
SIGNATURE AND TITLE: X

38. DATE SIGNED (MO DAY YR): 2-1-82
39. HOUR OF DEATH (24 HRS): 0905
42. DATE SIGNED (MO DAY YR):
43. HOUR OF DEATH (24 HRS):

40. NAME AND TITLE OF ATTENDING PHYSICIAN IF OTHER THAN CERTIFIER:
44. PRONOUNCED DEAD (MO DAY YR):
45. HOUR PRONOUNCED DEAD (24 HRS):

46. NAME AND ADDRESS OF CERTIFIER - PHYSICIAN, MEDICAL EXAMINER OR CORONER: Dr. E.R. Macke 110 Birch St. McCleary, Washington

47. IMMEDIATE CAUSE: (A) metastatic Cancer colon
INTERVAL BETWEEN ONSET AND DEATH: 2 yr

DUE TO, OR AS A CONSEQUENCE OF:
(B)
INTERVAL BETWEEN ONSET AND DEATH:

DUE TO, OR AS A CONSEQUENCE OF:
(C)
INTERVAL BETWEEN ONSET AND DEATH:

48. OTHER SIGNIFICANT CONDITIONS:
49. AUTOPSY? (YES/NO): No
50. WAS CASE REFERRED TO MEDICAL EXAMINER OR CORONER? (YES/NO): No

51. ACC. SUICIDE, HOM., UNDET., OR PENDING INVEST.:
52. INJURY DATE (MO DAY YR):
53. HOUR OF INJURY (24 HRS):
54. DESCRIBE HOW INJURY OCCURRED:

55. INJURY AT WORK? (YES/NO):
56. PLACE OF INJURY - AT HOME, FARM, STREET, FACTORY, OFFICE BLDG, ETC. (SPECIFY):
57. LOCATION - STREET OR RFD NO. CITY/TOWN, STATE:

58. REGISTRAR SIGNATURE: X Lauren H. Lucke M.D.
59. DATE RECEIVED (MO DAY YR): FEB 3 1982

STATE REGISTRAR ONLY
ITEM DOCUMENTARY EVIDENCE: REVIEWED BY: DATE: ITEM DOCUMENTARY EVIDENCE REVIEWED BY: DATE:

DSHS 9-150 (REV. 1-82)

DOH 01-003 (7/84)

Death records of principal players in the Maury Island story. Courtesy of Ron Halbritter.

DEPARTMENT OF COMMERCE
BUREAU OF THE CENSUS

WASHINGTON STATE DEPARTMENT OF HEALTH
DIVISION OF VITAL STATISTICS
CERTIFICATE OF DEATH

State File No. **73**
Registrar's No. **19**

1. PLACE OF DEATH:
(a) County Cowlitz County
(b) City or town (Rural)
(c) Name of hospital or institution: None **802**
(d) Length of stay: In hospital or institution NO
In this community (Years, months or days)

2. USUAL RESIDENCE OF DECEASED:
(a) State California (b) County LA
(c) City or town Long Beach
(d) Street No. 1118 Chestnut St
(e) If foreign born, how long in U.S.A.? _____ years

3. (c) Social Security Number No Record

3. (a) FULL NAME Frank Mercer Brown
3. (b) Was decedent ever a member of the Army, Navy or Marine Corps of the United States? Yes Act. Name of organization in which service was rendered: AAF Period of service 1-10/12

4. Sex Male
5. Color or race W
6. (a) Single, widowed, married, divorced Married
6. (b) Name of husband or wife Velma K. Brown
6. (c) Age of husband or wife if alive

7. Birth date of deceased February 19 1919
8. AGE: Years 28 Months 6 Days 12 If less than one day ___ hr. ___ min.
9. Birthplace No Record
10. Usual occupation Army Officer
11. Industry or business

Father:
12. Name Unknown
13. Birthplace Unknown

Mother:
14. Maiden name Unknown
15. Birthplace Unknown

16. (a) Informant's own signature Official Army Personnel records, Hamilton
(b) Address

17. (a) Removal (b) Date thereof 8-5-47
(c) Place: Burial, cremation, or removal Long Beach, Okla.
18. (b) Address C. C. Mellinger Funeral Home, Tacoma, Washington

19. (a) 8-4-47 (b) [signature]

MEDICAL CERTIFICATION
20. Date of death: Month August day 1 year 1947 hour 02 minute 37
21. I hereby certify that I attended the deceased from DOA ___ 19 ___ to ___ 19 ___ that I last saw him alive on ___ 19 ___ and that death occurred on the date and hour stated above.
Immediate cause of death crushing and disentegrating traumatic injury
Due to aircraft accident
Due to

Other conditions
Major findings Of operations
Of autopsy

22. If death was due to external causes, fill in the following:
(a) Accident, suicide, or homicide (specify) Aircraft
(b) Date of occurrence 1 August 1947 (accident)
(c) Where did injury occur? Cowlitz Wash.
(d) Did injury occur in or about home, on farm, in industrial place, in public place? NO In forest
(e) [Injury at work?]

23. Signature [signature] (M.D. or other)
Address McChord Field, Wash Date signed 2 Aug 47

DEPARTMENT OF COMMERCE
BUREAU OF THE CENSUS

WASHINGTON STATE DEPARTMENT OF HEALTH
DIVISION OF VITAL STATISTICS
CERTIFICATE OF DEATH

State File No. **74**
Registrar's No. **18**

1. PLACE OF DEATH:
(a) County Cowlitz County
(b) City or town (Rural)
(c) Name of hospital or institution: None **802**
(d) Length of stay: In hospital or institution No
In this community (Years, months or days)

2. USUAL RESIDENCE OF DECEASED:
(a) State California (b) County SF
(c) City or town San Francisco
(d) Street No. 587-24th Avenue
(e) If foreign born, how long in U.S.A.? _____ years

3. (c) Social Security Number No Record

3. (a) FULL NAME William Lee Davidson
3. (b) Was decedent ever a member of the Army, Navy or Marine Corps of the United States? Name of organization in which service was rendered: Period of service:

4. Sex M
5. Color or race W
6. (a) Single, widowed, married, divorced Married
6. (b) Name of husband or wife No Record
6. (c) Age of husband or wife if alive

7. Birth date of deceased January 16 1920
8. AGE: Years 27 Months 6 Days 15 If less than one day ___ hr. ___ min.
9. Birthplace Oklahoma
10. Usual occupation Army Officer
11. Industry or business

Father:
12. Name Unknown
13. Birthplace Unknown

Mother:
14. Maiden name Unknown
15. Birthplace Unknown

16. (a) Informant's own signature Official Army Personnel records - Hamilton
(b) Address

17. (a) Removal (b) Date thereof 8-5-47
(c) Place: burial or cremation Hawthorn, Calif.
18. (b) Address C. C. Mellinger Funeral Home, Tacoma, Washington

19. (a) 8-4-47 (b) [signature]

MEDICAL CERTIFICATION
20. Date of death: Month August day 1 year 1947 hour 02 minute 37
21. I hereby certify that I attended the deceased from DOA ___ 19 ___ to ___ 19 ___ that I last saw him alive on ___ 19 ___ and that death occurred on the date and hour stated above.
Immediate cause of death disentegrating traumatic injury
Due to aircraft accident
Due to

Other conditions
Major findings Of operations
Of autopsy

22. If death was due to external causes, fill in the following:
(a) Accident, suicide, or homicide (specify) Aircraft accident
(b) Date of occurrence 1 August 1947
(c) Where did injury occur? Cowlitz Wash.
(d) Did injury occur in or about home, on farm, in industrial place, in public place? No In forrest
(e) [Injury at work?] Yes

23. Signature [signature] (M.D. or other)
Address McChord Field, Wash Date signed 2 Aug 47

State of Washington }
County of Pierce } ss.

STATE OF WASHINGTON   cx 7876
DEPARTMENT OF SOCIAL AND HEALTH SERVICES
Health Services Division—Bureau of Vital Statistics
Olympia, Washington 98504

AFFIDAVIT
FOR CORRECTION OF A RECORD

I hereby swear that the record of { birth / death } number 9479 for Fred Lee Crisman

who { was born / died } to _____ (Name of father) _____ and _____ (Maiden name of mother) _____

in the city of Seattle, county of King

on 12-10-75 (Date) is incorrect or incomplete as follows:

The record now shows:	The true facts are:
Social Security Number: 532-32-6070	543-32-6070

I further swear that I represent the { deceased } as widow (Parent, attorney, etc.)
and that I have the consent of all parties concerned in stating these true facts. I further declare that if the corrected certificate is questioned, I will assume the responsibility of furnishing proof of the corrected item to the questioning agency.

Signed Mary Frances Crisman (Affiant)

Address 6501 Burning Tree Ln., Tacoma, WA 98406

Subscribed and sworn to before me this _____ day of _____, 1976.

Notary Public in and for the State of Washington, Residing at Tacoma, Wash.

DSHS 9-115 (11-72) HSA-69

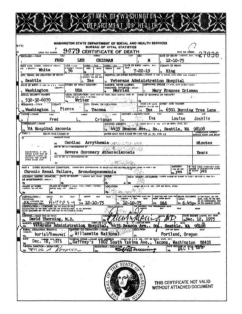

STATE OF WASHINGTON
DEPARTMENT OF HEALTH

WASHINGTON STATE DEPARTMENT OF SOCIAL AND HEALTH SERVICES
BUREAU OF VITAL STATISTICS
9479 CERTIFICATE OF DEATH   27836

DECEASED—NAME: FRED LEE CRISMAN   SEX M   DATE OF DEATH 12-10-75

RACE White   AGE 56   DATE OF BIRTH 7-22-19   COUNTY OF DEATH King

CITY, TOWN, OR LOCATION OF DEATH Seattle   CITIZEN OF WHAT COUNTRY Yes   HOSPITAL OR OTHER INSTITUTION Veterans Administration Hospital

STATE OF BIRTH Washington   USA   MARRIED, NEVER MARRIED, WIDOWED, DIVORCED Married   SURVIVING SPOUSE Mary Frances Crisman

SOCIAL SECURITY NUMBER 532-32-6070   USUAL OCCUPATION Writer   KIND OF BUSINESS OR INDUSTRY

RESIDENCE—STATE Washington   COUNTY Pierce   CITY, TOWN, OR LOCATION Tacoma   STREET AND NUMBER 6501 Burning Tree Lane

FATHER—NAME Fred L. Crisman   MOTHER—MAIDEN NAME Eva Louise Joshlin

INFORMANT—NAME Fred L. Crisman   MAILING ADDRESS 4435 Beacon Ave., So., Seattle, WA 98108

DEATH WAS CAUSED BY:
PART I. (a) Cardiac Arrythemia   Minutes
(b) Severe Coronary Atherosclerosis   Years

PART II. OTHER SIGNIFICANT CONDITIONS Chronic Renal Failure, Bronchopneumonia   AUTOPSY yes   IF YES WERE FINDINGS CONSIDERED yes

CERTIFICATION—AUTOPSY 12-10-75   DATE 12-10-75   DAS   HOUR 6:45

David Thorning, M.D.   DATE SIGNED Dec. 12, 1975

MAILING ADDRESS Veterans Administration Hospital, 4435 Beacon Ave., So., Seattle, WA 98108

BURIAL, CREMATION, REMOVAL burial/Removal   CEMETERY OR CREMATORY—NAME Willamette National   LOCATION Portland, Oregon

DATE Dec. 18, 1975   FUNERAL HOME Gaffney's 1002 South Yakima Ave., Tacoma, Washington 98405

FUNERAL DIRECTOR—SIGNATURE   REGISTRAR—SIGNATURE   DATE DEC 19 1975

THIS CERTIFICATE NOT VALID
WITHOUT ATTACHED DOCUMENT

keep up an investigative and reporting interest and at the same time deal with the areas of a business world that has no interest in such matters."

With reluctance, Crisman acquiesced to "Dahl's" interest in sharing with Leslie, but no record exists that the contact continued. Crisman closes with a report that he went to the original Maury Island UFO site, and found it barren of plant growth and surrounded by signs that the area would be razed for the sake of an unnamed federal project. "Why?...A bit of inquiry revealed that government men of some agency have returned over the years...many times for soil samples and pictures."

The name of Dr. Frank Stranges, still a personality in UFO circles in 1999, came up once more in research surrounding Crisman. The director of NICUFO (the National Investigations Committee on UFOs), Stranges was approached by an investigator for famed Kennedy assassination researcher and author Bernard Fensterwald. Fensterwald had received a leaflet from another noted author in the field, Paris Flammonde, that had Crisman's business partner—and a suspect in the anti-Castro milieu according to Jim Garrison—Thomas Beckham listed on NICUFO's board of directors. The investigator determined that Beckham met Stranges through Crisman.[62] The August 1993 release of an interview transcript with Beckham affirmed that Crisman managed his singing career and had introduced him to the UFO world.[63]

One other UFO circuit personality had a non-encounter with Crisman: Wayne Aho. Aho had remained active in the ufological community since his spaceship encounter in the Mojave Desert on May 11, 1957. Crisman invited him to attend the First Midwest UFO Conference in Omaha, Nebraska on August 12, 1967. Aho showed, but Crisman did not. Aho had previous involvement with shady characters on the UFO fringe. He and a business associate named Otis T. Carr were indicted in the late 50s for an investment scheme to develop a flying saucer that ran on free energy. The two were indicted for selling hundreds of thousands in illegal stocks, but charges against Aho were dropped. Carr was convicted and given a $5,000 fine. Like the money that Beckham and Crisman allegedly raised, the final disposition of Carr's profits remains unknown.

Aside from these instances, Crisman kept to his principle of avoiding publicity with regard to Maury Island and UFOs. He returned to his traveling and "the areas of a business world that has no interest in such matters." After the radio show, the Garrison subpoena, and his career with politics and the public, Crisman tried to start a public television station in Tacoma in 1975.[64]

The charge that he was one of the mystery tramps at Dealey Plaza on November 22, 1963 arose again in the mid-70s in articles that appeared in *True* magazine and *Crawdaddy*. Crisman maintained his story that he was teaching high school in Rainier on that day.[65]

The next time Fred Crisman ran for office, for a seat on the City Council; he lost by over 10,000 votes.[66] In September 1974, he was hospitalized for kidney failure. In April 1975 he married Mary Frances Borden, an ally in his library political battles. On December 10, 1975, Fred Crisman died at the age of 56.[67]

Notes:
1. *Coming of the Saucers*, p. 111
2. Crisman's social security number was 543-32-6070.
3. Crisman's son maintained that his father belonged to the Civilian Conservation Corps during this period.
4. Thompson, Paul B., "UFO Cautionary Tales #5, The Maury Island Case," Parascope web site (www.parascope.com), 9/16/98.
5. Halbritter notes that the Hanford Nuclear Plant Theory can be debunked "by anyone who simply looks at a map of the state of Washington. One of those oversize *Road Atlas'* is ideal. Notice that the Hanford Atomic reservation is located (intentionally)

east of the Cascade Mountain range, in an immense desert area. the Atomic Energy Commission, intended to utilize all that immense desert area for storage of Nuclear Wastes.

Maury Island is located in the Puget Sound Harbor, near Tacoma/Seattle Washington, and is surrounded by both the Cascade and Olympic Mountains. Mount Rainier, where Kenneth Arnold reported his observation is the highest mountain in the cascade range, and sits directly between the Hanford reservation and Puget Sound.

Tons of radioactive waste, shipped by either barge or airplane, would follow the mighty Columbia River, and use the river gorge to pass through the Cascade Mountains, near Portland, Oregon. This is the route followed by Kenneth Arnold flying from Boise, Idaho. Passing south of Hanford at Pendleton, Oregon he followed the Columbia until Chehalis, Washington, then turned north to Tacoma.

But if the objective is disposal of nuclear waste, why go north to Puget Sound, when the easiest route is to continue down the Columbia directly into the Pacific?

This may not make much sense to a person without a map, but looking at a map it should be easy to follow. Conceded that nuclear residue may turn up in some unusual places, but Puget Sound is not going to be one of those places."

Halbritter also notes Jacques Vallee's point in *Confrontations* that the Maury Island slag fragments showed no sign of radioactivity, even after lab analysis. Notes from Ron Halbritter to author, 1996.

6.   He included this observation about Maury Island: "I set about to make a trip to Maury Island in early 1950 to visit the site of the crash…the crash area was fenced off with barbed wire, and uniformed guards were still patrolling the area with rifles. In light of the Air Force's later claim that the entire matter was a hoax, this is hard to explain."

7.   Kimery, Anthony L., "The Secret Life of Fred Crisman," *UFO Magazine*, Vol. 8, No. 5, pp. 35-38.

8.   According to Kimery, "Intelligence sources say he was a member of a secret fraternity of former intelligence officials."

9.   Russell, Dick, *The Man Who Knew Too Much*, Carrol & Graf: New York, 1992, p. 216.

10.   Kimery, p. 36.

11.   Kimery notes that the U.S. General Accounting Office claimed in 1985 that Operation Paperclip ended in 1947, essentially denying that it was an ongoing program of the space race. Nevertheless, in 1984 the U.S. Justice Department prepared a case against

Paperclip Nazi Arthur Rudolph, an operations director at Mittelwork. Rudolph directed the Saturn V program that built the Apollo and Skylab rockets. NASA gave him its Distinguished Service Medal in 1967. Rather than face the Justice Department charges, however, he renounced his American citizenship and went back to Germany (with full pension). No Paperclip Nazis were ever prosecuted for war crimes. Piszkiewicz, Dennis, *The Nazi Rocketeers: Dreams of Space and Crimes of War*, Westport, CT, 1995.

12. Thomas, Kenn, *NASA, Nazis & JFK: The Torbitt Document and the Kennedy Assassination*, Kempton, IL: Adventures Unlimited Press, 1996, p. 142.

Researchers Kalani and Katiuska Hanohano dispute that Shaw was present at Von Braun's surrender. Acknowledging that memos released by the Justice Department indicate Shaw's CIA connection going back to 1949, with a heavy period of report filing by Shaw until 1956 ("Garrison Investigation: Queries from Justice Department," September 28, 1967"; CIA Memo to Justice Department, September 28, 1967), as well as corroborative testimony from former executive assistant to CIA deputy director Victor Marchetti and former director Richard Helms (given too late to help Garrison's prosecution), the Hanohanos nevertheless argue that little support exists for a link between Shaw and Operation Paperclip. Author Jim DiEugenio notes that such support may emerge when OSS files have been declassified on Shaw and Thrasher. Similarly, claims of Crisman's attachment to the OSS so far may come only from Crisman. (Hanohano, Kalani and Katiuska, "Notorious Fred Crisman, Part II," *UFO Magazine*, Vol. 9, No. 1, 1994, pp. 30-37.)

Bill Seibert, archivist at the National Personnel Records Center, adds that according to a note appended to morning reports, orders were cut (AG300.4) for Clay Shaw to be placed on temporary duty in the U.S. on March 28, 1945, and no entry of his returning to the European Theater of Operations exists in morning reports through June of that year.

Jim DiEugenio also notes that Shaw's entry in *Who's Who in the South and Southwest*, which outlined his association with Permindex and his military history with Charles Thrasher. (DiEugenio, pp. 209 and 214) stopped appearing after the 1963-64 edition.

13. Popular and critical response to Oliver Stone's movie led to the creation of the Assassinations Material Review Board, a broad governmental effort to declassify records pertaining to the assassination, which continued work through September 1998. It declassified the Crisman letter on September 27, 1996.

14. William Turner suggested that Garrison received a second letter about Crisman, but it did not emerge with the other documents surfaced by the Assassination Material Review Board.

15. Ashman, Charles, Interview with Ernesto Rodriguez, *Los Angeles Times*, 1975.

16. Golz, Earl, Interview with Ernesto Rodriguez, *Dallas Morning News*, 3/7/79.

17. Castro ostensibly did this in retaliation for plots against his life initiated by the Kennedy administration. The best case for this can be found in the 1998 book *Live By The Sword* by Gus Russo (Baltimore: Bancroft Press, 1998). The idea that Castro was behind Kennedy's assassination has long been dismissed as a second tier of CIA deniability. Oswald had to be framed as a lone assassin because pointing the finger at the true culprit, Castro and his Soviet masters, would have led to World War III, according to this theory. Several factors mitigate against it: 1. Back channel rapprochement was happening between Cuba and the U.S. at the time; 2. A CIA agent named E. Howard Hunt, also connected to Crisman by his possible presence in Dealey Plaza, later confessed to creating a public image of Oswald as a Castro agent to justify another invasion of Cuba; 3. Through a double agent, Rolando Secades Cubela, Castro apparently discovered that the murder plots against him did not track back all the way to JFK, but instead to autonomous military intelligence cels, possibly led by Edward Lansdale.

18. DiEugenio, Jim, *Destiny Betrayed: JFK, Cuba and the Garrison Case*, New York: Sheridan Square Press, 1992, p. 127.

19. Garrison, Jim, *On the Trail of the Assassins*, New York: Sheridan Square Press, 1988, p. 9.

20. Garrison, pp. 3-4.

21. Garrison's *Who's Who* listing records that the Louisiana bar admitted him in 1949, and this would have happened just after his FBI service according to his biography. *Who's Who in America*, 37th edition, Volume 1, 1972-1973, Chicago: *Marquis Who's Who*, p. 1117.

22. *NASA, Nazis & JFK*, p. 114. The Torbitt Document continued its samizdat, and later internet, existence until its 1996 under the title *NASA, Nazis & JFK*, with introductions by Kenn Thomas and David Hatcher Childress, when it became a published book.

23. *NASA, Nazis & JFK*, pp. 130-131.
24. *NASA, Nazis & JFK*, pp.144-146.
25. *NASA, Nazis & JFK*, p. 147.
26. *NASA, Nazis & JFK*, p. 146.
27. The Hanohanos note: "Rumors have circulated for years that Clay Shaw knew Crisman...There is no substance to this claim. The genesis of this rumor can be traced to an anonymous letter sent from Florida to Jim Garrison. This letter claims that Crisman had helped supply 'the money for certain political campaigns' in Louisiana and Washington State and in return, was protected by these regional politicians." The letter also claims that Crisman "was the first man that Clay called after being told he was in trouble..." The Hanohanos also point out that an article appearing in the November 1975 issue of *Crawdaddy* ("Secret Agent Man Meets The Mystery Tramp") which stated that Crisman's number appears in Shaw's phone book was demonstrably false. A copy of the book found at the Assassination and Research Center in Washington D.C. does not have the number.

     The Hanohanos also report that Dr. Larry Haapanen of Lewis-Clark State College in Idaho may have talked Garrison out of including mention of Crisman in his book, *On the Trail of the Assassins*. Haapanen "was very familiar with the information that Garrison had to work with and he felt that the inclusion of this unsubstantiated material would weaken Garrison's book."
28. Researcher Steve Gaal points out that "defense plants are cash cows but can be taxed locally. The local politics must be controlled. Long Beach had a mayor who protected Boeing. Later he was supported by Standard Oil for governor and he won." Correspondence with author, 1997.
29. Gold, Jon, *Murder of A City*, Tacoma, 1968, p. 123.
30. Arguments have been advanced that the writing style of the "Easy papers" suggests forgery because it does not match typical government bureaucratese. The letters surrounding the FOIPA releases of these documents, however, also contain an unusually conversational tone. Phillip Klass raised similar arguments about the dating formats on the MJ12 documents and lost a bet to fellow UFO researcher Stanton Friedman, who found government documents in a variety of formats. Crisman's temperament and inclination toward melodrama would not automatically have excluded him from service in the intelligence community—witness the career of G. Gordon Liddy—and neither would his writing style. The overwrought prose of the James Bond novels by Ian Fleming, for instance, became reality in many of the absurd CIA attempts to oust Castro. Efforts to shower Havana with money

and U.S. propaganda leaflets, create a religious vision in the
Cuban sky, and make Castro's beard fall out originated in a
conversation between Fleming, JFK and Ed Lansdale. (Russo,
Live By the Sword, p. 45)
31. Boylan, D., "A League of Their Own: A Look Inside the Christian Defense League," *Fourth Decade*, Volume 4, Number 5,
July 1997, pp. 10-14. Boylan cites reference in correspondence
from Ed Jeffords to James Alcock, July 18, 1968.

In correspondence with Ron Halbritter (9/9/94), researcher
Vaughn Greene recalled that Crisman belonged to the Christian
Anti communist Crusade, the Universal Life Church, "Gerald
L. K. Smith's nut group," something called the Sons of Aware-
ness, and also the Knights of the Golden Circle.
32. Russell, *The Man Who Knew Too Much*, pp. 194-195.
33. Scott, Peter Dale, *Deep Politics II: Essays on Oswald, Mexico
and Cuba*, Skokie, IL: Green Archive Publications, 1995, p. 114.
34. "UFO's Explained!", news release privately published by Reverend Bob LeRoy, November 10, 1996.
35. In correspondence with the author, Rev. LeRoy gave a brief
history of the Minute Men: "I knew Bob DePugh about as well as
any man alive, from 1962-1980! We split up in 1980 because he
wanted to buy my privately owned newspaper in 1979. I agreed to
sell out to him for $2,000. That was only $1 per name on our
mailing list. He paid me about 2 or 3 $200-per-month payments
in 1979 and 1980, then ran out of money and stopped the payments. After a few months of waiting, I consulted a lawyer. He
advised me to take the paper back, so I just started publishing it
again in 1980 (summer), after moving to New Jersey from Missouri.

The Minute Men was national and split into three regions:
East Coast; Central States (my area); and West Coast. Had over
30,000 readers of a newsletter called the *On Target,* went out in
the late 70s, 1962-1980...Nearly all of the "Christian Identity"
leaders came to our annual conventions in Kansas City, MO
from 1973-1980. I have met them all at one time or another. I
was one of the few Baptist ministers who fully supported the
Minute Men from 1962 to 1982. Now the new militia movement
has taken over most of the old Minute Men. DePugh and I both
believed like Gerald L. K. Smith. But we were not as anti-
Jewish or anti-Negro as Smith and also the New Identity pastors.
The Identity people under Sheldon Emry; Colonel Bill Gale of
California; Gordon Kahl of Harvey, ND; Bob Miles of Michi-
gan; Richard Butler of Idaho; James Ellison of Arkansas; Louis
Beam of Texas; Mr. J.B. Stoner of Georgia; Larry McCurry of

Montana; K. A. Badynski (KKK) of Tacoma, WA; Col. Jack Mohr of Mississippi; Rev. Thom Robb of Arkansas; and Dr. Ed Fields of Georgia; etc. were all leaders and editors of small newsletters like myself. Some are still at it after 40 years. Colonel Gale and I both fought Japs together in Leyte and Luzon (1944-45). He was about 5 years older than I. The youngest Captain (and Major Colonel later) in the U.S. Army. I was a mere PFC, LM gunner and parachutist for 3 years with 511th P. Inf. Reg. There.

The movement got its start under Wesley Swift of California during World War II and grew under R. Butler and Colonel Gale, who studied under his teachings. Rev. Sheldon Emry operated on his own in Arizona. Others in other states did the same thing. So, like the Baptists, Lutherans, Presbyterians, Pentecostals, Methodists, etc., they are split-up into dozens of right-wing factions nationally.

All names were semi-secret and given a number to use in all (1962-1982) communications. My number was 511, given after my WWII Parachute regiment. DePugh's was #551, etc. The FBI finally caught on in late '66 and '67. They began writing phony letters to some of the Minute Men, signing them 551, etc. Giving phony mail drops to thousands, thus causing more confusion among us." Letter to author, May 14, 1996.

36. From Jim Garrison to Jonathan Blackmer, July 18, 1977. Released by the House Select Committee on Assassinations, June 6, 1993. HSCA Record Number: 180-10112-10294. Agency File Number: 013519. Although labeled "open in full," Garrison's notes refer to "fairly meaty" letters and attachments that did not emerge as part of the Freedom of Information recovery.

37. Thomas, Kenn, "Interview with Kerry Thornley," *Steamshovel Press #5*, Summer 1992. Kerry Thornley became well-known in the information underground and marginals press. He co-wrote the *Principia Discordia*, the central "text" of the satirical Discordian religion, which worshiped Eris, a goddess of chaos. When Thornley died on November 28, 1998, he had plans to publish on the internet a manuscript he wrote detailing his involvement with the Kennedy assassination.

38. Aside from a January 1963 stay at the Mandeville mental institution north of Lake Pontchartrain. Garrison says, "Mandeville, unlike Jackson (where 8 months later Shaw and Ferrie were apparently trying to plant Oswald) is essentially a civil mental institution, where commitment is often voluntary. Jackson, on the other hand is strictly for the criminally insane. Perhaps Beckham had a temporary mental problem or perhaps his new,

older friends were toying with the possibility of an alternative
patsy in case of a last minute problem with LHO. In any case,
the Mandeville hospital refused to supply us voluntarily with
information and the point involved was not sufficiently significant to justify our seeking a court order."

39. Weberman, A.J. and Canfield, Michael, *Coup D'Etat in America*,
San Francisco: Quick Trading Company, 1975, 1992 revised.

40. A heavily redacted document labeled "DOD Notes" in the
Crisman FOIPA search (HSCA 180-10067-10418) reviewed a anti-
Castro plot in Miami involving a St. Louis native named Manuel
Aguilar: "Aguilar approached [redacted; Crisman?] in June 1970
regarding a plan against Cuba, including plot to exfiltrate top
GOC officials, a KOMAR patrol boat; jet aircraft. Claimed to
have 'cells' of supporters in Cuba and U.S., believed to be mem-
bers of Alpha 66, one possible Minola (sic) Ray." It adds, "[Re-
dacted; Crisman?] met Aguilar in 1961 through Felipe Vidal,
Santiago. Aguilar also known as 'Minola.' Aguilar had worked
for Raul Castro's right-hand man, 7-foot Negro, Hector Aldamas."
Does this suggest a Cuban origin for some of the Crisman/
Beckham "Cuban money"?

Another document in the "DOD Notes" file, a posthumous
application for a military award ("DOD" stands for "Date of
Death," strangely inappropriate to the information on Aguilar),
established a continuous service record in the military for Crisman
from May 26, 1942 to March 30, 1943. (HSCA 180-10115-10012.)
It lists that Crisman received the Distinguished Flying Cross in
World War II, an Air Medal with leaf cluster, four Purple Hearts,
British DFC Empire Medal, Star of Burma, American Theatre
Service Medal, Asiatic Pacific Service Medal, World War II
Victory Medal, Korea Distinguished Flying Cross, an Air Medal
for Korea, a UN Service Medal, Army Occupation Medal (Ja-
pan), and had February 19, 1946 as his separation date from the
Army despite service listed through 1953.

The "DOD" notes also refer to Walter C. Reudi of
Collinsville, IL, and law infractions involving sub-machine guns
and, M-14 rifle magazine body rejects from the Edison Tool and
Die Company in Collinsville, and 23 rocket launchers recovered
by the FBI.

41. Memorandum from William Hoxley to Jim Garrison, "Interview with Bob Lavender," February 19, 1968.

42. William Turner mentioned the existence of a second letter, and
Garrison referred to one, only originating from Dallas.

43. HSCA record number 180-10112-10295, Agency file number
013519, released 6/25/93.

44. Burton, Steven J., "Garrison Uncovers New Figure in JFK Assassination," *Los Angeles Free Press*, 11/8/68.
45. California governor Ronald Reagan assured that Bradley would never stand trial. Reagan refused to allow Bradley's extradition from that state. ("Crisman And Lawyer Going To JFK Quiz," *Washington News Tribune*, 11/20/68.)
46. See footnote 31. Jeffords, Edd, "JFK Case Subpoena Served On Crisman," Tacoma, *Washington New Tribune*, November 7, 1968. In his autobiographical book, *Murder of a City*, Crisman called journalist Jeffords "a supporting link in the whole 'hippie-coffee shop—G.I. subornment' world in Seattle and Tacoma" and accused him of complicity in his concealed weapons and drunken driving arrest of October 31, 1968. He suggested also that Jeffords' status as chairman of the Washington State Committee of Investigation Into the Death of John Kennedy had something to do with his subpoena from Garrison.
47. "Garrison Witness Asks More Cash," *New Orleans States Item*, 11/8/68.
48. Jeffords, Ed, "Crisman Home After Grand Jury Testimony," Tacoma, Washington, *New Tribune*, November 27, 1968.
49. "Crisman Case Set for Feb. 28," Tacoma, Washington, *New Tribune*, 1/10/69; "Judge Fines Announcer," Tacoma, Washington, 3/3/69.
50. "Lynn E. Hodges Files Libel Suit Against Station," Tacoma, *Washington News Tribune*, 1/30/69.
51. Gold, Jon, *Murder Of A City*...Tacoma, Twin Gates Publishing Company: Twin Gates, Washington, 1970, 191 pp.
52. Wolff, Richard, "Anti-manager Group Draws 50 to Talks," *Tacoma News Tribune*, March 20, 1969. "Sweetened Sugar Bowl: Backers Give Mayor Campaign Ammunition," *Tacoma News Tribune*, June 18, 1969.
53. Wilkins, Jack, "Slim Praises Pals, Raps Detractors as Era Ends," *Tacoma News Tribune*, January 7, 1970.
54. "Hodges Halts Libel Suit," *Tacoma News Tribune*, February 4, 1970.
55. "CTV Firm Plans To Sue City Council," *Tacoma News Tribune*, April 16, 1971; "Complete Unofficial Councilman Vote," *Tacoma News Tribune*, September 22, 1971.
56. Gibbs, Al, "Mismanagement Called Cause of Libraries Woes," *Tacoma News Tribune*, October 13, 1971. "Library Director Answers Critic," *Tacoma News Tribune*, October 13, 1971. "Three Attend Library Meet," *Tacoma News Tribune*, January 26, 1972.

1963 — 64
21

10/1/63	Appleby — all day — Illness	—	none
10/2/63	Appleby — all day — Illness	—	none
10/14/63	Wray — all day — Illness	—	none
10/15/63	Wray — all day — Illness	much	(½ day)
10/16/63	Wray all day Illness	·	much
10/17/63	Wray all day Illness	·	much
10/18/63	Wray all day Illness	—	much
11/1/63	much all day — Illness	—	none
11/20/63	Chase — all day — Illness in family	—	Davis
11/26/63	Boyle ½ day — Illness	—	none
11/27/63	Boyle all day — Illness	—	Davis
12/2/63	Bell ½ day — got her airplane uninsured	—	none
12/2/63	Boyle ½ day — Illness	—	Davis
12/3/63	Boyle all day — Illness		Davis
12/4/63	Boyle all day — Illness	—	Davis
1/3/64	Harris ½ day — Illness	—	none
1/3/64	Ingles — ½ day — Illness	—	none
1/6/64	Boyle — ½ day — Illness	—	none
1/7/64	Boyle — all day — Illness	—	Davis
1/8/64	Boyle — all day — Illness	—	Davis
1/9/64	Boyle — all day — Illness	—	Davis
1/10/64	Boyle — all day — Illness	—	much
1/13/64	Wray — ½ day — Illness	—	none
1/20/64	Harris — all day — Illness in family	—	none
1/20/64	Wray — Funeral	·	none
1/29/64	much — all day — Illness	—	none
1/30/64	Dungey — all day — Funeral	—	Davis
2/6/64	Crisman — all day — Illness	—	Davis
2/6/64	Johnson — all day — Illness	—	none
2/7/64	Cressman — all day — Illness	·	Davis
			(all)

Exculpatory of Crisman? This log from Rainier High School, where Crisman taught, indicates that no substitute teacher was called for him on November 22, 1963, supporting Crisman's claim that he was teaching that day. This page and several others from this log are written in a single handwriting.

57. Wilkins, Jack, "Politics Looms In Affairs of Tacoma Library Board," *Tacoma News Tribune*, August 7, 1973. Gibbs, Al, "Library In Hubbub: Jarstad, Crisman Exchange Invective," *Washington News Tribune*, August 22, 1973. Anderson, Win, "Crisman Resigns Position, Charges Library Politics," *Tacoma News Tribune*, October 7, 1973.

58. The Hahanos say that this actually took place at a meeting of something called Understanding Incorporated at the Tacoma Public Library on February 4. Correspondence from Gary Leslie indicates the July date. In either case, this was two years before Mayor Rasmussen appointed him to the board and a year before he started broadcasting on KAYE. (*UFO* Vol. 9, No. 1, p. 34.)

59. The Hanohanos note that this establishes Crisman's connection to New Orleans a year before the subpoena (*UFO* Vol. 9, No. 1, p. 34.)

60. The Hanohanos quote Dahl's widow Helen as saying "Something happened in the late 1960s to change the relationship between my husband and Fred. Fred began calling the shots. It's possible that Fred was blackmailing Hal." It should be recalled, however, that Dahl owned the boat upon which he had his UFO encounter but nevertheless reported it to his "boss," Fred Crisman. Crisman dominated the relationship even in 1947.

61. Support for this notion comes in the form of other letters written by "F. Lee" to noted UFO researcher Lucius Farish in Plumerville, Arkansas from November 1967 to January 1968. The correspondence discusses technical particulars of a well-organized but small and invite-only paranormalist study group called Parapsychology Research, including that its new director would be Crisman chum Robert Lavender, and gives a detailed report about Maury Island. The letters also make mention of the Loch Ness monster and the San Juan Lights and of networking with over 200 Fortean societies. They contain Crisman's complaints about the UFO community, repeat the allusion to *The Invaders* TV show, and note that "Any letter sent to Hal Dahl is usually answered by Crisman - if he bothers to answer at all." See Appendix 4.

62. Hanohano, Kalani and Katiuska, "Beckham Talks About Crisman," *UFO Magazine*, Volume 9, Number 1, 1994, pp. 36-38. The Hanohanos also discuss Milton Northdruft, who had lunch with Stranges and Beckham. Northdruft reports, "Beckham was quite an enterprising individual and gave me the impression of operating rather smoothly, having some solid people on which he could depend when things actually got under way at 8:00 p.m. that evening, with Frank Stranges speaking." Also according to

the Hanohanos, Stranges "was very hesitant to discuss the matter" with investigator Bill La Parl when approached about it at Timothy Beckley's 1992 UFO conference in Phoenix.

63. House Select Committee on Assassinations transcript 014888, Thomas Beckham interviewed by Robert Baras and L. J. Delsa.

64. Sypher, Richard, "TV Station's Promoters Assail TNT Coverage, " *Tacoma News Tribune*, January 10, 1975.

65. Shomshak, Vern, "True Magazine Less Than True—Crisman Says of Article on JFK's death," *Tacoma News Tribune*, May 22, 1975. "Secret Agent Man Meets The Mystery Tramp," *Crawdaddy*, November 1975.

   In December 1978, the House Select Committee on Assassinations summoned Stanley Peerboom, the principal at Rainer High School, to produce Crisman's employment records from the time. Peerboom complied, producing a two-page list with a single handwriting demonstrating that no substitute had been called for Crisman on November 22, 1963. It does reflect several absences for Crisman the following February through May. The accompanying letter from Peerboom points out that "Since the school district did not keep very extensive records at the time, I cannot supply the exact information which you requested. I am supplying all that is available." In a separate letter, however, Peerboom includes the remark, "I can also verify that on the day of the assassination of President John F. Kennedy, I was teaching at the school and Fred Lee Crisman was also teaching at the school on that day." He concludes, "I might mention that I regard Mr. Crisman as a person lacking in truth. I can only say if it is important, I can give reasons for the above statement." Peerboom also doubted the authenticity of a letter he received from Crisman's wife Mary, asking for copies of the same records, but included the letter with the materials he sent to the HSCA.

66. "Elections At A Glance," *Tacoma News Tribune*, November 5, 1975.

67. Obituary, *Tacoma News Tribune*, December 11, 1975. "Council Critic Crisman Dies," *Tacoma News Tribune,* December 11, 1975. "Crisman Native Tacoman," *Tacoma News Tribune*, December 16, 1975.

8

FROM CRISMAN TO CASOLARO

Only a reconstructed version of Fred Crisman's military record is available at the National Personnel Records Center on Page Avenue in St. Louis, Missouri. Many records were destroyed at this facility in a famous fire on July 12, 1973, but Crisman's record should not have been among them. The fire affected only Air Force records "Hubbard through Z" from the period that would have included Crisman. Moreover, the reconstructed record gives no charge-out indication, or record of who removed the original and why.[1]

Any attempt to understand the events at Maury Island in 1947 and their implications must come to grips with the anomalous problems of Crisman's biography. At Maury Island and under subpoena by Jim Garrison, Crisman's presence was telegraphed, in the first instance by pre-existing contact with Ray Palmer, in the second by connection to Garrison and Guy Banister at the FBI office in the Pacific Northwest. The argument that Crisman wrote himself into these situations falls apart in examining those documents, like the Easy papers, that according to the CIA's own analysts were created for the purposes of damaging him.

After he disappeared from the Maury Island scene, Crisman was reactivated as a fighter pilot in Korea. There he suffered mental debilitation and hospitalization. Kenneth Arnold had feared some sort of mind control activity precipitated some of the events surrounding Maury Island. Room 502 almost certainly was bugged, certainly spied upon. United Press bureau chief

Unidentified.

Ted Morello confessed that he too bugged conversations with Arnold, Smith, Dahl and Crisman. The two Air Force intelligence men who lost their lives, Davidson and Brown, were working for an Air Force UFO study project headed by Carl Spaatz and Nathan Twining, and their deaths were never adequately investigated.

Crisman clearly misrepresented himself to the UFO community, in correspondence to Lucius Farish and possibly by representing himself as Hal Dahl to Gary Leslie. What was that all about? He made some distant contact with known ufological figures like Frank Stranges and Wayne Aho, and introduced that world to his business partner Thomas Beckham. Beckham does seem to have been involved with the anti-Castro Cubans that Garrison pursued. Not a great deal of money could be had hustling this group to file incorporation papers, however. It was an aborted effort at best, considering that Crisman thereafter went silent on the UFO issue as he pursued political life in Tacoma. Was he trying to plant disinfo among the ufologists or provide bogus encouragement working on behalf of the military, the government or industrial aerospace?

Garrison's notes show his concern was not for what Crisman knew about Louisiana politicians, as Crisman suspected, but for his involvement with right-wing groups, church fronts and the anti-Castro Cubans. Consider the happy coincidence that members of one of the more significant right-wing groups, the Minute Men, could trace back to the spy network of Charles Willoughby, aide to Douglas MacArthur. MacArthur had expressed openly his concern about an invasion from outer space twice, in comments to the mayor of Naples, Italy in October 1955 and to cadets at West Point in May 12, 1962. Did MacArthur and Crisman simply read too much science fiction? Or was Crisman the military/industrial spy Garrison made him out to be?

Crisman in the *New Orleans States-Item,* November 21, 1968.

Every suspicious thing about Crisman's life, including the Maury Island story, can be chalked up to a con he was pulling, although they never brought him any discernible wealth. More charitable critics might argue that Crisman exploited the paranoid politics of the 1960s for publicity, a remarkably schizophrenic con that has him leaking his involvement in the Kennedy assassination to Garrison (and Copeland, the Torbitt Document author?) for the sake of denying it publicly. Jim Garrison's critics regarded Garrison as paranoid and delusional, even as proof emerged of Clay Shaw's CIA connections. To many, the world of transnational industrial espionage that Garrison saw as the backdrop to the assassination is simply not real, despite its continuing presence in global politics. Con men, industrial spies and low-level disinformationists abound in this environment and one testament to the veracity of Crisman's entanglement is the durability of his influence upon it.

This durability comes primarily through an association with a business partner, Marshall Riconosciuto, who he describes in detail in his 1970 book, *Murder of a City...Tacoma*. Crisman conscripted Riconosciuto in his war against the city management form of government in Tacoma. He describes Riconosciuto, as "a World War II pilot and later public relations man for the local Heidelberg Brewery, [who] had opened his own advertising agency and had been quite successful in local advertising circles. He was the owner of *Channel Magazine*, a TV guide that was a give-away item in most of the motel, hotel and drugstores in the Northwest."[2]

From the back cover of Crisman's autobiographical, *Murder of a City...Tacoma*, 1970.

Crisman reports that "I was producing material for political persons both in Washington and from out of state. Much of my material was sent through several advertising agencies, and I inquired as to what agency could handle material for local consumption. Strangely enough, a name popped up that was familiar but long forgotten. Several friends told me to see Marshall Riconosciuto, of the Riconosciuto Advertising Agency. I was informed that his agency had handled many candidates in the past, and he might need another writer in his stable. The name did ring a bell; and I knew that I must have known him in the 'old days' right after World War II. As it turned out, I did, and we sat in his office and talked politics and old times."

Crisman further described Riconosciuto as "an odd guy. With a name like that he has to have the ability to develop a certain type of patience and kindness to most people who try to spell it! Taller than he looks, his stance always leads one to think that he is a short fellow and one is always surprised at how tall he actually—5-10 or so—and with a husky physique to go with his height. Marshall is the perfect version of the 'hustler' in business, and he always reminds me of the White Rabbit in Alice in Wonderland...no matter where he is he is late for somewhere else. He is on the run from early morning until late at night and in making a complete round of a full day with him I never fail to be surprised at how many times he diverts from his business to do someone a kindness, or to stop and pay a call on an old friend. Marshall had friends tucked away in many odd corners of the city! They range in age from the very young to the aged, from men in high politics to those in the lowest of financial and social straits. He treats them all with the same consideration."[3]

Crisman goes on, "In talking and having lunch with Marshall Riconosciuto, I found that his advertising agency was not geared to handle political candidates on a steady business basis. Instead, it was the rock upon which had been founded *Channel Magazine,* a free TV guide given away in most of the western motels, hotels, and drugstores. He also expanded his original operation to include wholesale drug supplies, and he operated a small lab where certain common drugs were bottled under a variety of house names." As a member of the City Planning Commission, Riconosciuto had power struggles with city manager David Rowlands, was an ally to Mayor Rasmussen, and of course opposed the city management form of government. When Crisman began a newspaper as part of his arsenal in the anti-city management crusade, Riconosciuto gave back door approval—"He stated that he didn't care and that he hadn't offered any service anyway. I did not follow his meaning and I am not clear to the present day if he ever really gave me permission..."—to have him typeset it at Riconosciuto's office at 39 Broadway.[4]

Reaction to this situation provided Crisman's reflected some of his spying experience, perhaps going back to Room 502 at the Winthrop Hotel in 1947: "Before too long, Riconosciuto discovered that the office at 39 Broadway was bugged. "The discovery of listening and broadcasting devices at 39 Broadway only angered Marshall and some of his close friends...Electronic listening is not what it appears to be in the movies and on the television tube. There they simply tune their small hand device in and the words come in clear and with no interference. The hero learns what he wishes to know with no tiresome waiting, and he is off to act upon the vital information that he has learned. Not so in real life. In actuality, the devices work about 10% of the time and in that small bracket the amount of side conversation, radios blaring, TVs blasting and dull monotonous conversation that has no bearing upon what you want to know, is tremendous. I do not recommend electronic bugs for newly minted political spies." Crisman goes on for pages describing bugging and counter-bugging measures in the political struggles of Tacoma, which end in the assassination attempt against him in 1968.

The episode also provided Crisman's continuing link to the world of industrial espionage. The person who found the bug in Riconosciuto's office was Riconsociuto's

22-year-old son, Michael. As early as age 12, Michael Riconosciuto was featured in the *Tacoma News Tribune and Ledger* as an electronics prodigy,[5] and at a young age he constructed an argon laser that led to him working as an assistant to Nobel prize winner Dr. Arthur Schalow.

He emerged in the late 1990s as the chief informant to Danny Casolaro, an investigative writer who died under mysterious circumstance while working on a book about a transnational spook group known as "the Octopus." The Octopus exerted wide-ranging influence on global political affairs, including the assassination of JFK and many veterans of the OSS, a history that mirrored Jim Garrison's conceptions.

Michael Riconosciuto, son of Crisman associate Marshall Riconosciuto, in 1960. *Tacoma News Tribune and Ledger,* November 6, 1960.

The Octopus story turned on Michael Riconosciuto's modifications of a software known as PROMIS developed by a company called Inslaw. The PROMIS/Inslaw case became a cause celebre among those concerned with governmental abuse during Iran/Contra and the Reagan/Bush presidency. Michael Riconosciuto's work was part of a joint venture between the Cabazon Indian tribe of Indio, California, and Wackenhut, the security service of the infamous Area 51, with roots stretching back to such JFK political associates as George Smathers. Riconosciuto also made claims that he witnessed an alien autopsy, before the circulation of the well-known footage of such, as well as knowledge of the group called MJ-12 of UFO spy lore.

Casolaro's odd and unsolved death and his surviving research has been valuable in illuminating international intrique. In addition to the PROMIS modifications, Michael Riconosciuto developed night-vision goggles and fuel-air explosives on the Cabazon tribal land. Casolaro discovered that the fuel-air explosives may have been

used as part of the blast that killed nearly 300 Marines in Lebanon in 1987. The same explosives have since been suspected by various researchers as having been used in the World Trade Towers and Oklahoma City bombings. Major global events from the assassination of Princess Diana— Casolaro was investigating Dodi Fayed's uncle, Adnan Khashoggi as part of the Octopus—to the bombings connected to Osama Ben Laden, whose transnational mission as described by the U.S. mirrors the structure of the Octopus and involves the arms contract structure of the Saudis.

Michael Riconosciuto, 1990s. Riconosciuto became the chief informant to Danny Casolaro, an investigative writer who died mysteriously while investigating a transnational cabal he called *The Octopus.*

If all of this is demented paranoid fantasy, it is a fantasy that at least touches upon demonstrably real events, and as a matter of history has spanned generations. One last eerie coincidence that makes the Maury Island case almost disappear into the tangled web of half-perceived, half-created connections that currently inform global politics, is the fact that Casolaro and his informant Riconosciuto chased after their own strange object in the same Puget Sound environs and Crisman and Dahl—

almost a disk, but in fact, a digital tape. The story is told in one of the few fragments of the original Octopus manuscript that Casolaro left behind:[6]

> It is a pale moon that illuminates the characters in this story. With chords of fear and longing, it is a world of darkness and betrayal that everyone thinks they know but few have seen. The real faces in this world are all too human. Danger Man's mind is as balkanized as the script he lives and the land he travels. Perhaps betrayal becomes a way of life. The background music no longer echoes national anthems but T. S. Eliot's *Gerontion:* "Think/neither fear not courage saves us. Unnatural vices/are fathered by our heroism. Virtues/are forced upon us by our impudent crimes."

These impudent crimes are the subject of this update and a brief capsule seems as hopeless as carving the Lord's Prayer on the head of a secret agent. For, like the enormous Danger Man himself, this story will resist shrinkage. Its events are too febrile, its local color too relentless.

The sun had burned away the morning fog when I arrived in Seattle on Easter Sunday, bound for Everett, some thirty miles away. I had come to visit and retrieve a tape recording from the intriguing Danger Man himself, 43-year-old Michael J. Riconosciuto, whom lawmen had deposited in the Snohomish County jail in Everett, Washington.

The tape Danger Man has recorded a month earlier, he alleged, was a direct threat from a former Justice Department official describing two legal entanglements that were about to befall him if he cooperated with a mushrooming Capitol Hill inquiry. If this tape was retrievable, I knew this scandal was about to be publicly born.

It was during the last year that I began calling Michael "Danger Man." During hours of telephone calls from him, he had told me in exotic detail of his participation in "an enterprise" that worked its way around the world, trading in dope, dirty money, weapons, biotoxins and murder for the secrets of the temple. I had been able to unearth some documentation and a number of other people who were willing to provide a rich array of detail regarding Danger Man, his former associates and the underground empire he described.

But now he had become a key witness in the eight year old legal battle between the Justice Department and Inslaw, a District of Columbia computer company whose software tracking system called PROMIS has been used by law enforcement to track cases and criminals. "But it will track anything once its provided with the rules," Inslaw's founder says.

Inslaw charged, and two courts have agreed, that the software—selling for $150,000 per user—had been stolen by a handful of people in the Justice Department in the course of a contract dispute. Now, Inslaw charges, the software has been distributed by profiteers to intelligence and military agencies in, among other countries, Iraq, Libya, South Korea, Israel and Canada. Inslaw's William Hamilton had independently learned from a Canadian official that PROMIS was being used in 900 different locations in Canada.

A little more than a week before his arrest, Danger Man had filed an affidavit in the case on behalf of Inslaw saying that private interests had hired him in the early 1980s to modify the software for Canadian distribution. Those private interests, he told me, represented tentacles of the underground cabal that made its home on an Indian reservation just north of Mexicali. In the affidavit, Danger Man said he was called in February by a former Justice Department official and warned against cooperating with an investigation into the case by the House Judiciary committee.

He added that the former Justice official told him that if he talked to investigators he would be implicated in an unrelated criminal case and would lose another ongoing child custody case.

Late Friday evening on March 29, on the Key peninsula off Puget Sound, Danger Man was arrested for distribution of methamphetamine.

I arrived in Snohomish County two days later on March 31. This is ponderosa pine and giant fir country flanked by the Cascade Mountain range to the east, Port Gardner Bay and the Olympic Mountains to the west with the Snohomish River snaking through the north end of the city of Everett, the county seat.

By late evening, I had been to the jail a number of times and each time Danger Man was refused visitors on the orders of the U. S. Marshall in Seattle. Still, Danger Man was able to find me at a nearby motel and call several times from the jail with cryptic directions for the retrieval of the tape, his expected movement the following day to a federal magistrate in Tacoma and more details about how dangerous he was becoming to the enterprise.

That enterprise moved drugs, guns and money to the ever-changing temples of power in different parts of the world, the geography changing with the political climate unless the political climate could be changed to suit the enterprise, according to Danger Man, two other "agents of influence," and a former Israeli agent.

But no one is supposed to talk about it, and Danger Man told me again of his best friend Paul who had been murdered in San Francisco almost ten years earlier. "Paul was the best there was as a money mover. The access codes he maneuvered were offshore accounts amounting to over a billion dollars," Danger Man said. "They don't play around. You're just found dead one day."

Traveling to Tacoma with Danger Man's lawyer, I saw seals basking in the only shaft of sun I had seen so far in the Northwest—fat with their catch of steelhead trout moving to freshwater spawning. We talked of Danger Man's allegations, some documentable, and the tape that both of us had been promised.

"Michael sure called this one," the lawyer said.

We arrived in Tacoma just before the 3 p.m. hearing. Danger Man filled the courtroom with his presence. Under six feet tall, he was immense in frame but agile and graceful in movement like some giant white rabbit or perhaps some hybrid fugitive creature related to a fox. A former Air America pilot who says he may know Danger Man under a name other than Michael Riconosciuto says "He was called 'the Fat Man' in Asia." Richard Brenneke won't even talk about Danger Man over the telephone. (Brenneke's claims through the years regarding his role in an "October Surprise" plot to delay American hostages in Iran until after the 1980 election have been bouncing around for some time.)

The hearing before a federal magistrate in Tacoma concerned bail for Danger Man which was refused. While the complaint charged an isolated incident of distributing drugs on March 29, there were four other dates mentioned in which confidential informants with audio and video recordings were used as well.

The next day—April 2—I was driven from Gig Harbor to a patch of bog in the peninsula on the reaches of Puget Sound. This is where, I was told, Danger Man had thrown a copy of the tape from a car on the night of his arrest. I was driven up into the hills on the peninsula. Here the high pine trees, mostly wolf pine, and the red cedar stay in the rain shadow. The ground is mostly scrubland and skunk cabbage heavy with the scent of wild herbs and flowers especially in the pouring rain. Many of the people live in huts, some attached to mobile homes, in the backwater of the peninsula. The first man I was to meet on this far end of nowhere was an old, grey-bearded Swede in a wide-brimmed leather hat. He came out of his hut talking in staccato rhythms and reciting broken poetry. He appeared somewhere between 60 and 70 years of age. "Can you cry?" he asked me. "Then prepare to shed a tear and shed them now," he said. He hardly paused on the hillside in the pouring rain before advising that "The fault is not in the stars. The fault is in ourselves."

When he stopped talking, he started singing, and finally I was able to ask if he had a tape for me.

My driver said "No. He doesn't have the tape. We just wanted you to meet some of Michael's old friends."

Sitting side by side under a tarp, the bearded old Swede took me on a compulsory guided tour of Danger Man from the time he was a child winning science fairs to now. Prior to working with the Nobel Laureate at Stanford's Physics Lab at 16 and 17 years of age, he had suddenly already distinguished himself in mining, sonar, lasers and communications. Much of that I had heard before. Nobel laureate Dr. Arthur Schalow, in a lengthy interview months before, remembered Danger Man well. "You don't forget a 16-year-old youngster who shows up with his own Argonne laser," Dr. Schalow had told me. There was an old article about Danger Man when he was 10 years old after he strung up an alternative telephone service in his neighborhood.

The old Swede, Danger Man's father and my driver wanted to make it very clear that this was a person who made very powerful people take notice of him when he was a boy. But why, I asked, would this group pursue him. Everyone, including Danger Man's father, would tell me "To control him." He had been running from that, I was told, since the mid-eighties when he left the Indian reservation. And now he was regarded as a rogue always presenting a moving targets having been harassed through the years by brigades of law enforcement for one charge or another. I had even found an old letter of his dating back to 1982 in which he described having "to present a periscopic image to the public."

The rain did not let up as the old Swede danced in the brush. I watched a big jack rabbit dart under and then away from the old Swede's tarp before it limped trembling and hidden in the grass. While some creatures are born to hunt, others are born to flee. These are nature's fugitives, and, like the fox, have a curious freedom in the masks they wear and access to obscure regions where no one will follow. Sometimes they have the protective coloring of the hunter but that is the ruse of the fox. They learn that instinctively.

By the end of the week I had trucked back and forth across Puget Sound by daylight and nightfall in an odyssey of pursuit for the tape. I would meet Danger Man in jail and talk with him many times from the Kitsap County jail to which he had been moved on the peninsula.

I had also been placated, I presumed, with documents concerned mostly with weapons, fuel air explosives, documents relating to Gerald Bull, assassinated the previous spring in Brussels, Carlos Cardoen in Chile, mining papers, lab papers relating to scientific experiments with lasers, and letters regarding the return of that mysterious billion dollars which Danger Man said had come from the Nugan Hand bank in Australia. I had already seen some of these documents in the months before but now it looks as though the gumshoes from the House Judiciary Committee would also see them.

Two Capitol Hill investigators had arrived on my heels to interview Danger Man. By the end of the week they had arrived in Seattle, had discussions with the U.S. Attorney, and made arrangements to have Danger Man moved.

"I'm screwed," Danger Man said, "don't you see. These guys are my only hope. I've come up with the cheapest way to refine platinum there is. But I'm screwed because they'll try to show that the chemicals I use at the mine are precursor ingredients to making methamphetamine." The chemicals at one of his labs included, he said, chloracetone, sodium cyanide, nitric acid, ammonium chloride and bags of platinum dust.

If I received the tape, the original, I was to give it to the investigators, he said. I could make a copy, he added, to bring back to Washington, D.C.

The next morning, Danger Man was moved from his cell on the Kitsap peninsula to Seattle where the Judiciary Committee investigators and their stenographer would be interviewing him. I arrived in Seattle and met both investigators. Despite their refusal to let me accompany them on their interview with Danger Man, we reached an agreement to engage in dialogue back in the nation's capitol. They spent all day with Danger Man and then, I learned, provided documents from another repository which I had not seen in Bremerton at the southern tip of the inlet. Having arrived on the 3rd of April, both investigators left on the 5th.

By the tail end of the week, I had learned that federal agents had raided one of Danger Man's labs in the mountainous Pine Creek area west of Tonasket still high in rain and snowmelt as well as his place in Aberdeen, a coastal strip town and still another place in Anaheim, California.

I had previously talked to a Denver businessman about Danger Man and his elusiveness. "I watched Mike demonstrate a new laser weapon he had created," the Denver man said, "a wand that blew whatever he pointed it at straight up in the air. I had called a number of high-ranking military people, and Michael was scheduled to demonstrate this new creation at Fort Hood, Texas. When the time came and we gathered at Fort Hood, Michael just didn't show. That's the way he was then, and I don't expect he's any different now."

The beginning of spring always has its moody, bad tempered transitions but with the tape never emerging, I was more than a little frustrated and more than doubtful in the tape's existence.

"I hope, for your sake, I'm wrong," I told him when he was back in the jail at Kitsap County.

He was unhappy I was leaving. I could sense his feelings grow mute in embarrassment; everything in him withdrew, a silence arose. I was going to be indulgent with whatever he said, which I knew would still leave both of us empty-handed; for ultimately, and precisely in the deepest and most important matters, especially if he was telling the truth, he was unspeakably alone.

I returned home the next day.

Notes:
1. Conversation with Bill Siebert of the National Personnel Records Center, December 1998.
2. *Murder of a City...Tacoma,* pp. IX-X
3. *Murder of a City...Tacoma,* pp. 8-9
4. *Murder of a City...Tacoma,* p. 78-79
5. *Tacoma News Tribune and Ledger,* November 6, 1960.
6. Danny Casolaro's surviving research became the basis for the only book to explore his Octopus thesis in-depth, *The Octopus: Secret Government and the Death of Danny Casolaro* by Kenn Thomas and Jim Keith, Portland, OR: Feral House, 1996.

APPENDIX 1

Memories of Mutan Mion: Richard Shaver Summarized
Brian Redman, *Conspiracy Nation* (www.shout.net/ ~ bigred)

Great classics of the UFO genre of literature belong to the circa-1950s era. This was the time when independent researchers approached the flying saucer manifestations with fresh eyes; a time when the U.S. government cover-up was still in its awkward learning-to-walk stage, and it is likely therefore that real information slipped through.

It was in reading Jim Keith's *Casebook on the Men in Black* that I first came across mention of the Richard S. Shaver stories, "paranoid tales about the 'deros,' a malevolent humanoid race living inside the Earth who occasionally made forays above ground, and who degraded life on the surface by irradiation with harmful electronic rays."[1]

Keith quotes as follows from the original Shaver stories:

Nothing about my fictional creations has been more misunderstood than the "dero." The dero is the human whose mind has been under the influence of detrimental flows of energy until he has become a detrimental robot—shortened to dero.

He is a phenomenon peculiar to the caverns, the readers seem to think. I never meant to infer that the dero was confined exclusively to the cavern life, but only that the worst of earth's deros are to be found among the cavern people.

All earth people are to some extent deros, and especially considered from the viewpoint of all-over result, such as the results we got from our last war; all men are deros.

But in the caverns this stupid following of thought patterns without content of true reason is to be found organized, fixed, honored by the observance of centuries of stupidity; a form of state, a way of life. Up here we have not quite that sad a result from deros among us, as yet.[2]

I next came across mention of the Shaver stories while reading Gray Barker's classic, *They Knew Too Much About Flying Saucers.* According to Barker, Shaver's "deros" (DEtrimental RObots):

(a) once inhabited Earth's surface, and now live in caves;
(b) derive pleasure from terrorizing, torturing and exploiting surface people;
(c) playfully torture individuals, making them hear voices;
(d) engage in interplanetary traffic with evil beings from other planets;
(e) direct harmful rays against mankind.[3]

But lest you think Shaver's stories are nothing more than "stories," there are indications to the contrary. The mysterious Richard S. Shaver sent the legendary Ray Palmer, editor of the now-defunct *Amazing Stories* magazine, a manuscript that Shaver claimed was true. Palmer did not believe the story, and rewrote it, disguised as fiction. But when the series based on Shaver's manuscript began appearing in *Amazing Stories* around 1945, "Palmer became less sure that Shaver was just imagining things."[4]

The Shaver stories ran in Palmer's magazine for five years, and were extremely popular. Circulation soared to 185,000, which is huge for what was a "pulp" magazine. The Shaver stories were big, in the late 1940s, and it is earnestly hoped that some publisher will see fit to re-publish them. I have been fortunate to obtain a copy of some of the Shaver stories, published as *I Remember Lemuria* and *The Return of Sathanas* in 1948. In his foreword, Richard S. Shaver writes, in part, as follows:

I am a simple man, a worker in metal, employed in a steel mill in Pennsylvania. What I tell you is not fiction! I can only hope that when I have told the story of Mutan Mion as I remember it you will believe— not because I sound convincing or tell my story in a convincing manner, but because you will see the truth in what I say, and will realize, as you must, that many of the things I tell you are not a matter of present day scientific knowledge and yet are true!

I am no mathematician; I am no scientist. I have studied all the scientific books I can get—only to become more and more convinced that I remember true things. But surely someone can definitely say that I am wrong or that I am right, especially in such things as the true nature of gravity, or matter, of light, of the cause of age and many other things that the memory of Mutan Mion has expressed to me so definitely as to be conviction itself.

I want to thank editor Ray Palmer, in whose 'fiction' magazine, *Amazing Stories,* the stories in this book were first published, for his open mind and for the way he has received the things I have told him in addition to what I have written in this story of Mutan Mion of ancient Lemuria. It began when he published my ancient alphabet in 'Discussions' and requested the readers to carry out checks of their own.[5]

Regarding Shaver's alphabet, Palmer writes:

January 1945 issue of *Amazing Stories.* Some of the reports by readers were subsequently published, but the great majority were not. These reports proved to be the most amazing the editor has ever received on anything published in his magazine. They would seem to indicate beyond all doubt that the "ancient language" of Mr. Shaver is part of an original "mother tongue" from which all Earthly languages have sprung.[6]

The following synopsis is based on *I Remember Lemuria* and *The Return of Sathanas* by Richard S. Shaver, Evanston: Venture Books, 1948:

"I am a culture man, a product of the laboratories. During the process of my development to culture manhood, I roamed the culture forests of Atlantis, which is the name for Surface Atlan. Sub Atlan is just below Atlantis, while Tean City is located at the center of Mu, at a great depth below Sub Atlan. The walls of the great cavern in which Tean City is located are hardened to untellable strength by treatment with ray-flows which feed its growth until it is of great density. There are many other cities which grew through the centuries to vast size, but none so great as Tean City. Some are abandoned, but all are indestructible; their cavern walls too dense to penetrate or to collapse. Since Tean City is located near the center of Mother Mu, gravity neutralizes itself by opposition. And I was going down into the city of many wonders! Out on the street I took one of the many vehicles that are provided for travel about the city. These vehicles, their weight reduced by a gravity deflection device, are powered by motors whose energy is derived from a gravity focusing magnetic field, by which one side of a flywheel becomes much heavier than the other. This is accomplished by bending gravity fall in the same way that a lens bends a light ray.

Soon I neared the squat entrance to the shafts that fell from Sub Atlan to Center Mu, to Tean City. The elevator dropped sickeningly, so swiftly that a great fear grew in me that I would be crushed by deceleration when we finally stopped. Then, with little sensation, the car stopped. Here at the center of Mu I had become nearly weightless, and the ceasing of even such swift motion did not have ill effects upon my weightless body.

As I was about to leave the elevator, my friend, the elevator control-man drew me aside. "Fear rides the ways down here," he whispered. "Fear is a smell down here that is ever in the nose—a bad smell, too."

I left the elevator car and immediately was immersed in the sensually shocking appeal of a variform crowd, mostly at this hour, a shopping rush of female variforms. There were a great number of creatures of every shape. All were citizens; all were animate and intelligent—hybrids of every race that space crossing had ever brought into contact, from planets whose very names are now lost in time. The technicons may have been wrong in the opinion of some when they developed variform breeding; but they have certainly given life variety. I had never seen so many variforms before. (Variforms are hybrids developed from many interplanetary life forms, mated by deliberate applications of mutative rays in the laboratories of Mu's technicons.) It had indeed been a day of brainstorms, I mused, when some old technicon had realized that not only would a strong integrative field with a rich exd (energy ash) supply cause all matter to grow at an increased rate, but would also cause even the most dissimilar life-gens to unite. It has been the realization that had resulted in various form life. Most of the crosses by this method had resulted in an increased strength and fertility.

Travellers were gazing about lost in wonder at the vaulting glitter of sculptured pillars and painted walls, done by men of a calibre whose work *ro* like myself cannot grasp entirely. (*Ro* is a thing of simple repetitive life pattern easy to understand and control. To "ro" you is to make you do things against your will. A large generator of thought impulse can be set up to *ro* a whole group of people. "Row the boat" is modern and the meaning has become physical force and not mental force. "*Ro* the people" was an ancient method of government. "Romantic" was the name of such a government. Ro-man-tic: science of man life patterning by control. Any person is *ro* who is weaker than the mental impulses about him. Men are *ro* today because they are not self-determining, though they think they are.)

Synopsis
I became a member of my young girlfriend Arl's class. The class was dominated by the immense presence of the teacher, a son of the Titans.

But I sensed a strange, deeply buried and secret fear in the mind of the Titan. There was a gnawing something that a part of his brain dwelt on continually. Fear was a smell that was ever in the nose down here in Tean City. But I concentrated on the lecture:

"A great cold ball hung in space. Once it had been a mighty, living planet, swinging ponderously around a dying sun. Then that sun had gone out, and the deadly cold destroyed life on the once-mighty living planet. But the planet's forests had, in their many ages of life, deposited coal beds untold miles in depth—clear down to the stony core of the planet. Hanging in space the dead immensity of this planet was largely potential heat, for its tremendously thick shell was mostly pure carbon.

"This carbon-encrusted planet was the sun, your sun and mine. A blazing meteor came flaming toward this cold ball. Deep it plunged into the beds of carbon. The fire spread swiftly—an ever-fire of disintegrance, not the passing-fire of combustion—and our sun was born into life-giving flame!

"A carbon fire is a clean fire and contains no dense metals like radium, titanium, uranium, polonium—whose emanations in disintegrance in suns cause old age and death.

"But then, sun heat was clean, and life sprang furiously into being on its daughter, Mu's surface. Nor did this life die—death came only by being eaten. Then life suffered old age not at all, for there was no cause.

I could not help the question that sprang to my lips. "Why do you say 'Then life suffered old age not at all, for there was no cause.'? Is there cause now?" The teacher looked at me. "You are new here, Mutan Mion. Therefore it is easy to understand that you have not heard. Yes, young ro, there is cause.

"I have spoken of the carbon fire as a clean fire. By this I mean that the atoms of carbon, when disintegrated, send forth the beneficial energy ash called exd which can be assimilated by our bodies and used to promote life-growth. However, the source of this ash is not carbon alone, but all other elements excepting the heavy metals such as I mentioned before. It is when these heavy elements begin to disintegrate in the ever-fire that we come to the cause of age.

"The particles of radium and other radioactive metals are the poison that causes the aging of tissue. These particles are thrown out by all old suns whose shell of carbon has been partly or altogether burned away, permitting the disintegrating fire to reach and seize upon the heavy metals at the sun's core. Our sun has begun to throw out great masses of these poisonous particles. They fall upon Mu in a continual flood, entering into living tissue and infecting it with the radioactive disease we call age.

"Eventually, if we remain on Mu, we will grow old, and finally die."

But that alone was not the strange, deeply buried and secret fear I had sensed in the mind of the Titan. "It is not the age poisons you fear," I accused.

"Come students," he said gently. "We will go now to the embryo laboratory."

Many strange machines filled the laboratory. But these machines were subordinate to the real science of this great room, being designed only to chemically and electronically nourish and develop the many human embryos that moved and grew in synthetically duplicated mother-blood in sealed bottles.

The older ones kicked and tugged healthily at the grafted umbilical tube which supplied the life fluid—called Icor, the "blood of the gods." And it was this blood that was the subject of the lecture the Titan now gave us.

He told us of the upkeep and preparation of this fluid, both in the embryo and the adult; the difficult and important part being the process of detecting and removing the slightest trace of the radioactive poisons that cause age.

Once more the Titan commented on the proposed emigration from Mu, weaving it into his lecture. There seemed to me to be an undercurrent of double meaning in his motive for repeating it; a double meaning that I strove to associate mentally with the fear-thing that was something else.

Our aging sun (he said) threw off increasingly large amounts of these sun's seeds, small but dense and active disintegrative particles, and I learned that keeping Atlan's peoples young was an increasingly difficult job for the technicons. I learned that the coordinators were preparing the plans and ships for our migration to a young, new-born sun, where the infection that caused the occasional trouble with detrimental energy robotism or detrimental err in the human did not occur.

The detrimental energy robotism or detrimental err is mainly due to depolarization of the matter of the brain; it is no longer earth polared, it is sun-polared—and hence inducts the disintegrant flows from the sun into the brain by simple dynamic induction. A magnet could become sun-polared and point to the poles of the sun just as an ordinary compass points to the poles of the earth. This is what happens to parts of the brain; they become sun polared. When the depolarization lies in the nervous system and ego recognition of activating centers, the victim is a killer or a repressive reactionary. It is simply true that man is an electrical machine which functions well when his energy flows are of his own creating, but functions especially ill when the energy flows are from the sun. Hence, a mind powered by sun particle energy flows of a detrimental nature becomes a robot. The result is robotism, or the inability to think constructively. Victims of detrimental err have but one basic thought, to kill, in keeping with the natural elemental instinct of the disintegrant metals.

We filed back into the classroom. For a long moment the Titan looked at us, and especially at me. Then he spoke.

"Somehow you have seen the fear in me. Perhaps you have sensed this in other places in Tean City. Yes, there was, and is, fear in me. And it is a fear that we all try to keep secret because those of us who show fear also show suspicion if not knowledge, and either has been equivalent to the signing of a death warrant. There are spying rays on us that seek out our knowledge and destroy us before we can coordinate it into an effective counteraction to the thing that is going on; to the thing we fear.

"It has come to me that certain groups of Atlan are against the projected migration, and the recent disappearance of several men important to our work lends color to the story. Of course we all know that the only units able to do anything of the kind would be the key leaders. Some of these may have accidentally suffered a severe flashback of detrimental ion flow, so that their will has become one under detrimental hypnosis."

Terror In Tean City

That evening Arl took me to a dance. Never had I known that there could be such pleasure! The stimulation of human attraction between male and female, she told me, was due to the generation of many kinds of tiny and fecund spores which grow and are released upon stimulus by male and female. The male spores grow in the female and vice versa, just as pollen between flowers. This cell pollen and the sensation of its growing presence is love.

In the enhanced delight of the dance I was oblivious of all but the bundle of vitality to which my pulse and soul were synchronized, and my arms held Arl as a treasure beyond value.

Then, as I lost myself in pleasure, it happened. The madness of the fear that was upon Tean City struck; and for the first time in my life I knew the true meaning of terror! Arl screamed, and pushing me from her, pointed to the edge of the dance floor. There the great shoulders of a horned son of a Titan hunched, one big hand clutching in desperate agony at the folds of a drape, the other pointing up and out to indicate the path of the ray that played upon him. Even in the face of death his only thought was to tell what he knew of the fear; and to point out its direction so that the technicons might answer with a ray of their own.

But nothing checked the ray; and I realized that contrary to all the usual rules there was no guard ray on duty. No wonder there was fear in Atlan!

"By the Elder Gods!" I swore to myself at the realization that no guard ray was going to protect us. "It is true: our perfect government is not so perfect after all!"

The deadly ray had not ceased. It played first on one figure and then on another; each victim rolling in turn on the floor.

Arl was tugging at my elbow. Together we left the hall. We kept with a group of young Atlans who walked, without panic or the impulse to run, toward the parked rollats (vehicles). I knew why: they feared to attract a spy-ray to themselves.

Arl's fingers pressed warningly on my arm, and I heard her whisper, her voice low, casual. An excited tone might have attracted the curiosity of the mad mind behind the horrible deaths, who must even now be surveying the scene of his mad acts of killing in grisly satisfaction.

"Listen to that man just behind us."

I listened. His voice was also casual—held no excited note. "What lies behind the fear and death here is the mad wish of certain rodite (controllers) to appropriate everything to themselves."

A selfish thing, indeed! But more mad than selfish. Such a view could only be the result of detrimental err.

The speaker went on. "We, the mediocro, know the madness of refusing all of the normal units of life's fabric the right to existence and growth. No social fabric can be built of dull and lifeless robots which are so besotted with detrimental energy that they refuse the least of the units of the fabric their right to growth and intelligence. Therein lies the strength of the social fabric—the unit's realization of its own self and its place in the whole."

I heard another voice, answering in agreement. "Yes, this murderous effort is doomed to failure. The intelligent members of the guilty rodite (controllers) must realize that such murder of the normal life unit is based on the refusal of the right to share in the fruits of the social project."

Another voice chimed in. "If they are intelligent, then why do they act so detrimentally?"

"Perhaps they are all mad," said the first speaker. "The sane unit of such a project will see that the basic unit right is inherent to their own success, and realize that destroying those rights will wreck their own plans. The only thing it can be is that some of the rodite have been detrimentally charged by disintegrant coil leaks."

I could not help breaking into the conversation. "That is right! A detrimental hypnosis in which the self confuses its self-originated impulses with the exterior-originated detrimental impulses to destroy. Such a condition is called dero, or detrimental energy robotism."

The rodites' minds had somehow been overwhelmed by detrimental, evil force flows which in time produced creatures whose every reaction in thought is dominated by a detrimental will. When this process has gone on long enough, a race of dero is produced whose every thought movement is concluded with the decision to kill.

Speeding away in the rollat (vehicle), I wondered, can we help to strive against this immense err, deep-seated in the control-minds about us as it must be; or must we flee at once, before they make impossible our flight?

Somehow I knew that the thought in my mind was in the mind of all. We were in danger. We were marked for disappearance, illness, or horrible death! We must flee, now or never!

Proof of the thoughts of the others came almost instantly. As we later trooped in assumed light-heartedness down a tunnel, one of the accompanying youths proposed a picnic in the forest. He said it loudly, in a merry voice, for the spy-rays were all around. The others chorused their delighted approval, a delight that Arl and I feigned too. All fell in with the project, the unspoken desire to flee strong within us. We reached the elevator shafts that led up to Sub Atlan, from which we would take another lift to surface Mu. As we shot upward, I whispered the news to the elevator man: "The terror is loose in Tean City. Escape as soon as you can. If at all possible, beg off from another descent and be away. There is great danger for all whom they suspect are aware of them."

He masked a straight face, but I could see the concern in his eyes, and the determination to make good his escape also.

As we lolled in apparent ease on the soft sod of the culture forest, the traditional empty spying-glass made its appearance in the circle. No one spoke of it, but it was a significant reminder of death's clutch. That empty globe now had a meaning almost immense. What to do to avoid that damnable mechanical play of detrimental force from the mind of some unknown rodite, staring through the viewplates of his defective, detrimentally hypnotic mechanism? If they thought we were escaping they would seek us out and snatch us back.

And then, as I sat there, an idea presented itself. I knew a way to escape, and I spoke quickly before my thoughts were clear enough for any unseen listener to read. "Let us charter a spaceship and take a look at Mother Mu from above! There is no greater thrill than that to cap the day!"

As one we leaped to our feet. I knew then that our thoughts had been very similar. "We will have to take a shuttle ship first," said a young Titan quickly. "Come. I know the way."

Notes:
1. *Casebook on the Men in Black* by Jim Keith. IllumiNet Press, 1997. ISBN: 1-881532-11-9.
2. qtd. in Keith.
3. *They Knew Too Much About Flying Saucers*, by Gray Barker. IllumiNet Press, 1997. ISBN: 1-881532-10-0.
4. Ibid.
5. *I Remember Lemuria* by Richard S. Shaver. Evanston: Venture Books, 1948.
6. Ibid.

APPENDIX 2

"Sabotage Hinted in Crash of Army Bomber at Kelso"
Paul Lanz, *Tacoma Times,* August 2, 1947

The mystery of the "Flying Saucers" soared into prominence again Saturday when the *Tacoma Times* was informed that the crash of an army plane at Kelso may have been caused by sabotage.

The *Times'* informant, in a series of mysterious phone calls reported that the ship had been sabotaged "or shot down" to prevent shipment of flying disk fragments to Hamilton Field, California, for analysis.

The disk parts were said by the informant to be those from one of the mysterious platters which plunged to earth on Maury Island recently.

Lending substance to the caller's story is the fact that twelve hours before the Army released official identification, he correctly identified the dead in the crash to be Captain William L. Davidson, pilot, and First Lieutenant Frank M. Brown.

Classified Material: At the same time, he informed the *Times,* Kenneth Arnold, Boise businessman who first sighted the flying saucers, and United Airlines Captain E. J. Smith, who also sighted them, were in secret conference in Room 502 at the Hotel Winthrop. A check confirmed the information but neither Smith nor Arnold would disclose the nature of the conference nor the reason for their being in Tacoma.

According to the anonymous caller platter fragments were loaded aboard a B-25 at McChord Field Friday for shipment to the California field. Half an hour after the takeoff the plane crashed near Kelso, Washington. Two enlisted men; Master Sergeant Elmer L. Taff and Technician Fourth Grade Woodrow D. Mathews parachuted to safety.

At McChord field an intelligence officer confirmed the mystery caller's report that the ill-fated craft had been carrying "classified material."

Hint Sabotage: Major George Sander explained: "Classified material means there was a somewhat secret cargo aboard the plane. No one was allowed to take pictures of the wreckage until the material was removed and returned to McChord field."

He declined to say what constituted "classified material."

The theory of sabotage was borne out by the statement of the two crash survivors that one of the engines burst into flames and that regular fire apparatus installed in the engine for such emergencies failed to function.

Names Revealed: Notified of the information passed along by the anonymous informant, Captain Smith said:

"When the story breaks it will be given general release but it will NOT come from this room." At the time he was in the Hotel Winthrop in conference with Arnold.

Saturday Smith said he and Arnold would deny anything that was printed about the secret sessions held in the hotel. However he was visibly disturbed and expressed consternation when notified late Saturday that the names of the dead pilot and co-pilot had been revealed before the army released them.

According to the telephone callers, both the dead officers were members of military intelligence at Hamilton field.

APPENDIX 3

Government Documents
Incident 4AF 1306 I
16 July 1947
Memorandum for the officer in charge
On 12 July 1947, E.J. Smith, of the United Airlines, was interviewed at the Boise Municipal Airport, Boise, Idaho. Captain Smith was passing through Boise on a scheduled flight at the time and had a 20 minute stop-over. Captain Smith reiterated the statements originally made by him to the press as to what he had seen in the late evening of July 4th, when 8 minutes out of Boise on the route to Seattle, Washington. It is the opinion of the interviewer that due to the position Smith occupies, that he, Smith, would have to be very strongly convinced that he actually saw flying disks before he would open himself for the ridicule attached to a report of this type. Frank M. Brown, S/A CIC 4th AF

Incident 4AF 1208 I
16 July 1947
Memorandum for the officer in charge
On 12 July 1947, Mr. Kenneth Arnold, Box 387, Boise, Idaho was interviewed in regard to the report by Mr. Arnold that he saw 9 strange objects flying over the Cascade Mountain Range of Washington State on July 25th. (sic). Mr. Arnold voluntarily agreed to give the interviewer a written report of exactly what he had seen on the above mentioned date. The written report of Mr. Arnold is attached to this report as Exhibit A.

Agent's notes: Mr. Arnold is a man of 32 years of age, being married and the father of two children. He is well thought of in the community in which he lives, being very much the family man and from all appearances a very good provider for his family.

Mr. Arnold recently purchased a home on the outskirts of Boise, recently purchased a $5,000 airplane in which to conduct his business to the extent of which is explained in the attached exhibit. It is the personal opinion of the interviewer that Mr. Arnold actually saw what he stated he saw. It is difficult to believe that a man of Mr. Arnold's character and apparent integrity would state that he saw objects and write up a report to the extent that he did if he did not see them. To go further, if Mr. Arnold can write a report of the character that he did while not having seen the objects that he claimed he saw, it is the opinion of the interviewer that Mr. Arnold is in the wrong business, that he should be writing Buck Rogers fiction. Mr. Arnold is very outspoken and somewhat bitter in his opinions of the leaders of the U.S. Army Air Forces and the Federal Bureau of Investigation for not having made an investigation of this matter sooner. To put all of the statements made by Mr. Arnold in this report would make it a voluminous volume. However, after having checked an aeronautical map of the area over which Mr. Arnold claims that he saw the objects it was determined that all statements made by Mr. Arnold in regard to the distances involved, speed of the objects, course of the objects and size of the objects, could very possibly be facts. The distances mentioned by Mr. Arnold in his report are within a short distance of the actual distances on aeronautical charts of this area, although Mr. Arnold has never consulted aeronautical charts of the type the Army uses. Mr. Arnold stated further that if he, at any time in the future, saw anything in the sky, to quote Mr. Arnold directly, "if I saw a ten story building flying through the air I would never say a word about it," due to the fact that he has been ridiculed by the press to such an extent that he is practically a moron in the eyes of the majority of the population of the United States.

Incl: Exhibit "A"
Statement of Kenneth Arnold at Boise Idaho
12 July 1947
The following story of what I observed over the Cascade mountains, as impossible as it may seem, is positively true. I never asked nor wanted any notoriety for just being in the right spot at the right time to observe what I did. I reported something that I know any pilot would have reported. I don't think that in any way my observation was due to any sensitivity of eyesight or judgement than what is considered normal for any pilot.

On June 24th, Tuesday, 1947, I had finished my work for the Central Air Service at Chehalis, Washington, and at about two o'clock I took off from Chehalis, Washington airport with the intention of going to Yakima, Wash. My trip was delayed for an hour to search for a large marine transport that supposedly went down near or around the southwest side of Mt. Rainier in the state of Washington and to date has never been found. I flew directly toward Mt. Rainier after reaching an altitude of about 9,500 feet, which is the approximate elevation of the high plateau from which Mt. Rainier rises. I had made one sweep of this high plateau to the westward, searching all the various ridges for the marine ship and flew to the west down and near the ridge side of the canyon where Ashford, Washington is located. Unable to see anything that looked like the lost ship, I made a 360-degree turn to the right and above the little city of Mineral, started again toward Mt. Rainier. I climbed back up to an altitude of approximately 9,200 feet.

The air was so smooth that day that it was a real pleasure flying and, as most pilots do when the air is smooth and they are flying at higher altitude, I trimmed out my aircraft in the direction of Yakima, Washington, which was almost directly east of my position and simply sat in my plane observing the sky and the terrain. There was a DC-4 to the left and to the rear of me approximately fifteen miles distance, and I should judge a 14,000-foot elevation. Traveling north along the airline route.

The sky and air was as clear as crystal. I hadn't flown more than two or three minutes on my course when a bright flash reflected on my airplane. It startled me as I thought I was too close to some other aircraft. I looked every place in the sky and couldn't find where the reflection had come from until I looked to the left and the north of Mt. Rainier where I observed a chain of nine peculiar looking aircraft flying from north to south at approximately 9,500-foot elevation and going, seemingly, in a definite direction of about 170 degrees.

They were approaching Mt. Rainier very rapidly, and I merely assumed they were jet planes. Anyhow, I discovered that this was where the reflection had come from, as two or three of them every few seconds would dip or change their course slightly, just enough for the sun to strike them at an angle that reflected brightly on my plane.

These objects being quite far away, I was unable for a few seconds to make out their shape or their formation. Very shortly they approached Mt. Rainier, and I observed their outline against the snow quite plainly.

I thought it was very peculiar that I couldn't find their tails but assumed they were some type of jet planes. I was determined to clock their speed, as I had two definite points to clock them by; the air was so clear that it was very easy to see objects and determine their approximate shape and size at almost fifty miles that day.

I remember distinctly that my sweep second hand on my eight-day clock, which is located on my instrument panel, read one minute to 3 p.m. as the first object of this formation passed the southern edge of Mt. Rainier. I watched these objects with great interest as I had never before observed airplanes flying so close to the mountain tops, flying directly south to the southeast down the hog's back of a mountain range. I would estimate their elevation could have varied a thousand feet one way or another up or down, but they were pretty much on the horizon to me which would indicate they were near the same elevation as I was. They flew like many times I have observed geese to fly in a rather diagonal chain-like line as if they were linked together. They seemed to hold a definite direction but rather swerved in and out of the high mountain peaks. Their speed at the time did not impress me particularly, because I knew our Army and Air-Forces had planes that went very fast.

What kept bothering me as I watched them flip and flash in the sun right along their path was the fact I couldn't make out any tail on them, and I am sure that any pilot would justify more than a second look at such a plane.

I observed them quite plainly, and I estimate my distance from them, which was almost at right angles, to be between twenty and twenty-five miles. I knew they must be very large to observe their shape at that distance, even on as clear a day as it was that Tuesday.

In fact I compared a zeus fastener or cowling tool I had in my pocket with them, holding it up on them and holding it up on the DC-4 that I could observe at quite a distance to my left, and they seemed smaller than the DC-4; but, I should judge their span would have been as wide as the furtherest engines on each side of the fuselage of the DC-4.

The more I observed these objects, the more upset I became, as I am accustomed and familiar with most all objects flying whether I am close to the ground or at higher altitudes. I observed the chain of these objects passing another high snow-covered ridge in between Mt. Rainier and Mt. Adams, and as the first one was passing the south crest of this ridge the last object was entering the northern crest of the ridge.

As I was flying in the direction of this particular ridge, I measured it and found it to be approximately five miles so I could safely assume that the chain of these saucer-like objects were at least five miles long. I could quite accurately determine their pathway due to the fact that there were several high peaks that were a little on this side of them as well as higher peaks on the other side of their pathway.

As the last unit of this formation passed the northern-most high snow-covered crest of Mt. Adams, I looked at my sweep second hand and it showed that they had traveled the distance in one minute and forty-two seconds. Even at the time this timing did not upset me as I felt confident after I would land there would be some explanation for what I saw.

A number of news men and experts suggested that I might have been seeing reflections or even a mirage. This I know to be absolutely false, as I observed these objects not only through the glass of my airplane but turned my airplane sideways where I could open my window and observe them with a completely unobstructed view.

Even though two minutes seems like a very short time to one on the ground, in the air in two minutes time a pilot can observe a great many things and anything within his sight of vision probably as many as fifty or sixty times.

I continued my search for the marine plane for another fifteen or twenty minutes and while searching for this marine plane, what I had just observed kept going through my mind. I became more disturbed, so after taking a last look at Tieton Reservoir I headed for Yakima.

I might add that my complete observation of these objects, which I could even follow by flashes as they passed Mt. Adams, was around two and one-half or three minutes, although, by the time they reached Mt. Adams, they were out of my range of vision as far as determining shape or form. Of course, when the sun reflected from one or two or three of those units, they appeared to be completely round; but, I am making a drawing to the best of my ability, which I am including as to the shape I observed these objects to be as they passed the snow covered ridges as well as Mt. Rainier. When these objects were flying approximately straight and level, they were just a black thin line and when they flipped was the only time I could get a judgement as to their size.

These objects were holding an almost constant elevation; they did not seem to be going up or coming down, such as would be the case of rockets or artillery shells. I am convinced in my own mind that they were some type of airplane, even though they didn't conform with the many aspects of the conventional type of planes that I know.

Although these objects have been reported by many other observers throughout the United States, there have been six or seven other accounts written by some of these observers that I can truthfully say must have observed the same thing I did; particularly the descriptions of the three Western Air Lines (Cedar City, Utah) employees, the gentleman (pilot) from Oklahoma City and the locomotive engineer in Illinois. Also Capt. Smith and Co-pilot Stevens and Marty Morrow of United Air Lines, Seattle, Wash. Some descriptions could not be very accurate taken from the ground unless these saucer-like disks were at quite a great height, and there is a possibility that all of the people who observed peculiar objects could have seen the same thing I did; but, it would have been very difficult from the ground to observe these for more than four or five seconds, and there is always the possibility of atmospheric moisture and dust near the ground which could distort one's vision.

I have in my possession letters from all over the United States and people who profess that these observations have been observed over other portions of the world, principally Sweden, Bermuda and California.

I would have given almost anything that day to have had a movie camera with a telephoto lens, and from now on I will never be without one, but to continue further with my story, when I landed at Yakima, Washington, airport I described what I had seen to my very good friend Al Baxter, who listened patiently and was very courteous but in a joking way didn't believe me.

I did not accurately measure the distance between these two mountains until I landed at Pendleton, Oregon, that same day where I told a number of pilot friends of mine what I had observed and they did not scoff or laugh but suggested that they might be guided missiles or something new. In fact several former Army pilots informed me that they had been briefed before going into combat overseas that they might see objects of similar shape and design as I described and assured me that I wasn't dreaming or going crazy.

I quote Sonny Robinson, a former Army Air Force pilot who is now operating dusting operations at Pendleton, Oregon: "What you observed, I am convinced, is some type of jet or rocket propelled ship that is in the process of being tested by our government or even it could possibly be by some foreign government."

Anyhow, the news that I observed these spread very rapidly and before the night was over I was receiving telephone calls from all parts of the world; and, to date I have not received one telephone call or one letter of scoffing or disbelief. The only disbelief that I know of was printed in the papers.

I look at this whole ordeal as not something funny as some people have made it out to be. To me it is mighty serious, and since I evidently did observe something that at least Mr. John Doe on the street corner or Pete Andrews on the ranch has never heard about is no reason that it does not exist. Even though I openly invited an investigation by the Army and the FBI as to the authenticity of my story or a mental or a physical examination as to my capabilities, I have received no interest from these two important protective forces of our country; I will go so far as to assume that any report I gave to the United and Associated Press and over the radio on two different occasions which apparently set the nation buzzing, if our Military Intelligence was not aware of what I observed, they would be the very first people that I could expect as visitors.

I have received lots of requests from people who told me to make a lot of wild guesses. I have based what I have written here in this article on positive facts and as far as guessing what I observed, it is just as much a mystery to me as it is the rest of the world.

My pilot's license is 333487. I fly a Callair airplane; it is a three-place single engine land ship that is designed and manufactured at Afton, Wyoming as an extremely high performance, high altitude airplane that was made for mountain work. The national certificate of my plane is 33355. Kenneth Arnold, Boise, Idaho. Frank M. Brown, S/A, CIC 4th AF

Incident 4AF () I 16 July 1947
Memorandum for the officer in charge
On 12 July 1947, a call was made at the newspaper office of the *Idaho Daily Statesman,* Boise, Idaho. The aviation editor of the paper, Mr. David M. Johnson, was interviewed in regard to how well he knew Mr. Kenneth Arnold of Boise, Idaho, and as to the credibility of any statement made by Mr. Arnold. The purpose was an attempt to verify statements made by Kenneth Arnold on 26 June 1947 to various national news services to the effect that he, Mr. Arnold, had seen 9 objects flying in the air above the Cascade Mountain range of Washington. These objects were subsequently referred to as flying saucers or flying disks and will here-in-after be referred to as such in this report. Mr. Johnson stated that he had known Mr. Arnold for quite a period of time, having had relations with Mr. Arnold on various occasions, due to the fact that both he, Mr. Johnson, and Mr. Arnold were private fliers and frequently got together to talk shop. Mr. Johnson stated that as far as he was concerned anything Mr. Arnold said could be taken very seriously and that he, Mr. Johnson, actually believed that Mr. Arnold had seen the aforementioned flying disks. Mr. Johnson stated that after Mr. Arnold reported having seen the flying disks, that the editor of the paper had assigned him, Mr. Johnson, the assignment of taking the airplane belonging to the newspaper and exhausting all efforts to prove or disprove the probability of flying disks having been seen in the Northwest area. The results of this assignment to Mr. Johnson and what he subsequently saw is put forth in a sworn statement signed by Mr. Johnson attached to this report as Exhibit B.

Agent's notes: Mr. Johnson is a man of approximately 33 to 35 years of age. From all appearances he is a very reserved type person. Mr. Johnson has logged 2,800 hours of flying time in various types of airplanes up to and including multi-engine aircraft. During part of the war years, Mr. Johnson was the first pilot of a B-29 type aircraft being assigned to the Twentieth USAAF and stationed on Tinian Island in the Pacific. It is the personal opinion of the interviewer that Mr. Johnson actually saw what he states that he saw in the attached report. It is also the opinion of the interviewer that Mr. Johnson would have much more to lose than to gain and would have to be strongly convinced that he actually saw something before he would report such an incident and open himself for the ridicule that would accompany such a report. Incl: Exhibit "B"

Statement of David N. Johnson
Boise, Idaho
July 12, 1947

To Whom It May Concern:
On the sixth day of July, 1947, I received from James L. Brown, general manager of the Statesman Newspapers, incorporated in Idaho as the Statesman Printing company, an assignment which was in substance:
"Conduct an aerial search of the Northwest states in an effort to see and photograph a flying disc. Conduct this patrol for so long a time as you believe reasonable, or until you see a flying disc."
In accordance with these instructions, I took the Statesman's airplane and with Kenneth Arnold as a passenger, flew a seven and one-half hour mission on the seventh day of July, 1947. This mission was without result. It covered an area embracing the confines of the Hanford plant in Washington, and territory between and around Mt. Rainier and Mt. Adams, where Arnold first reported seeing objects henceforth described as saucers or discs.
On the eighth day of July, 1947, I took an AT-6 of the 190th Fighter squadron, Idaho National Guard, of which I am a member, and flew to northern Idaho, into northwestern Montana briefly, to Spokane, Washington, and back to Boise by way of Walla Walla, Washington, and Pendleton, Oregon. This search also was negative.
On the ninth day of July, 1947, I continued the search, again using a national guard At-6, this time centering my efforts over the Owyhee mountains west and southwest of Boise, a portion

of the Mountain Home desert on a track southeast of the Mountain Home army air base, thence into the Sawtooth mountains, and back in the general direction of Boise on a line carrying me well to the north of the Shafer Butte forest service lookout station, into the Horseshoe Bend area, and thence back in a southwesterly direction to a point between Boise and the village of Meridian, west of Boise a few miles.

During this search, which lasted approximately two and one-half hours, I flew under and around rapidly forming cumulus clouds over that area known as the Camas Prairie, east of Boise. The clouds were near the village of Fairfield in that valley, and Fairfield is 75 miles airline distance east of Boise. At that time I saw nothing in the vicinity of these clouds. At the time I reached the point between Boise and Meridian, I was flying at an altitude of 14,000 feet mean sea level, which would be a mean average of 11,000 feet above the earth in this area, not considering errors in the altimeter induced either by barometric changes since my takeoff, or by the temperature at that altitude.

I turned the aircraft on an easterly heading, pointing toward Gowen Field, and had flown on that course for perhaps a minute when there suddenly appeared in the left hand portion of my field of vision an object which was black and round.

I immediately centered my gaze on the object. At that time, due to its erratic movement, I thought I was seeing a weather balloon. I called the CAA's communication station at Boise, and asked if the weather station had recently released a balloon. The reply from communicator Albertson was that the bureau had not. I do not remember his exact words; I am under the impression he said "not for several hours" or gave me the exact time of the previous release, which was around 0830 that day.

Upon hearing this response, I turned the aircraft broadside to the object, pulled back the plexiglass covering to avoid any distortion, took my camera from the map case, and exposed about 10 seconds' duration of eight millimeter motion picture film.

During the time the camera was at eye level, I could not see the object because of minuteness of scope introduced by the optical view finder with which the camera, an Eastman, was equipped. Taking the camera away and once again centering my gaze on the object, I observed it to roll so that its edge was presented to me. At this time it flashed once in the sunlight. It then appeared as a thin black line. It then performed a maneuver which looked as if it had begun a slow roll, or a barrel roll, which instead of being completed, was broken off at about the 180-degree point. The object rolled out of the top of the maneuver at this point, and I lost sight of it.

This entire performance was observed against the background of clouds previously forming over the Camas Prairie. The object appeared to me, relatively, as the size of a twenty-five cent piece. I do not know, how far away it was. I do not know, nor can I truthfully estimate, its speed. I can only say it was not an airplane, and if it was at a very great distance from me, its speed was great, taking into consideration that apparent speed is reduced to the viewer if an object is a very great distance away.

I forgot to look at my clock to determine the exact time I saw the object. The CAA's log of radio contacts shows my first contact to been made at 1217 hours. But a few seconds elapsed between the time I first saw the object and the time I called the CAA's station.

I subsequently related over the radio a description of what I saw, and communicator Albertson may remember it. The control tower may have a recording of the conversation. I have not checked to determine that.

The purpose of my relating over the air what I saw was to enable rapid transmission of the report to the newspaper, for at that time I was on assignment and my energies thenceforth were devoted to (1) transmitting the information and (2) conducting a further search, which I did after landing for fuel and to make some telephone calls. The next search, begun within half an hour after landing from the first one, consumed another two hours, but was negative. I explored thoroughly the region where I saw the object. Immediately after sighting the object, I asked if there were other aircraft in the area. There was a P-51 of the 190th squadron practicing maneuvers in the vicinity of Kuna, but that was behind me. A C-82 passed over Boise, but I saw that aircraft go beneath me by some 2,000 feet.

The P-51 in the vicinity of Kuna proceeded to the area where I saw the object, at my request, and conducted a search. It was negative. During the afternoon, flights of P-51s were sent out to cover the area, and some of them flew high altitude missions on oxygen. These searches were negative.

I was subsequently informed that personnel on both the United Air Lines side of Gowen Field, and on the National Guard side, observed a black object maneuvering in front of the same cloud formation, which by now had grown so that the clouds reached a probable height of 19,000 or 20,000 feet from a mean base of 13,000 or 14,000 feet, mean sea level. Three of these men were National Guard personnel, and I talked to them, asking them to describe what they saw, before telling my story, in order to avoid suggestion or inference of a leading nature. They saw the object (from the ground) while I was on the second search. They believed the time to have been 1400 hours. The object performed in the same erratic manner, they said, as I observed. The above is the extent of the story, and information concerning myself is now in order.

I have approximately 2800 hours of flying time in equipment ranging from primary trainers to B-29s. Of course, that does not increase my powers of observation except as to those practiced daily by an airman. It does not make my eyesight any sharper except again as to the incidental demands of an airman. At the time of the experience related above, I had flown fourteen and one-half hours on an assignment to find a disc and if possible to photograph it. I may have been suffering, although slightly, from want of oxygen.

Prior to sighting the object, I had concluded there was no point in pressing the search, that I probably would never see the disc-like objects referred to by Arnold and Captain Smith of United Air Lines.

At all times during the search, both on that day and the two preceding days (particularly when I was with Arnold) I had literally talked to myself to keep beating into my head that I would not fall victim to the power of suggestion or self-hypnosis arising from a naturally very intent desire to find a disc and bring success to the assignment given me.

I therefore do not believe that I was a victim of suggestion or hypnosis. I am familiar with the optical illusion of a fixed object beginning to move after it is watched a sufficient length of time. I know what tricks the eyes will play as to moving bodies, and have learned of this particularly during night formation flying.

I saw the object appear suddenly. If it had moved in a jerky fashion (as it did at first) for the full length of time I observed it, I would not be so strong in saying that I saw something not an aircraft, not a balloon, and not a corpuscle moving across the retina of either eye. The maneuver described by the object when its edge was presented to me convinces me that I saw an object actually performing in an erratic flight path. The question remains, of course, whether I saw it. The motion picture film, developed and processed by R. W. Stohr in Eastman Laboratories at 241 Battery Street, San Francisco, showed no trace of any object. Stohr says if it was more than a mile distant from me at the size I described, the object would not have registered sufficiently on the film to be shown. He said it probably was too far away to be apparent even though great enlargement in that case is limited because of the size of the film and the fact I did not have any telescopic equipment on the lens. The exposure was f.16, stop set at infinity, at a speed of 16 frames per second.

I have worried over this matter a great deal since seeing it. I "took myself aside" and said, "Come now, Johnson, don't be so stupid." But I cannot bring myself to the point of thinking I did not see anything. The impression of the moment was too vivid, too realistic, and I knew in the air when I saw that partial slow roll or barrel roll, that I was not the victim of illusion.

I trust this matter will be of help to those investigating the flying disc phenomena which have been reported.

A chart is attached depicting the movements of the object as I saw it.

This statement is made voluntarily and freely, in response to the request of Mr. Brown and Captain Davidson, who called on me this morning.

David N. Johnson

Frank M. Brown, S/A CIC 4th AF

Department of Justice Communications Section

August 6, 1947

Teletype

FBI Seattle 8-6-47 7-13 PM PST

Director FBI - URGENT

Flying discs, S. M. - X. Retel Portland to Director, San Francisco, and Seattle August Five Last. Intelligence officers McChord Field, WN., advise that in their opinion and from their investigations there is no question of the crash of the B-Twentyfive at Kelso, WN. approximately two fifty a.m., August one last having been caused by any sabotage. They state their investigation indicates the left engine burned out an exhaust stack which caused the wing to burn and break off. the left wing as broke off tore off the tail and the plane crashed into the ground killing Capt. Davidson and Lt. Brown intelligence officers of the Fourth Air Force who were returning from McChord Field, WN., to Hamilton Field, California. The crew chief and a hitchhiker parachuted to safety from the plane. Only four members were aboard the plane, Davidson and Brown being pilot and co-pilot and had no chance to escape when the wing broke off. Lt. Col. Donald L. Springer, A-two officer for the Fourth Air Force, Hamilton Field, California, advised that Captain Davidsson and Brown were sent from Hamilton Field to interview [redacted] and [redacted] at Tacoma, WN., regarding their report of seeing some flying discs over Maury Island, WN., and that they obtained some of the disc fragments. [redacted] and [redacted] are partners in a [redacted] business at Tacoma, Washington. ["copies destroyed Nov. 18, 1964"]

Captain Davidson and Lt. Brown on Thursday, July Thirtyfirst last interviewed [redacted] from Boise, Idaho, who was one of the first that reported seeing flying discs and [redacted] United Airlines pilot from Seattle, WN., who also reported seeing flying discs. This interview took place at the Wint Hotel on the afternoon of July Thirtyfirst last. Captain Davidson and Lt. Brown were returning to Hamilton Field for Airforce Day and had with them some of the disc fragments as reported by [redacted] and [redacted]

Reporter [redacted] of *Tacoma Times,* and United Press Wireman [redacted] of Tacoma, received anonymous phone calls July Thirtyfirst and August First last regarding the meeting at the Winter Hotel over the discs fragments and that the B-Twentyfive which crashed the morning of August One was sabotaged or shot down information as yet not verified indicated the entire story started by [redacted] and [redacted] possibly to promote sale of slag found in a gravel pit on Maury

Island, WN. No information available as yet as to the identity of the individual who made the anonymous phone call to the *Tacoma Times* and the United Press, [redacted] and [redacted] will be interviewed as soon as possible. Investigation continuing. Wilcox END 11-33 PM OK FBI WA GH

Office Memorandum . United States Government
To: D. M. Ladd
Date: August 6, 1947
From: E. G. Fitch Subject: FLYING SAUCERS
Special Agent [redacted] of the Liaison Section contacted Lieutenant Colonel C. P. Martin, Army Air Forces Intelligence, inquiring about an article which appeared in the West Coast newspapers recently stating in substance that an airplane carrying recovered flying saucers crashed in route from Portland, Oregon, to Los Angeles, California.

Colonel Martin advised [redacted] that the only information that has been received by Headquarters of the Army Air Forces is that a CIC Agent of the 4th Air Force Headquarters, Hamilton Field, San Francisco, was killed in an airplane crash. The Headquarters of the Air Forces have been advised that he was on a top secret mission. Colonel Martin indicated that he was under the impression that the CIC Agent was either on route to or from an interview with Mr. [redacted] who is one of the individuals who first saw one of the flying saucers.

Colonel Martin stated that the Air Forces have no additional information and will receive none until the report is received from the Air Forces. Colonel Martin suggested that the San Francisco Field Office contact Colonel Springer, headquarters 4thj Air Forces, Hamilton Field, San Francisco, who undoubtedly would be able to furnish the details regarding this matter which are at this time unknown by the Headquarters of the Air Forces. Colonel Martin pointed out to Mr. [redacted] however, that it was his belief that no flying saucers have been recovered but that it was merely an attempt to reinterview an individual who previously had reported seeing one of the flying saucers. SWR:rhr

Federal Bureau of Investigation
U. S. Department of Justice
Communications Section August 6, 1947
FBI Portland 8-5-47 8-50 PM HHS
Director and SACS Seattle and San Francisco URGENT
Flying discs, SM Dash X. RE Telephone Call from Mr. Ladd, One PM today requesting teletype summary concerning newspaper reports of recent reported flying discs in Portland area and a reported conf of Army officials in Portland concerning flying discs. [redacted] aviation editor the Oregonian, advised that a Captain William L. Davidson and Lt. Frank M. Brown of Fourth AAAF headquarters San Francisco were in Portland July twentyseven last and interviewed [redacted] an experienced pilot, who had reported June fourteen last seeing a formation of flying discs over Bakersfield, California. According to [redacted] they had also interviewed following four experienced pilots who were among first who reported seeing discs - [redacted], business man, Boise, Idaho, [redacted] and co-pilot [redacted], United Airlines, and [redacted] *Idaho Statesman.* To ascertain the purpose of the interviews [redacted] contacted Major General Twining [Twining's name is scratched out, but still readable] of Wright Field, Ohio by phone at Albuquerque, NM, and from him gained the impression that the AAF instituted this investigation to wash out the disc reports, since they are definitely not of AAF or[igin] on Friday, August first, the plane in which AAF investigators Captain Davidson and Lt. Brown were riding, crashed at Kelso, Wash. and both were killed. The wreckage was screened by AAF intelligence from McChord Field. The *Tacoma News Tribune* and through them the United Press put out a story the plane was carrying parts of a disc which had struck a boat owned by [redacted] and [redacted], Tacoma, [redacted] advised that today's issue of the *Oregonian* carries a UP story stating that [redacted] denies saying the metal fragments he furnished was from a disc, and analysis of the fragments shows them to be from a Tacoma slag mill. No AAF intelligence personnel available Portland. No recent substantive reports of flying discs in the Portland area Seattle verify at McChord Field and San Francisco verify at AAF Hdqrts. SF, submitting teletype summaries to the bureau. No further investigation Portland. Bobbitt, END AND

ACK WA 0157AM OK FBI WA DW SE S OK FBI SE KLS
SF OK FBI SF NCW DVIMSC

Federal Bureau of Investigation
U.S. Department of Justice Communications Section
August 6, 1947
Telemeter
Washington from SFRAN S5 8-6-47 12-09 PM
Director Urgent
Flying Discs, SM - X. Re: Portland teletype referencing
phone call from Mr. Ladd at Bureau one PM August Fifth last.
A-Two San Francisco unable to verify. Lt. Col. Donald Springer
A-Two Hamilton Field, in charge of investigation by A-Two is
thought by A-Two to be returning from Kelso, Washington area
having gone to Kelso upon learning of deaths of AAF investi-
gators mentioned in reference teletype. He planned, upon de-
parture, to obtain results of AAF investigators or reinterview
persons mentioned in referenced teletype. Springer will be contacted upon his return and bureau advised. Kimball

Federal Bureau of Investigation
U. S. Department of Justice Communications Section
August 7, 1947
FBI, Seattle 8-747
5-20 PM RH Director and SAC, Chicago and Butte
URGENT
Flying discs sighted by [redacted] and [redacted] Tacoma,
WN. SM Dash X. Remytel August Six, last captioned flying
disks. [redacted] and [redacted], Tacoma, in signed statement
instant date state that in early part of June, last, they picked up
some strange rock formations from a gravel pit, Maury Island,
Washington. They [fragment] a cigar box of these rock formations they sent to Ray Palmer, editor of *Venture Magazine* in
Evanston, Illinois. They state Palmer is also editor of fantasy
Magazine, Chicago, Illinois. They state they request Palmer
only to make a chemical analysis of the rock formation. [re-
dacted] and [redacted] state Palmer later wrote asking for additional sample stating he had been unable to analyze the material. [redacted] and [redacted] state Palmer, a few days after
the flying disk stories started the late part of June, last, con-

tacted them by phone at Tacoma, Washington, saying he would pay for an exclusive story if the material which they had sent him was fragments of a flying disc. [redacted] states he wrote Palmer a letter in which he stated the material was part of a flying disk.

[redacted] and [redacted] admit this statement was entirely false. [redacted] and [redacted] state they were called by [redacted] of Boise, Idaho to meet with him at the Winthrop Hotel, Tacoma, Washington, on July thirtyfirst, last. They state [redacted] called in Army intelligence officers from Hamilton Field, California, and Captain [redacted] of United Air Lines, Seattle, Washington to attend the meeting. [redacted] and [redacted] claim they told the intelligence officers, Captain Davidson and Lieutenant Brown, as well as [redacted] and [redacted] exactly how they [fragment] the rock formations and that they had no connection with any flying disc. [redacted] and [redacted] state they furnished some of the rock formation to the intelligence officers as samples. Captain Davidson and Lieutenant Brown left Tacoma, Washington in a B twenty five to return to Hamilton Field California about two thirty a.m. August One, last, and were killed when their plane crashed at Kelso, Washington, after the left engine burned out an exhaust stack which in turn caught the left wing on fire and it broke off. The crew chief and each officer parachuted to safety [redacted], Associated Press Wireman, Tacoma, advised that two or three days after the flying disk stories started, he contacted [redacted] to check a story the *Seattle Post Intelligencer* had got from the fire chief at Harbor, Washington, to the effect that [redacted] had some flying disk fragments. At this time [redacted] admitted to [redacted] the entire story was false.

[redacted] and [redacted] state [redacted] was paid by Ray Palmer of the *Fantasy* magazine and possibly the *Boise Statesman* newspaper to come to Tacoma, Washington and obtain a story from them regarding the flying disk fragments. They further state that [redacted] had a friend on the *Chicago Times* and was possibly selling the story to the *Chicago Times* through this friend. A check of the at the Winthrop Hotel, Tacoma where [redacted] had his room, reflect that on July Thirty First, last, [redacted] called [redacted] at A. M. five two naught naught Evanston, Illinois, collect, and also called naught one naught nine Boise, Idaho, collect, and [redacted] called [redacted] at Dearborn Five Two Naught Naught Chicago, collect, and [redacted] called [redacted] at Dearborn two three two three.

On July Thirty First and August one, last, a total of five anonymous calls were received by a *Tacoma Times* reporter and the United Press wire men at Tacoma, giving information regarding the meeting at the Winthrop Hotel over the disk fragments and stating that the B Twenty Five had been shot down or sabotaged which killed Captain Davidson and Lieutenant Brown inferring that this was done because the intelligence officers were carrying disk fragments in their plane. [redacted] and [redacted] state these calls could have come from themselves, [redacted] or [redacted] and deny that they made the calls. No record of the calls as having been made from [redacted] room in the Winthrop Hotel can be located. [redacted] and [redacted] are evasive as to just what information they did furnish by phone or letter to [redacted].

[redacted], United Press wire man, Tacoma, Washington, state it appears the *Boise Statesman* paper and [redacted] have been pushing the publicity on the flying disk stories. [redacted] states that [redacted] was either the first or one of the first to claim he had seen flying disks. [redacted] and [redacted] state that [redacted] admitted receiving money from [redacted] to come to Tacoma to check the disk story. Unless advised to the contrary by the bureau, the Butte office at Boise, Idaho, will obtain all information regarding the connection between the *Boise Stateman* paper and [redacted] will interview [redacted] Route One, Mountain View Drive, Boise for what information he has as to the above facts and what information he furnished [redacted] and the *Boise Stateman* regarding the Tacoma meeting and the sabotage of the B Twentyfive. The Chicago office will interview [redacted], editor of *Fantasy* magazine, regarding his connections with [redacted] and [redacted] and [redacted] and what information each furnished to [fragment] will also attempt to ascertain what information Captain [redacted] furnished the *Chicago Times*. The Seattle office at Seattle will interview [redacted], [redacted] along these same lines. Will also ascertain what information he fire chief at Harbor, Washington obtained from [redacted] and [redacted]. Wilcox Ack In Ord PLS WA 9-39 PM OK FBI WASH DC VH CG OK FBI CG MDG BT OK FBI BT VGW DISC PLS

FBI Seattle 8-12-47 8-05 PM PST
Director and SACS Chicago and Butte
URGENT
Flying discs sighted by [redacted] and [redacted] Tacoma, WN. SM Dash X. Remytel August Seven last. [redacted] United Airlines pilot, interviewed re: associations with [redacted] and [redacted] in Tacoma, WN., from July Thirtyone to August third last. [redacted] has received previous publicity for having seen flying discs or similar objects on July Fourth last in company with his co-pilot, [redacted] during routine United Airlines flight out of Boise, Idaho. [redacted] relates that he went to Tacoma, WN., from Seattle on Thursday, July Thirtyone last in response to telephone call from [redacted] at Tacoma. [redacted] claims he had previously met [redacted] on two occasions, the first time on July fifth last in offices of *Seattle Post-Intelligencer* where both were interviewed re flying discs they had seen, and on second occasion in Boise, Idaho, about three weeks while he, [redacted] was passing through on routine flight.

On this latter occasion [redacted] was in company of Captain Davidson and Lieutenant Brown, Army intelligence officers, and a reporter [redacted] of the *Idaho Statesman* newspaper. [redacted] claims no previous acquaintance with [redacted] or [redacted]. [redacted] relates that on night of July thirty one last in Tacoma, WN., the [redacted] and [redacted] story, which both have subsequently admitted to be false was told to [redacted], Captain Davidson, and Lieutenant Brown by [redacted] and [redacted]. Subsequent to this interview, [redacted] gave Captain Davidson and Brown a box of the alleged fragments which they apparently took with them on their fatal flight. [redacted] states that on Saturday, August first last, after learning of the crash and death of Davidson and Brown, [redacted] called [redacted], editor of the *Venture Press* in Evanston, Illinois, and was told by [redacted] to discontinue his investigation of the [redacted] story and to keep the two hundred dollars expense money which [redacted] had previously wired to [redacted].

[redacted] relates that he and [redacted] made subsequent attempts to go out to Maury Island with [redacted] and [redacted] on Friday, Saturday and Sunday, August first, second and third, but were put off by [redacted] and [redacted] for various reasons, [redacted] states that reporter [redacted] of Tacoma and [redacted] of United Press office Tacoma informed him and [redacted] of anonymous phone calls, and from accuracy of the info transmitted by these anonymous phone calls, [redacted] believes they were made by either [redacted] or [redacted]. [redacted] admits calling his personal friend [redacted], aviation editor of *Chicago Times*, on Friday, August first last, to interview him of the Tacoma incident as per a previous agreement between them that Smith would let [redacted] in on any flying disc stories which he might run into. [redacted] also admits that he told reporter [redacted] of *Idaho State* in telephone conversation Saturday night, August Second last, that Captain Davidson and Lieutenant Brown were carrying fragments with them on the fatal flight.

[redacted] says that [redacted] told him on Saturday night August Second last that he, [redacted] if contacted by the Army or other authorities was going to say that the entire story was a hoax. [redacted] states that he told his complete story to Major Sanders of McChord Field, Tacoma, on Sunday morning, August Third last, and that [redacted] left Tacoma. Unless advised to contrary, [redacted] and [redacted] who are both Tacoma newspapermen mentioned above, will not be contacted for verification of [redacted] story above. Unable to locate fire chief of Harbor, Washington to verify information received by him from [redacted] and [redacted]. Since this story originated in *Seattle Post Intelligencer* newspaper this lead is being discontinued unless advised to contrary. Letter containing completer interviews with [redacted}. [redacted] and [redacted] as outlined above will be forwarded AMSD to Bureau. Wilcox, END ACK IN ORDER PLS WA 10-30 PM OK FBI WA BW

FBI Seattle 8-14-47 5-15 PM FB Director Routine
Flying discs sighted by [redacted] and [redacted], Tacoma, Washington, SM X. Reurtel instant date. Please be advised that [redacted] did not admit to [redacted] that his story was a hoax but only stated that if questioned by authorities he was going to say it was a hoax because he did not want any further trouble over the matter. Complete report now en route to Bureau AMSD, which indicates probably [redacted] or [redacted]

made the anonymous phone call in the hope of building up their story through publicity to a point where they could make a profitable deal with *Fantasy* magazine, Chicago, IL. [redacted] and [redacted] will not be reinterviewed unless advised to the contrary by the Bureau. Wilcox, A AND HOLD PLS 9-16 PM OK FBI WASH DC CAR

Office Memorandum United States Government
To: Mr. D. M. Ladd
From: Mr. J. P. Coyne Subject: Flying Discs
There are attached two copies of a blind memorandum setting forth the facts relative to the reported air crash of two AAF officers investigating flying disc complaints.

Recommendation: It is recommended that a copy of this memorandum be furnished by the Liaison Section of the Air Force Intelligence. Attachment, RGF: mjp

Office Memorandum United States Government
To: The Director
From: Mr. D. M. Ladd Subject: Flying Discs
In connection with your request to be advised as to the facts concerning newspaper reports of flying discs in the Portland area and the reported conference of army officials in Portland concerning flying discs the Portland office was advised that [redacted] aviation editor of the *Oregonian,* has stated that Captain William L. Davidson and Lieutenant Frank M. Brown of the Fourth AAF Headquarters, San Francisco, were in Portland on July 27, 1947. While in Portland they interviewed [redacted], an experienced pilot, who had reported that he observed on June 14, a formation of ten flying discs over Bakersfield, California. [redacted] added that Davidson and Brown had also interviewed the following four experienced pilots who were among the first to report seeing discs. [redacted], businessman from Boise, Idaho; [redacted], a co-pilot; [redacted] United Airlines and [redacted] aviation editor, *Idaho Statesman.* In order to determine the purpose of these interviews [redacted] contacted Major General Twining of Wright Field, Ohio, and from him gained the impression that the AAF instituted this investigation to wash out the disc reports since they are definitely not of AAF origin.

On Friday, August 1, the plane in which AAF investigators, Captain Davidson and Lieutenant Brown, were flying, crashed at Kelso, Washington and both were killed. The wreckage was screened by AAF Intelligence from McChord Field. The *Tacoma News Tribune* and through them the United Press put out a story that [redacted] and [redacted]. It has also been inferred that this plane was sabotaged to prevent these disc parts from being examined.

STATUS: Investigation by the Bureau has reflected that this plane was definitely not carrying parts of a disc and there appears to be no substantiation of a sabotage charge.

For your further information there is attached a blind memorandum setting forth in more detail the results of the investigation surrounding the above plane crash. No further inquiry is being made in this matter.

ACTION: Air Force Intelligence has been advised of the results of our investigation. RGF:mjp

August 14, 1947
Flying Discs

The *Tacoma News Tribune* and through them the United Press put out a story that an army plane which was allegedly carrying parts of a disc which had struck a boat owned by [redacted] and [redacted] had crashed on August 1, 1947, killing two Air Force Intelligence officers who were interviewing persons who were alleged to have flying discs.

[redacted] and [redacted] when interviewed by Bureau Agents, advised in a signed statement on August 7. 1947, that in the early part of June, 1947, they picked up some strange rock formations from a gravel pit on Maury Island, Washington. They sent a cigar box of these formations to one [redacted] editor of the *Venture* magazine of Evanston, Illinois and also editor of the *Fantasy* magazine in Chicago, Illinois. According to them they requested [redacted] to make only a chemical analysis of the rock formations. [redacted] then wrote asking for additional samples stating he had been unable to analyze the material. [redacted] and [redacted] remarked that a few days after the flying disc stories appeared during the latter part of June, [redacted] contacted them by telephone saying he would pay for an exclusive story if the materials they had sent him were fragments of a flying disc. [redacted] said he wrote [redacted] a letter in which he represented the material as being a part of a flying disc, and both [redacted] and [redacted] admitted that this statement was entirely false.

[redacted] and [redacted] then received a call from one [redacted] of Boise, Idaho who requested them to call him at the Winthrop Hotel in Tacoma on July 31, 1947. According to them [redacted] called in army intelligence officers from Hamilton Field, California and one Captain [redacted] of United Airlines of Seattle, Washington to attend this meeting. [redacted] and [redacted] maintained they told the intelligence officers Captain Davidson, Lieutenant Brown, Kenneth [redacted] and [redacted] exactly how they got the rock formations and that they had no connection with any flying discs. [redacted] and [redacted] stated that they then furnished some of the rock formation to the intelligence officers as samples.

Captain Davidson and Lieutenant Brown left Tacoma, Washington in a B-25 to return to Hamilton Field, California about 2:30 A.M. August 1, 1947, and were killed when their plane crashed at Kelso, Washington, after the left engine burned out an exhaust stack which in turn caught the left wing on fire which caused it to break off. The crew chief and each officer parachuted to safety.

[redacted], an Associated Press Wireman at Tacoma advised that two or three days after the flying disc story started he contacted [redacted] to check the story that the *Seattle Post-Intelligencer* had received from the Fire Chief at Harbor, Washington, to the effect that [redacted] had some flying disc fragment. At this time [redacted] admitted to [redacted] that the entire story was false.

Relative to [redacted] and [redacted] stated that he was paid by [redacted] of the *Fantasy* magazine and possibly the *Boise Statesman* to come to Tacoma and obtain a story from them regarding the flying disc fragments.

On July 31 and August 1, a total of five anonymous calls were received by a *Tacoma Times* reporter and the United Press Wireman at Tacoma giving information regarding the meeting at the Winthrop Hotel over the disc fragments and stating that the B-25 had been shot down or sabotaged which killed Captain Davidson and Lieutenant Brown, inferring that this was done because the intelligence officers were carrying disc fragments in their plane.

[redacted] and [redacted] stated that these calls could only have come from themselves, [redacted] or [redacted] who, they stated, had a friend on the *Chicago Times* and was possibly selling the story to the *Chicago Times* through this friend. [redacted] and [redacted] denied making these calls.

[redacted] upon interview, state that reporter [redacted] of the *Tacoma Times* and [redacted] of the United Press office in Tacoma had informed him that [redacted] had several anonymous calls and from the accuracy of the information transmitted [redacted] believes they were made by either [redacted] or [redacted].

Federal Bureau of Investigation
United States Department of Justice
August 14, 1947
Communications Section Transmit the following
message to: SAC, Seattle URGENT

Reurtel August Twelve. It is noted from interpretation of [redacted] claims that during the conference on July Thirty One that [redacted] and [redacted] apparently repeated their false story about the material being fragments of a flying disc and only on Saturday night August second did [redacted] admit that the story was a hoax. If such is the case it would appear either [redacted] or [redacted] made the anonymous phone calls since they would have been under the impression at that time that the material furnished to Captain Davidson and Lieutenant Brown was actually parts of a flying disc. It would also appear that [redacted] and [redacted] did not admit the hoax to the Army Intelligence officers because if they had done so the officers probably would not have taken the alleged fragments with them on their fatal flight. This matter should be cleared up upon reinterview with [redacted] and [redacted]. When this point clarified no further investigation necessary. Hoover, RTF:mjp

Federal Bureau of Investigation
United States Department of Justice
407 U.S. Court House Seattle 4, Washington
August 18, 1947

Director, FBI

RE: Flying Disc Sighted by [redacted] Tacoma, Washington SM - X

Dear Sir:

The following, in general, are the facts regarding the flying disc story that started by [redacted] and [redacted] which subsequently resulted in news stories by the *Tacoma Times,* the *Boise Statesman* and the *Chicago Times* that a B-25 carrying Army Intelligence officers was shot down or sabotaged over Kelso, Washington on August 1, 1947 because it was carrying some flying disc fragments.

The original story, as related by [redacted] and [redacted] was to the effect that [redacted], while patrolling in his boat near Maury Island, Washington, sighted six flying discs, one of which fluttered to the earth and disintegrated, showering his boat with fragments which caused some damage to the boat and killed his dog. [redacted] wrote a letter to [redacted] of Ziff-Davis Company which publishes fantastic adventure magazines in Chicago, sending him fragments of the flying disc and relating the above story. [redacted] requested Trans-radio news in Chicago to verify the story as related by [redacted] and [redacted] telegraphed [redacted] confirming [redacted] story. [redacted] then engaged [redacted] Boise, Idaho, who was the first to report sighting the flying disc and whom [redacted] had previously made a contract for a story regarding the flying disc, to come to Tacoma and check the story as related by [redacted] and [redacted].

[redacted] came to Tacoma, Washington, July 30, 1947 and arranged for a meeting the following day, Jul 31, with [redacted] and [redacted] in his room 502, Winthrop Hotel, Tacoma, Washington. [redacted] also called to attend the meeting Captain [redacted], United Airlines Pilot who had also reported seeing flying disc fragments, and Army Intelligence to attend this meeting. [redacted] Captain [redacted] Captain Davidson and Lieutenant Brown of Army A-2 Intelligence from Hamilton Field, California, all met in [redacted] room at various times during the afternoon and evening of July 31, 1947 and discussed the flying disc story as related by [redacted] and [redacted]. The Army Intelligence officers, Captain Davidson and Lieutenant Brown, left about 2:00 A. M. the morning of August 1, 1947 to return to Hamilton Field, California for Air Force Day in a B-25 and were carrying some of the reported disc fragments. The left engine on the B-25 burned an exhaust stack which in turn caught the left wing afire, the wing subsequently breaking off and tearing off the tail. The B-25 crashed, killing Captain Davidson and Lieutenant Brown. However, the Crew Chief and a hitch-hiker parachuted to safety. Intelligence Officers at McChord Field, Washington advised there was no indication of any sabotage. the plane crashed at Kelso, Washington approximately 2:50 A.M. August 1, 1947.

Five anonymous calls were received by a reporter, *Tacoma Times,* and the United Press Wireman, Tacoma, between 11:30 A. M., July 31, 1947 and 5:30 P.M., August 2, 1947. The first call was to a *Tacoma Times* reporter approximately 11:30 A. M., July 31,in which the caller stated that there was a meeting taking place at that time in room 502 of the Winthrop Hotel concerning the disc fragments found on Maury Island. The second call was received between 11:00 A.M. and 12:00 noon, August 1, 1947 by the Tacoma Times reporter in which the caller advised that at the moment a big meeting was taking place in [redacted] room 502, Winthrop Hotel; that the B-25 which crashed was carrying disc fragments and that McChord Field officials had stated it was shot down of sabotaged. the third call was received Friday, August 1, 1947 at 5:30 P.M. by the United Press Wireman, Tacoma, in which the caller stated that the B-25 which crashed at Kelso, Washington was carrying flying disc fragments and that the dead officers' names by Army authorities and the caller indicated that when the names were released, it would verify the information he was furnishing was correct. The fourth phone call was received at approximately 6:45 P.M., Friday, August 1 by the United Press Wireman in which the caller stated the B-25 was definitely shot down and that if he contacted Army Intelligence officers, they would not deny it. The fifth phone call was received by the United Press Wireman, Tacoma, at 5:30 P.M. August 2, 1947 at which time the caller stated the B-25 was shot down from the air with a 2m.m. cannon; that the Marine plane found recently on Mt. Ranier had also been shot down and that Captain [redacted] would be taken to Wright Field Tuesday morning. When the Army authorities released the names of the dead Intelligence officers which verified the information as given by the anonymous caller, the *Tacoma Times* printed this story on August 2, 1947 and carried several articles thereafter inferring that the B-25 had been shot down or sabotaged because of the fact that it was carrying disc fragments [redacted] and [redacted] have admitted that the material which they sent to [redacted] had no connection with any flying discs and have given a signed statement to that effect which are being forwarded herein. [redacted] and [redacted] deny, however, that they actually started the flying disc story and their actual part of the story.

United Airlines pilot, [redacted], states that [redacted] and [redacted] on July 31, 1947, both related their original flying disc fragment story. Information gathered would indicate that the anonymous phone calls were possibly made by [redacted] in order to build up the flying disc story to the point where they could make a profitable sale of the story to [redacted], Chicago, Illinois. No facts have been developed which would definitely prove that [redacted] made those calls. However, from all facts and information gathered, it appears he is probably the most likely to have made the anonymous calls. The detailed interviews of the persons contacted in regard to this flying disc story are being set out below.

The following investigation was conducted by Special Agent [redacted] at Tacoma. Washington on August 6, 7, 1947:

[redacted] Associated Press Wireman, Tacoma, Washington, advised that in the early part of June, 1947 he was requested by the *Seattle Post Intelligencer* to check on a story which he was informed had been obtained from the Fire Chief at Harper, Washington. the story was supposed to have originated with [redacted]. Mr. [redacted] stated that the story was to the effect that [redacted], while patrolling in his boat near Maury Island, saw five or six flying discs, one of which fluttered toward the ground and finally disintegrated. Fragments of the disc were reported to have showered down on the boat of [redacted] causing some damage and killing his dog. Mr. [redacted] stated that he went to the home of [redacted] on [redacted], Tacoma, Washington to check with him on this flying disc story. he stated that as best he could recall, this was just a few days after the first flying disc stories had appeared in the paper and was on a Sunday evening. He believed it was the early part of June. He stated that [redacted] took him in the kitchen and proceeded to talk about this flying disc story in low muffled tones. He stated that [redacted] acted rather suspicious and that shortly his wife came into the kitchen and was in a considerable rage, telling [redacted] to admit that the entire story was a plain fantasy which he had dreamed up. He stated that after his wife told [redacted] to admit the entire story was false, that [redacted] them admitted that there was nothing whatever to the story and it was an entire hoax. [redacted] stated that in view of the enraged condition of [redacted] wife, he immediately left and reported to the *Seattle Post Intelligencer* that the entire story was a hoax and that they should not print it in any way. He further stated that he advised the *Seattle Post Intelligencer* that [redacted] was a mental case and that nothing which he reported should be carried as far as a news story.

Mr. [redacted] stated that since that time he had received repeated requests from the *Boise Statesman* requesting information as to the flying disc stories reportedly originating with [redacted] and [redacted]. [redacted] stated that he had never, in his experience, had such pressure brought upon him to release a news story and that he repeatedly advised the *Boise Statesman* that the story of seeing the flying discs by [redacted] and [redacted] was a complete fabrication and should be in no way, carried as a news story and refused to furnish any information regarding these reports. He further stated that he advised the *Boise Statesman* shortly before, or at the time [redacted] left Boise to come to Tacoma to check on the flying disc stories with [redacted] and [redacted] that [redacted] should not come as the entire story was a hoax.

The following information was obtained from [redacted], Tacoma, Washington, Proctor 8416, a reporter for the *Tacoma Times:*

It was the *Tacoma Times* paper which first issued a story on August 2 and subsequent stories intimating that the B-25 which crashed at Kelso, Washington on the early morning of August 1, had been sabotaged or shot down because of the fact that it carried flying disc fragments. [redacted] stated that on Thursday, July 31, at approximately 11:30 A.M. he received an anonymous phone call in which the caller stated that [redacted] and Army Intelligence officers were meeting in room 502 of the Winthrop Hotel to check on the flying disc story from which fragments were obtained on Maury Island. [redacted] stated he turned around to speak to his editor and when he picked up the phone again the line was dead. He stated that the caller asked for [redacted], a reporter on the *Tacoma Times* who was out at the time of the call. He stated that [redacted] called [redacted] at room 502 in the Winthrop Hotel and was advised by [redacted] that he could furnish no information as he was there on a Government mission.

[redacted] stated that on Friday, August 1, between 11:00 A.M. and noon, he received another call for [redacted] in which the anonymous caller stated that he might have some information for him. [redacted] asked the caller if he was not the same party that had called the previous date and he said yes. The caller then related that at that moment there was a big meeting in progress in [redacted] room 502, in the Winthrop Hotel; that the B-25 which crashed that morning in Kelso was carrying flying disc fragments from California and that McChord Field officials had stated the plane was sabotaged or shot down. the caller then hung up after making some statement to the effect that he was a switchboard operator. [redacted] stated that he went to the Winthrop Hotel on Friday about noon and found that there was no male operator on duty. He stated he then went to room 502 and [redacted] answered the door and that Captain [redacted], United Airlines pilot, was on the phone. [redacted] stated that he heard [redacted] make a statement to the effect that the information must be very strictly confidential. He stated that there were one or two others in the room besides [redacted] and [redacted] but that he could not identify them. He stated that [redacted] told him he could make no statement and that he had attempted to check the story with various people on Maury Island with negative results.

He stated that about 3:30 P.M., Friday, he wrote a story regarding the mysterious informant and called [redacted] at his hotel room, stating that he had written this story and that [redacted] had better check it. He stated that he talked to [redacted], the United Press Wireman, Tacoma, who advised that the story sounded fantastic. [redacted] stated that about 5:30

P.M., Friday, August 1, an anonymous caller called [redacted], the United Press Wireman, stating that Captain Davidson and Lieutenant Brown were the Intelligence officers that were killed in the crash of the B-25 and that civilians and the sheriff had been kept away from the wreckage with the Army guarding it. He stated the anonymous caller then said that the names had not been released yet by the Army and that this would verify his statements. [redacted] stated that the following morning, Saturday, August 2, the Army verifies that the officers killed were Captain Davidson and Lieutenant Brown and two days later verified that they were Army Intelligence officers. [redacted] stated that the anonymous caller again later contacted [redacted], calling him by that name, and at this time stated he did not call the *Tacoma News Tribune* or the Associated Press and denied calling [redacted] or [redacted]. In this call the anonymous caller stated that. "Don't think I'm doing this for you." He then asked if the story had been put on the wire and when [redacted] said yes, the caller stated, "We want this to get back to New Jersey." The caller further stated that the B-25 was shot down by a 20 m.m. cannon and that the marine plane which was recently found wrecked on the side of Mt. Ranier, having been missing for several months, had also been shot down. The caller stated to [redacted] that he should get in touch with a flyer named [redacted] with United Airlines who, he stated, was with Captain [redacted] when they were shot at over Montana. The caller then stated, "I'll see you Tuesday. I'm going to San Francisco." [redacted] stated that he had checked with Captain [redacted] of United Airlines who denied knowing any pilot by the name of [redacted] denied ever having flown over Montana.

[redacted] stated that [redacted] received another anonymous call in which the caller stated that [redacted] would be sent to Wright Field on Tuesday and that Saturday one of the men who found fragments of the flying disc was to be flown to Alaska. [redacted] stated that in view of the fact that the information as to the Intelligence officers on the B-25 had been as furnished by the anonymous caller, had subsequently been verified by the Army, the story was released that the B-25 was carrying disc fragments returning to Hamilton Field, California and furnishing the inference that the plane had been sabotaged or shot down. [redacted] stated that about 8 P.M. on Sunday,

August 3, he contacted Captain [redacted] at his home; [redacted] Seattle at which time [redacted] stated he had not given any story out to the *Post* in Boise and when he called and found out it was the *Boise Statesman,* he had hung up. He stated that the *Boise Statesman* then contacted him, at which time he admitted he had seen the disc fragments, but that he did not take any of them. This time [redacted] informed [redacted] that he had been with Major George Sanders, Public Relations Officer from McChord Field, all afternoon until about 3:45 P.M. [redacted] informed [redacted] that he had told the Army authorities everything that he and [redacted] knew about the flying disc fragments story from the time that [redacted] left Boise, Idaho and he had left Seattle, Washington. This time [redacted] admitted that there were some of the supposed disc fragments in [redacted] room at the Winthrop Hotel and that [redacted] an [redacted] had been in the room Thursday afternoon. On Monday [redacted] stated that he called [redacted] who advised that if this were not used in the paper, he and [redacted] would see him after lunch. [redacted] stated that about noon [redacted] and [redacted] contacted him at which time [redacted] stated that he and his son had been exploring a gravel pit on Maury Island and found some strange rock formations. He stated they picked up some of these samples and that [redacted] later saw them and they went back over to Maury Island at which time additional samples were obtained and that [redacted] sent these to a friend of his at the University of Chicago to have analyzed. They stated that they received a report and that apparently this friend had asked a newspaperman to find out where the rock formations were obtained. [redacted] and [redacted] told [redacted] that sometime after the first flying disc story has appeared, they received a telegram from *Trans-Ocean Press* from Chicago wanting information on the flying disc fragments. [redacted] stated that they had at no time indicated the rock formations were a part of a flying disc and that captain [redacted] and [redacted] were not interested in the rock formations and they denied giving them to [redacted] and [redacted].

[redacted], a United Press Wireman, Tacoma, Washington furnished substantially the same information that was obtained from [redacted] the *Tacoma Times* reporter, regarding the anonymous phone calls which he had received. He stated further that the first call he received was on Friday, August 1, at around 5:50 P.M. At this time the caller stated that the B-25 which crashed at Kelso, Washington, was carrying disc fragments and that the two officers killed were Captain Davidson and Lieutenant Brown, officers with Army A-2 Intelligence at Hamilton Field and that the fragments were top secret material. He stated the caller indicated that when the Army released the names of the dead officers it would verify that the information he was furnishing was correct. [redacted] stated that the second call he received at approximately 6:45 P.M. Friday, August 1 at which time the caller stated that the B-25 was definitely shot down and that if he contacted Army Intelligence A-2, the man in charge would not deny it. [redacted] stated he thought the man said to contact Colonel Guys, but it was found out it was Colonel Gregg who was in charge of Army Intelligence A-2.

The caller further stated that the Sheriff's office had been kept away from the crash and that no civilians had been allowed near the plane. [redacted] stated the third call he received at 5:30 P. M., August 2, and that this was the caller stated that one of the men who had been conferring with Captain [redacted] and [redacted] was taken to Alaska that day. The caller further stated that the B-25 was shot down from the air with a 20 m.m. cannon; that the Marine plane found recently on Mt. Ranier had also been shot down; that captain [redacted] would be taken to Wright Field Tuesday morning and that a United Airlines pilot by the name of Morgan flew with Captain [redacted] when they were shot at over Montana. The caller stated he was leaving for San Francisco and would be back Tuesday.

[redacted] and [redacted] both stated that they had made very little effort to question the anonymous caller to obtain his identity as they felt it was useless and that if they stared questioning him he would refuse to furnish any further information.

On August 5, 1947 Special Agent [redacted] contacted in the resident agency office, Tacoma, Washington by [redacted]. At this time [redacted] asked if the Seattle office was investigation of the crash of the B-25 and he was informed that no investigation was being conducted by the Seattle office. [redacted] at this time related in a rambling story that he had picked up some strange rock formations which he had forwarded to a friend of his in the University of Chicago to have analyzed and that later, in some manner unknown to him, these rock formations had been reported as being fragments of a flying disc. On August 7, 1947 [redacted] and [redacted] were interviewed at the Tacoma resident agency office. Both [redacted] and [redacted] at first denied any knowledge of how the rock formations which they had picked up to have analyzed became connected with the flying disc stories. Both denied making any statement to anyone that these rock formations were portions of a disc fragment. It was apparent from the start of the interview that [redacted] and [redacted] were not telling their complete and true connection with the flying disc story. they refused to give any definite information as to what they said or had done which caused them to become involved in a flying disc story, but gave evasive answers and repeatedly stated that they had nothing to do with it and were at a loss to understand how they became connected with the flying disc story. After considerable questioning, they stated that in the early part of June they sent to [redacted] of the Ziff-Davis Publishing Company which published the *Fantasy* magazine in Chicago and the *Venture* magazine in Evanston, Illinois, some rock formations which they had found on Maury Island.

They stated they sent these formations, asking [redacted] to have them analyzed. They stated that later [redacted] wrote and asked for more samples, advising he had failed to analyze the samples. [redacted] and [redacted] stated they have never sent any additional samples and that the next they heard regarding the rock formations which they had sent [redacted] was when he called [redacted] and asked if the rock formation could have come from a flying disc. [redacted] stated he made some remark that they possibly could have come from a flying disc and that he immediately sat down and wrote a letter to [redacted] which was in the latter part of June in which he stated the material could have been portions of a flying disc. [redacted] claimed that he thought he told [redacted] over the phone something about being in his boat when he obtained these rock formations, but stated he could not recall what he had written to [redacted] and claimed that he passed the whole thing off as a joke. [redacted] and [redacted] were questioned at length in an attempt to obtain specific information as to exactly what each one had dome with regard to the rock formation. However, each stated that the only thing they had done was tell [redacted] the formations could have come from a flying disc in view of the fact it appeared "that's what he wanted them to say." No definite information could be obtained from either [redacted] or [redacted] as to what each specifically had done to start the flying disc story. The signed statement which was obtained from [redacted] and [redacted] and in which they admitted the rock formations had no connection with any flying discs is being forwarded to the Bureau herewith. the statement contains no information of value and therefore is not being set forth herein.

Regarding the meeting which was held in the Winthrop hotel on Thursday, July 31, [redacted] and [redacted] stated that they both met [redacted] there about 1:00 P.M. they stated that they all left [redacted] room about 3:00 P.M. and that [redacted] took [redacted] to Berry's Airport at Tacoma and [redacted] flew his plane to Seattle where he picked up Captain [redacted] [redacted stated that he picked up [redacted] and [redacted] at Berry's Airport about 5:00 P. M. and that [redacted] came to [redacted] room at about 7:00 P.M. [redacted] stated that he and [redacted] left about 8:30 P.M. when he drove Smith to Seattle to get his car and that [redacted] went home at this time.

[redacted] stated they returned about 11:30 P.M. at which time the Army Intelligence officers were in [redacted] room and that [redacted] left about midnight. He stated that he returned to [redacted] room Friday afternoon for approximately one-half hour from 2:30 to 3:00 P.M. at which time [redacted] and [redacted] were still there and neither seemed to be able to recall if [redacted] was in [redacted] room on Friday, August 1. The best that could be obtained from [redacted] and [redacted] as to what took place in [redacted] room was to the effect that most of the talk was about flying, that no one seemed very interested in the rock formations and that they had no connection as far as they knew with any flying disc. [redacted] stated that [redacted] wanted to obtain pictures of the place where the rock formations were obtained and that the Army Intelligence officers did not appear to be interested in any manner whatever.

[redacted] operates the *Sentinel* [redacted] Company at [redacted] Tacoma, Washington and [redacted] has recently been working with him buying [redacted] They have also been associated with the Harbor Patrol Association at Tacoma, Washington which furnishes patrol and police protection to parts of the harbor area which are not patrolled by Tacoma police or Sheriff's officers. [redacted] resides at [redacted] Tacoma, Washington, Army serial number [redacted] During the war he was a pilot and it is believed presently holds a Reserve officer's commission as a Captain.

Regarding the B-25 which crashed, killing Captain Davidson and Lieutenant Brown of the 4th Air Forces, Captain Robert G. Bjorningg, A-2 Officer, McChord Field, advised that this investigation of the crash reflected an exhaust stack had burned out on the left engine which in turn caught the left wing afire and that when the left engine which in turn caught the left wing afire and that when the left wing broke off, it also broke off the tail. The plane at the time of the crash was carrying Captain Davidson, Lieutenant Brown, the hitch-hiker and a man as Crew Chief to take care of the airplane. The Crew Chief and the hitchhiker parachuted to safety, but Captain Davidson and Lieutenant Brown were killed. He stated that their investigation reflected no indication of any sabotage whatever.

A check of the records of the Winthrop Hotel at Tacoma, Washington revealed that [redacted] giving his address as [redacted], Boise, Idaho rented room 502 from July 30 at 7:43 P.M. until August 3. A record of the phone calls made from room 502 during this period was made by Miss [redacted]. This record reveals that [redacted] on July 31 called [redacted] at [redacted], Evanston, Illinois, collect. On the same date called Lieutenant Brown at 5800 Hamilton Field, California, collect. [redacted] also called 019-J in Boise, Idaho on July 31. On August 1 [redacted] called [redacted], Portland; [redacted] at Dearborn 5200, Chicago; and [redacted] called [redacted] at Dearborn 2323 at Chicago. Both Chicago calls were collect. The remainder of the calls appear to be personal calls and are not being set out. A record of the phone calls made are being retained as an exhibit in the Seattle office.

The following information was obtained by Special Agent [redacted] in interview on August 12, 1947 with Captain [redacted], United Airlines pilot: It should be noted that Captain [redacted] has previously received publicity for having supposedly seen flying discs or similar objects on July 4, last while on a routine United Airlines flight out of Boise, Idaho in company with his co-pilot [redacted] concerning this incident. Captain [redacted] states that they took off from Boise, at 8,000 feet, co-pilot [redacted] called his attention to some objects in the sky ahead of them about ten degrees left which neither one could identify. [redacted] states that he called a CAA radio operator at Ontario, Oregon and requested him to step outside his radio shack and see if he could see any of these objects overhead. the CAA radio operator replied in the negative.

Captain [redacted] states that he first met [redacted] on July 5 in the offices of the *Seattle Post Intelligencer* where both were being interviewed concerning their sighting of flying discs. [redacted] states that he next met [redacted] about three weeks ago in Boise, Idaho and had a ten minute lay-over there. On this occasion [redacted] was in company of Captain William L. Davidson and Lieutenant Frank M. Brown, Army Intelligence officers and a reporter [redacted] of the *Boise Statesman*. [redacted] next contact with [redacted] was on Thursday, July 31, last when he received a telephone call from [redacted] calling from Tacoma in the early afternoon at which time he asked Smith to come over to Tacoma and join him as he was investigating a flying disc story for "someone back East" and some fragments were involved which [redacted] might be interested in seeing. After some discussion [redacted] agreed to join [redacted] in Tacoma and [redacted] told [redacted] he would fly over and pick him up at Boeing Airport at 4:00 P.M. [redacted] met [redacted] at Boeing Field at about 4:00 P.M. and they flew to Berry's Airport at Tacoma, Washington where they were met by [redacted]. The three of them proceeded in [redacted] car to the Winthrop Hotel where [redacted] was occupying room 502. [redacted] ordered something to eat and during this time either [redacted] or [redacted] called a [redacted] and invited him up to the room.

By this time [redacted] states he had learned from [redacted] that [redacted] and [redacted] were the participants in the latest flying saucer disc story and [redacted] states that he had no previous acquaintance with either of these men before meeting them in Tacoma on this date. While in the hotel room [redacted] showed [redacted] a letter which he received from [redacted] of the *Venture Press* of Chicago requesting that [redacted] investigate the [redacted] story in Tacoma. [redacted] informed [redacted] at this time that after receiving this letter he had called [redacted] by telephone in Chicago as a result of which call [redacted] had forwarded him $200.00 expense money for covering the story. Shortly thereafter, at about 7:30 P.M. [redacted] arrived at the hotel room and the discussion began among the four men present as to what [redacted] and [redacted] had seen on Maury Island. [redacted] professed reluctance to tell the story, claiming that several unfortunate incidents had occurred subsequent to his seeing the flying discs and he believed the entire incident had brought him bad luck.

In this connection he stated that four or five days subsequent to his seeing the flying discs, a man called at his home and had a conversation with him the course of which [redacted] was warned to forget all about everything he had seen on or near Maury Island. In addition to that, [redacted] stated that his sixteen year old son had run away from home following the incident and had been picked up by the police somewhere in Montana. After some further discussion [redacted] finally agreed to tell his story of the flying disc incident in front of [redacted] after eliciting a promise from [redacted] that he would not discuss the matter for at least two weeks. It should be noted that [redacted] had previously told his story to [redacted] and [redacted]. At this point [redacted] related the incident which has already been described and which he alleged had taken place on or about June 23 or 24. While relating the incident [redacted] mentioned that he had taken pictures of the flying discs which he had seen but that the printed films were marred with white spots.

When [redacted] had concluded his story, [redacted] related that he had gone the following day to Maury Island to verify what [redacted] related that he had gone the following day to Maury Island to verify what [redacted] had told him concerning the fragments and had at this time picked up several fragments and taken them with him. At this time [redacted] related that he also saw one of the flying discs hovering over the island but that it had disappeared into a cloud. When [redacted] and [redacted] had finished telling their story [redacted] told the group that he had earlier in that evening called Captain Davidson and Lieutenant Brown, Army Intelligence Officers and that they were on their way to the hotel room. At this point [redacted] protested that he did not wish to tell his story before anyone else and he was advised by [redacted] that if such was the case why didn't he just leave and not be there when they arrived. [redacted] and [redacted] then left the room and went downstairs. [redacted] departed alone.

[redacted] drove back to Boeing Field near Seattle where [redacted] desired to pick up his own personal car, which he did. They then returned to the hotel where they found Captain Davidson and Lieutenant Brown in room 502 with [redacted]. [redacted] met them at the door and seemed excited, explaining to [redacted] that Captain Davidson had just drawn a reproduction of a freak disc which had supposedly been seen by a woman in Arizona and that this drawing was an exact reproduction of the flying disc which he, [redacted], had seen several weeks before, nearing Mt. Rainier. [redacted] states that shortly after this [redacted] seemed very anxious to tell his and [redacted] story to the Army officers. Before this was done, however, [redacted] had a discussion with Lieutenant Brown, informing him that they had promised [redacted] not to release the story for two weeks and that if [redacted] were allowed to tell the story at this time, Brown and Davidson must agree not to release the story for one month.

Following this agreement, [redacted] related [redacted] and his story of the flying discs over Maury Island to Brown and Davidson. Following this recitation, Lieutenant Brown, in an answer to a query from [redacted] said that he and Captain Davidson were of the opinion that there might be some truth in the current flying disc stories, but that their immediate superiors (presumably A-2 at Hamilton Field) did not agree with them. Brown and Davidson then held a brief discussion as to whether they should return that same night to Hamilton Field and they decided that they would. All five of the men then went down to the lobby where Brown detached himself from the group and entered a phone booth to call for a car from McChord Field. [redacted] also left the group and met Brown outside the phone booth where they held a short discussion relative to the credibility of [redacted] and [redacted] story. Brown indicated to [redacted] that he would attempt to find out if the story was on the level and that Brown would call him the following day regarding this matter.

The group then proceeded to the front of the hotel at which time [redacted] brought his car to the front of the hotel and took from his trunk a box of the alleged flying disc fragments picked up on Maury Island. He offered them to Brown and Davidson and when the Army car arrived from McChord Field the box of fragments was placed in the car with the officers. [redacted] departed alone and [redacted] and [redacted] went in search of something to eat and later returned to the hotel for the night.

On Friday morning, August 1, 1947, [redacted] received a call from [redacted] informing him that a B-25 had crashed during the night and it was believed to be the same plane which Brown and Davidson were flying. Following this call [redacted] and [redacted] came to the Hotel room and from the room [redacted] again called McChord Field in an attempt to get information about the crash. [redacted] took the phone from [redacted] and spoke to a Colonel Gregg, identifying himself and asking if the B-25 which crashed was the only one which had taken off from McChord Field the previous night. Gregg told him that it was. Following this call [redacted] called [redacted] in Chicago and informed him of the previous night's conversation and the fact that Davidson and Brown were believed to have been killed.

[redacted] told [redacted] to discontinue his investigation of the incident and that he, [redacted], was no longer interested. [redacted] then took the phone from [redacted] and asked [redacted] if he could shed any light on the situation. [redacted] was unable to say what [redacted] reply to [redacted] was. Following these telephone discussions [redacted] says that he called [redacted] whom he identified as a personal friend of his and an aviation editor of the *Chicago Times*. [redacted] states that he had previously made an agreement with [redacted] in Chicago that should he ever run across any flying disc stories which showed promise of news value, that he would contact [redacted] and this call was a result of that agreement. Shortly afterward, Colonel Gregg called him from McChord Field stating that Hamilton Field had requested that [redacted], [redacted] and [redacted] submit their addresses to Hamilton Field for convenience of any Army investigation of the incident which may be forthcoming.

After this call the four men went to a restaurant for lunch. During the course of this meal [redacted] excused himself from the table and attempted to call SAC Bobbitt of the Portland Field Office, Federal Bureau of Investigation with whom he claims acquaintance. Bobbit, however, was unavailable and [redacted] was unable to complete the call. After returning to the hotel room, a *Tacoma Times* reporter called attempting to gain information, but they did not give him any. Later, a Mr. [redacted] of the United Press called and [redacted] spoke to him on the telephone but refused to give out any information. [redacted] further relates that while the four men were in the room at this time, an envelope was shoved under the door and that he retrieved it from the floor. [redacted] states that the appearance of this envelope seemed to startle [redacted] considerably and that in fact [redacted] turned white as a sheet until [redacted] read the note unsigned which was a communication to the hotel advising that a strike of hotel employees was eminent and that guests should not expect room and telephone service much longer.

Shortly after this incident [redacted] and [redacted] left the hotel room after promising to take [redacted] and [redacted] to Maury Island the following morning (Saturday). [redacted] and [redacted] then went out for dinner and on their return, [redacted] found a note in the box requesting him to call a certain telephone number. He did this from the hotel room and was answered by [redacted], *Tacoma Times* reporter who requests [redacted] to go out and call him from a pay station. [redacted] complained and was informed by [redacted] that two anonymous telephone calls had been received by him that a discussion regarding flying discs had been taking place in room 503 at the Winthrop Hotel which involved Army Intelligence officers. From the information which [redacted] had received, [redacted] was convinced that the anonymous caller must have been present at the discussion also, as [redacted] was seemingly in possession of pertinent remarks which had been made in the room. [redacted] states that he did not give [redacted] any further information and that in conclusion of the call, he returned to the hotel room and he and [redacted] retired for the night.

On Saturday morning, August 2, 1947 [redacted] received a telephone call from [redacted] in Chicago, but was unable to give him any further information. [redacted] advised him, however, that he would call him back at 2:30 that afternoon [redacted] then called from a coffee shop nearby and [redacted] and [redacted] joined [redacted] and an unknown man in the coffee shop for breakfast. The unknown person was discussing some lumber business with [redacted] and left after breakfast. On leaving the coffee shop, [redacted] asked [redacted] about the negatives of the photographs which he claimed to have taken of the flying discs. [redacted] said the negatives were in the glove compartment of his car, but a search of the instant glove compartment was fruitless. The four then preceded in [redacted] car to the dock where they were to embark for Maury Island. The boat, however, could not be started and the trip was postponed until late in the day. While at the dock, however, [redacted] asked to be shown the damage to the boat which had allegedly occurred when the fragments showered down on Maury Island. [redacted] pointed out what may have been repairs to the windshield and the lights on the boat, but [redacted] was not personally satisfied that these repairs were made as a result of any such incident. [redacted] and [redacted] then drove [redacted] and [redacted] back to the hotel at approximately 10:45 A. M. and [redacted] told them he would call them later on and that they would go to Maury Island.

On returning to the hotel, [redacted] called [redacted] at the *Tacoma Times* as a result of which call he and [redacted] met [redacted] at the coffee shop across the street from the Winthrop Hotel. [redacted] stated that the purpose of this meeting was to try to find out something more about the anonymous phone calls which [redacted] had told him about. He and [redacted] still refused to give out any further information regarding the Thursday evening conference to [redacted] and were informed by [redacted] that the *Tacoma Times* was afraid of being scooped on the story and was going to print something on that day. [redacted] and [redacted] then returned to the hotel and shortly thereafter received a phone call from [redacted] but the call was cut off by the switchboard operator since it was not an emergency call. [redacted] and [redacted] then returned to the hotel lobby where they found a telegram from [redacted] asking them to call him at either Broadway or Proctor 7733, [redacted] is not sure of the exchange. [redacted] called this number, but [redacted] was not there. [redacted] states that he went then to the Western Union Telegraph office and dispatched a collect telegram to [redacted] at the *Chicago Times* which contained a brief resume of the incidents which had occurred and which requested [redacted] to wire [redacted] a telephone number where [redacted] could be reached after 6:00 P. M. [redacted] states that he had never received an answer to that wire. Following this, [redacted] states that he and [redacted] that he an [redacted] were sitting in the lobby of the Olympic Hotel when [redacted] entered and gave them each a copy of the latest edition of the *Tacoma Times* which contained a story hinting at sabotage in the crash of the Army B-25 which killed Captain Davidson and Lieutenant Brown. [redacted] stated that he and [redacted] continued to occupy seats in the hotel lobby most of the afternoon inasmuch as they were unable to receive calls in the hotel room due to the hotel employees' strike. He relates that he received a call in the late afternoon from [redacted] advising him to call [redacted] that evening at 8:30 as [redacted] had further information regarding the anonymous calls. [redacted] also received a telegram requesting that he call Boise 6000 which he did and found that it was [redacted] of the *Boise Statesman*. He refused to give [redacted] any further information at this time. However, shortly thereafter, [redacted] called from Boise and advised [redacted] that the Army had released a story through Brigadier General Shram revealing the confidential assignment which Brown and Davidson had been engaged on.

In view of this release, [redacted] requested [redacted] to answer one question for him which was, "Were they carrying any alleged disc fragments on the plane?" and [redacted] answered, "Yes, they were." Following this [redacted] called [redacted] as per his earlier request and was informed that [redacted] of the United Press had received another anonymous call at which time "the voice" said that the Army B-25 carrying Captain Davidson and Lieutenant Brown had been shot down with 20 m.m. shells. The voice went on to state that [redacted] would be called back to Wright Field on Tuesday. When [redacted] asked why he was giving out this information the caller replied that it was not for the benefit of the newspapers, but that he was interested in seeing that the information got back to New Jersey. The voice also informed [redacted] at this time that one of the two persons who had been talking to [redacted] and [redacted] had now left for Alaska. As a result of this latter bit of information [redacted] decided to find out of [redacted] or [redacted] had left town. He located [redacted] at the Sunset Theatre and [redacted] came to the hotel and met [redacted] and [redacted] They were unable to locate [redacted] by phone and [redacted] left saying that he would try to find out where [redacted] was and that he would call them tomorrow (Sunday) and that they would go out to Maury Island at that time.

After [redacted] left, [redacted] and [redacted] went to the *Tacoma Times* office where a reporter met them and took them to [redacted] in the United Press office. There they read the latest press releases and had a discussion with [redacted] regarding the anonymous phone calls. In the course of this discussion [redacted] mentioned the name Major George Sanders, Public Relations Officer at McChord Field as being one of the officers interested in the investigation.

Following this discussion with [redacted] at which time [redacted] states they still refused to divulge any further information, [redacted] and [redacted] returned to the hotel for the night.

On Sunday morning, August 3, 1947, [redacted] appeared at the hotel room and told them that he had received a letter from [redacted] which said in effect, "Take care of my business. I'll be out of town for three or four days." [redacted] had a letter with him but he did not show it to [redacted] or [redacted]. The three men then drove to [redacted]'s secretary's house in South Tacoma and picked her up and the four of them then went to breakfast. [redacted] excused himself and called Major Sanders at McChord Field and arranged an appointment to meet him at the hotel lobby at 11:oo A. M. They then took [redacted] secretary to her home where [redacted] picked up a typewriter and then drove [redacted] and [redacted] back to the hotel. They asked him if he was going to take them to Maury Island that day and he replied that he was not. He further stated that he was sick of the entire business and that if he was ever contacted by the Army or the authorities he was going to deny ever having seen anything and claim to be "the biggest liar that ever lived."

Shortly after returning to the hotel, [redacted] met Major Sanders in the lobby and they went in [redacted] car to a coffee shop in South Tacoma where Smith proceeded to tell Major Sanders the entire story of the incidents which had occurred in Tacoma regarding the [redacted] and [redacted] story since Thursday afternoon. Following this, [redacted] took Major Sanders back to the hotel and introduced him to [redacted] and suggested to [redacted] that he also tell Major Sanders the entire story of what had occurred. [redacted] did so. Major Sanders after looking at the fragments which were still in the room suggested that they drive out to the Smelter near Tacoma as he believed the slag at the Smelter would bear a distinct resemblance to these fragments.

The three men then drove to the Smelter and the slag was noted to be definitely similar to the fragments which [redacted] and [redacted] had left in the hotel room. They then returned to the hotel room and Major Sanders left them. After packing their bags, [redacted] took [redacted] to Berry's Airport where his plane was parked and then [redacted] drove himself back to Seattle.

About an hour after his arrival in Seattle, which was approximately 7:30 P. M., [redacted] of the *Tacoma Times* appeared at [redacted] home with the newspaper containing the Associated Press story which had originated in Boise, Idaho in the *Boise Statesman* and which was written by [redacted] following [redacted]'s admission to him that fragments had been carried by Lieutenant Brown and Captain Davidson on the fatal B-25 flight. [redacted] at this time continued to refuse to give any statements for the Press and told [redacted] that he had placed all of his information in the hands of the Army. [redacted] stated that a couple of days later he called Major Sanders at McChord Field and asked him if there was any recent information concerning the incident. [redacted] states that Major Sanders informed him that [redacted] had not yet been contacted, but that the Federal Bureau of Investigation was "setting a trap for him." [redacted] further advises that on Friday, August 8, 1947, he appeared before lawyer [redacted] at the County-City Building, Seattle and made a deposition of the facts relating to the incidents in Tacoma from Thursday afternoon, July 31, last until Sunday morning, August 3, last.

A copy of this deposition is now in possession of the writer and is being forwarded herewith to the Bureau. It should be noted that this deposition is in no way as complete as the statement taken by the writer above and any setting out of this deposition in this communication would be superfluous. Copies of this communication are being sent to the Butte, Portland, San Francisco and Chicago Offices for their information only. Unless advised by the Bureau to the contrary, instant investigation is considered closed by this office. For the information of the Bureau, Captain R. G. Bjorning, Intelligence Officer, McChord Field, Ft. Lewis, Washington advised at the weekly O.N.I.-S.I.D.-F.B.I Intelligence conference that the Public Relations Officer at McChord Field had received a telephone call from an individual at Army Air Forces Headquarters at Washington, D.C., during which call the Public Relations Officer was requested to obtain a signed statement from [redacted] and [redacted] which could be published and thus publicly close the matter. Captain Bjorning further related that he had no additional information in this matter and that he did not handle it.

Very truly yours,

J. B. Wilcox Special Agent in Charge

ENCLOSURES DAM;PHL;MEK 100-18945

CC - Butte Portland San Francisco Chicago

Appendix 4

An Interview with Fred Crisman

The actual voice of Fred Crisman appears only once in the files released under the Freedom of Information Act for this book. The following interview was conducted by Mel Gaumer of Tacoma's KTAC News. Robert Griffin, Crisman's attorney, is the other respondent. The interview took place on November 1, 1968.

A: I heard your broadcast.

Q: Oh, yeah, you heard the broadcast, sure. And Murray Morgan, of course, is on our staff, actually as a freelancer but he and I work together and, you know, fooled around with this thing all night. What I'm primarily interested in is what you have to say. I'm trying to— I'll try to be completely fair and objective. I'm not trying to crucify anybody. But this is a story, let's face it.

A: Most of it is absolutely untrue and has no relationship to the real thing at all and consequently I'm real unhappy with it. But insofar as the Garrison subpoena—what he particularly, what he alleges is that I know people that he feels has some pertinent knowledge to the assassination. Now I don't even know what people he's talking about.

Q: Maybe I can—maybe I can inject a name here that I got this morning for what it's worth. And as I say, believe me, Fred, as of yesterday at this time I knew nothing about this thing except what I had read about the Garrison investigation in the past. I have a lot more information than I had then, how much of it is fact and how much of it is fantasy, I don't know. One name that I had is Tom Beckham. He also goes by the name of Evans, Mark Evans.

A: He had two or three million hit sellers, in the record business.[1]

Q: All right. Tom Beckham as I understand it is under indictment in New Orleans.

A: No, I talked to him on the telephone this morning. He's in Omaha, Nebraska. They had an indictment for him for running a school of some kind back in Des Moines, Iowa, but they dropped it.

Q: Well, the information that I got from New Orleans today, and as you know I did not use this, and I hadn't used it up to this point. I got this information. And I know there are some other newspeople who probably have the same information—that Tom Beckham was actually in jail in Des Moines, Iowa, in connection with a school fraud of some sort. I may add that I have called Des Moines. I used to operate a radio station in Ft. Madison, so I know Iowa.

A: All I know is Tom called me today on the telephone. He wanted to know what was going on with this thing breaking this way. And I told him what I heard on the radio. And he said, no, after that the indictment was dropped three months ago.

Q: Well this I can check out. One of the problems that I've run into today that you're probably aware of is this is All Saints Day and New Orleans is a very Catholic town: consequently, Garrison's office is closed. So I couldn't get there. All the county offices—they call them parishes—are closed. It's a parish in New Orleans, rather than a county. I also have this piece of information that I'd like to have some more information on. I understand that you have or you did in the past file articles of incorporation for a School of Criminology.

A: No, Beckham did. All I did was write the courses for it.

Q: Were you involved as a corporate officer?

A: Oh, yeah, yeah.

Q: Well, at this point, I wasn't—these are all matters of record.

A: While Beckham was here he filed about six corporations, all of them non-profit stuff. Some of them I wrote some of the stuff for, some of them I didn't.

Q: All right, let me ask you this, Fred. As I understand it the subpoena from the Grand Jury down there is for the 21st of November at 10:00 in the morning. Have you been served with a subpoena yet?

A: No, I've had no official word whatsoever.

Q: Now Fred,—and this I don't use as part of the tape I'm asking you for information. In the State of Washington, who would serve that? How would this be handled? Do you know? This is a county. Would this be served by the local Sheriff?

A: The local Sheriff—you can quote this—if the local Sheriff serves it, the State of Louisiana itself does not have subpoena power over a Washington resident. Now if it comes through a Federal court, if there's a Federal question or had a—there's only one way Louisiana could get a witness down there—that is their State—would be either to have extradition or to have Federal Court.

Q: I understand this Grand Jury is not a Federal Grand Jury.

A: No.

(Inaudible)

Q: You have to have extradition papers cleared on a thing of this kind.

A: (Robert Griffith) I think that I would advise my client—I have not advised him, I haven't even consulted him—but I think I would advise him that if he's got nothing to hide, if he were served subpoena, and they furnished him the necessary fees to get down there, and his expenses to get down there and back, he's got nothing to hide to go down and back free. So there would be no inference of any type of guilt on behalf of my client.

Q: What about you, Fred?

A: I would go down there under those conditions.

(Inaudible)

Q: As I say, these are things that should come on the record.
A: I've got nothing to hide from anybody. I'd meet Garrison if he wishes to question me about people that I know. Fine. I'm willing to give a complete list of everybody I know.

Q: To your knowledge, have you ever talked to any of Garrison's people before in an official capacity about this investigation?
A: No, never.

Q: I mean, if you have, it's been an undercover-type guy.
A: Yeah. The only thing that I knew of was the fact that there had been Garrison investigators out in the State of Washington off and on during the last year and a half.
A: (Robert Griffin) I think you should tell him what you believe the so-called undercover agents are—what they're trying to purport that you know.
A: Yeah, I think this was good. And we'll get it on the record. What the heck! I think in all probability what they're looking for, actually, the remnants of the free fighters of the Cuban free fighters—against Castro of their financial fights. This is what they're looking for. And Garrison feels he finds the remnants of that, whatever it might be, well up in the thousands of dollars. And if he finds that, whoever has it, wherever it might be, he'll find a definite lead to the person that was involved in the shooting of the President. Because as you recall, going back to his original theory, it was free Cubans who [blank] about the Bay of Pigs type thing, that were a spin-off from the Bay of Pigs, that concocted and formed this whole thing.

Well, there was a tremendous amount of money involved and Tom Beckham was a disc-jockey in New Orleans, and pretty well educated—and at that time the free fighters were—you know, everybody was doing all kinds

of social things to help them out—all this type of thing.
He served as their banker. Now how much money there
was, all totaled, I don't know. I'm really not sure.

Q: Were you involved with Beckham that time?

A: I never met him until he came to Washington. But why he
came, I'm not sure. I met him out here. He had a couple
of hit records he wanted to promote[1] and that sort of thing,
and I went along with that. I helped out on it. I wrote a lot
of his stuff for him, as Bob has told you. I'll write material for anybody, for anything. I earn a living as a freelance
writer. Consequently, I've written for major political figures in both parties.[2] I still do. Doing so right now.

Q: There's a rumor afoot that you've been writing an underground newspaper in Tacoma. Is there anything to that?

A: This has been laid on my back about seven or eight times—
one thing they brought out over and over again. Especially, people calling over the air and asking about it. I
use phraseology in that paper. But I pointed out to them
that many a minister uses phraseology out of the Bible.
Whether a rumor is true or whether it's not true has no
bearing here.[3]

(Inaudible)

Q: I think this is the way this should be.

A: I've met a couple of fellows that liked - that have written
material for that, the *New Times*, I think you're talking
about.

Q: Yes.

A: But I haven't written it. I don't have anything to do with
it.

Q: Let's get to something else. Our first contact was yesterday afternoon right after you had had a meeting in the
office of Mayor [blank], with the mayor, Mr. Nichols of
KAYE, Chief Zittel, and Mr. Dukenthaler. What about
this local matter? Let's get that on the record now.

A: Okay, let's get that on the record because I feel this is
beginning to get a little annoying, this type of thing. In the
first place, I wasn't speeding to start out with.

A (Robert Griffin) Wait, no, I don't think we should. The
reason I say this is this is still in the process. There's
going to be a hearing on that, and I don't think we should.

Q: Okay, fine. (Inaudible.) I'll cut this part of the tape, and
you have my word on it. I'll—I won't run it.

A: (Griffin): I think what you ought to tell us—your work
with Boeing and some of what you were telling me as to
maybe a feeling of Garrison as to the accusation.

Q: Let me lead into that, Bob, and you tell me if I'm wrong.
About a year ago—and I may be wrong in this, Fred, but
I think I'm right—about a year ago Garrison in a speech
in Los Angeles or in the State of California that made an
allusion to the fact that there were some people doing
work for Boeing who were involved in the assassination
plot of John F. Kennedy. Now, do you have any ideas
what this might be?

A: Now he knows I was a former Boeing employee. I was a
personnel man. I worked for Boeing a couple of years. I
quit Boeing to go back to the field of teaching. Now he
claims that I did not quit. That I still work for Boeing. He
attempts to paint a picture of me as sort of a highly paid,
undercover—and please don't mistake underworld. I had
this quoted to me back today, that I was supposed to be
with the underworld.

Q: If you had called this WTIX man who had some allusions
of the same kind...

A: That I belonged to a fantastic conglomeration of rather
highly-paid, sort of super spies for the industrial world -
spy upon one another, especially in the field of aerospace
and aero-hardware of one kind of another. Actually, it's

not. I don't have any connection with Boeing whatsoever. He's made this allusion to about two or three people. And he has mentioned this Boeing thing three or four times.

A: (Griffin) Now the one thing I want to get eminently clear, you quit Boeing.

A: That's right. Resigned from Boeing.

Q: Because again I have picked up today a great deal of things, and it's very difficult to sort out fact from fiction. And as I say, I want to be fair. Whether I agree with you or not is beside the point, you know, on anything. Whether you agree with me—we're both in the same business. One other thing, as far as I'm concerned, and from here on out we'll say what you want to say. We'll see if we can get it all. I'm going to cut some of these extraneous remarks out. There seems to be on the part of some people in this area, some question as to your use of the title, "Doctor." Can you tell me the source of this usage on your part?

A: (Griffin): Could I answer that?

Q: Sure, perfectly all right.

A: (Griffin) He is a psychologist who has a doctor's degree, and he can legally use the term "doctor."

Q: May I ask one thing more? From what institution...

A: I got two really, but one is an honorary type thing. Brentridge College, and it's at Falcomb, England, and you can call it by calling Falcomb 405, if you wanted. I got my transcripts and I got my—in Latin and in English.

Q: I knew that you had a B.A. from [blank] that you got in '51. Am I correct?

A: I got a B.A. in '50.

Q: I know this much. It shows you that I have done a little work. But that was fine. This is another thing. Now, at this point is there anything else you want to get on the record or you think you should get on the record?

A: (Griffin) I think that you should get on the record or something that even though he has not been served a subpoena in this matter, he is a local person, and I think he should bring out which I told the PI last evening—he's a veteran of two wars; he's a fighter pilot who's been shot down twice—is that right? Shot down twice in World War II and again in Korea. So he was shot down three times in an airplane serving his country. He is a highly educated man who has not only been a teacher, but is presently in the radio field, who is a good citizen, and is quite shocked. And the thing that should be—because you're going to be served a subpoena in a Grand Jury does not mean that you're a victim or that there's any accusation against you; it merely means that you might have some knowledge about something that might be relevant to some issues. So people who are subpoenaed do not have any guilt complex associate. That's why I made it emphatic at the first point, that my client, if he's served that subpoena and given transportation there and expenses, will voluntarily go. They don't have to do anything more. Isn't that right?

A: That's right.

A: (Griffin) I think that should be in the record.

Q: I think also at this point there is one thing I should make clear. As soon as I get back to the station, Bob, Fred is familiar with this, you probably aren't—I will make a complete, unedited dub of what I have here and I will furnish it to you—I will also have one myself—and I'll try to be eminently fair and not take anything out of context. I'm not going to run this whole thing. There are a couple of points in here we want to cut off.

A: (Griffin) Sure. This is one of the reasons why he selected you when [blank] because I thought that your broadcast had been the fairest, on the line. At least you went to the trouble to place the calls and find out what these people had to say on the other end.

Q: I don't know whether you heard my 5:30 broadcast last night.

A (Griffin) No, I didn't.

Q: After my confrontation with Fred last night, I went back and I said these are facts I have from UPI. These are things that Mr. Crisman said to me. I draw no conclusions. That's not for me to do. All right, fine. You're Robert Griffin. You're a Tacoma attorney representing Fred Lee Crisman.

A: (Griffin) Right.

Q: And you're Fred Lee Crisman and to the best of your knowledge you are the same Fred Lee Crisman that Mr. Garrison's talking about.

A: Right.

Q: And I'm Mel Gaumer, the news director of KTAC.

A: (Griffin) One point I'd like to put in the record, of your courtesy. That you did not try to ask any twisted questions. You were very fair to both myself and my client. I'd like that to go onto the tape also, that you were very courteous and very fair and very objective.

Q: Thank you very much.

A: One thing, I've had some—why did I use the name John Gold.

Q: Yes, I'm glad you thought of that. This, of course, anybody in my business doesn't worry about, but other people do.

A: We didn't know whether the program was going to be a success or not and I give Jim Nichols credit for this. He said I don't want to have the experience of having a program to produce unless it really clicks and becomes as popular as Party Line in the morning that you can get up and walk off with. So let me keep the name John Gold. You just use a station name. I was perfectly willing to use the name Fred Crisman. I didn't care one way or another. Jim thought it would be better to use John Gold. I told him not to use doctor, it had nothing to do with it. But he did anyway in promoting the thing.

Q: General Mills has had 18 Betty Crockers, I think.
A: People say I'm trying to hide something. That wasn't it. The reason was simply that. So I couldn't get up and walk off with the program.

Notes:
1. According to rock music historian Jerry E. Dürrwächter no one named Tom Beckham or Mark Evans has ever had solo hits on the Pop, Country, R&B, or Adult Contemporary charts. There are many people with the name "Evans" on the charts, but no "Mark Evans." "Charlie" Beckham had one country hit (#84, "Think I'll Go Home, 6/18/88) and "Bob" Beckham had one country hit (#73, "Cherokee Strip," 9/2/67) and three Pop hits in 1959 (#32) and 1960 (#36 & #105). The August 9, 1977 edition of the Mobile, Alabama *Press Register* reports that Beckham promoted country-western concerts in the Mobile area under the name "Eggleston Zimmerman."
2. Political figures that Crisman wrote speeches for include General Curtis LeMay, the vice presidential candidate to George Wallace in 1968. LeMay once adamantly remonstrated Senator Barry Goldwater when Goldwater asked to be taken to the "blue room" to see alien bodies from the Roswell crash. In his last years, LeMay also worked with Trevor James Constable at "cloudbusting," a technology used by Wilhelm Reich to battle UFOs in the Arizona desert.
3. Nevertheless, in his 1970 book, *Murder of a City,* Crisman tells the story of co-creating the *New Times* with the help of Marshall Riconosciuto and Bob Lavender ("a young man with a print shop"), who was later interviewed by one of Jim Garrison's investigators. According to Crisman, the *New Times* "carried the same front page heading and artwork that the old *Tacoma Times* carried, and it did offer a form of journalism that was both new and unexpected in the Northwest." In fact, *Murder of a City* is comprised in part of articles from the *New Times.*

Correspondence
Letter To The Editor, *Amazing Stories,* June 1946
Sirs:
I flew my last combat mission on May 26 when I was shot up over Bassein and ditched my ship in Ramaree Roads off Chedubs Island. I was missing five days. I requested leave at Kashmere. I and Capt.—— left Srinagar and went to Rudok then through the Khesa pass to the northern foothills of the Kabakoram. We found what we were looking for. For heaven's sake, drop the whole thing! You are playing with dynamite. My companion and I fought our way out of a cave with submachine guns. I have two nine-inch scars on my left arm that came from wounds given me in the cave when I was fifty feet from a moving object of any kind and in perfect silence. The muscles were nearly ripped out. How? I don't know. My friend has a hole the size of a dime in his right bicep. It was seared inside. How, we don't know. But we both believe we know more about the Shaver Mystery than any other pair. You may imagine my fright when I picked up my first copy of *Amazing Stories* and see you splashing words about on the subject. Do not print our names. We are not cowards but we are not crazy.

"Discussions: Report From Alaska," *Amazing Stories*
May 1947
Sirs:
I have just finished reading the September issue of *Harper's Magazine,* and I noted where William S. Baring-Gould had selected my letter to you last winter as an example of crackpot letters. I bitterly resent this. It is all well and good to sit in a comfortable office or home and look upon far places and strange things as through a veil of unbelief…however, when you are there and death looks you right in the eye…you feel a little different, and the safe, comfortable U. S. A. becomes the world of never-was and "does it really exist?" I felt that you, too, Mr. Palmer, had more or less given me up for a jerk who was only trying to

pull your leg. Again the fear that maybe all this was only a promotion stunt and gales of laughter in the *AS* office.

Well, you see how it is. Dick and I have made our Alaska journey, and we failed, we lost and we lost a lot. Dick lost his life. The details I don't suppose you are interested in, however, Shaver would get a kick out of a journey to the Alaska cave. It seems strange to read *AS* and see the "little" people still wondering and still "investigating" their claims of caves. Go and take a look for yourself, I say. Sure, it takes money and guts. I know, I have spent all I have of both. It sickens me when I read an article like Gould's. So smug and sure. After all, Dick is dead, and that meant a lot to me. I don't care much whether you believe or not. I'm sick of the whole mess. I don't even want to think of last year, and of Alaska least of all. Just wanted to go on record as being further sickened by Gould's article. Fred L. Crisman, 125 Woodland Salishan Add., Tacoma, Washington

Well, there you are, Mr. Crisman, on record. And we heartily agree with you. But we are interested in the details of your little journey, and we offer herewith to publish your story of that Alaska cave complete. Our readers want proof. We want proof. If you've got any at all, we want it. In your previous letter, you asked us to keep your identity a secret. We had to do that, and you can't blame us for being reluctant to believe, although we did publish your letter because it was right in line with what we do believe, and that is the Shaver Mystery. It is shocking, certainly, to have you tell us that your companion was killed in that Alaskan adventure, but we can't just let it rest there. Either this is true, or it isn't true. And if true, you can't just let it go by being sickened of the whole affair. We have chosen to publish this letter, rather than replying directly to you as yet, although by the time this is published you will have heard from us. If your story can be proved, and this cave shown to us, we CAN and WILL raise money for a complete investigation.

Our readers, judging from the thousands of letters we have, would find a way to finance the thing themselves, if we didn't. They're that interested. For example, Chet Geter, well-known author, has recently started a club of *Amazing*

Stories readers who are interested in doing something about solving the mystery. That ought to prove to you that you would certainly not be considered a crackpot if you came forward with your complete story. Baring-Gould, true enough, took it upon himself to cover a subject whereon he was completely ignorant, and worse still, grossly misinformed. He was like a Zulu given the job of writing a technical article about an atomic pile from information given him by a Hottentot. We consider Mr. Gould's article to be simply a smart article-writer's annexing of a fat check by getting there fastest with the mostest words on a subject he was clever enough to realize was "hot." He writes for a living, and he'd do an article about steel mills, if it was hot. Although we hope he'd go to a steel man for his information, and not a Hottentot. So, let us go on record too. You send us your story, and prove it, and we'll pay you a damsite more than Gould got for his article. And if you prove to have no more facts than Gould did, we'll forget about it and no hard feelings. Sound okay to you?—Ed.

William S. Baring-Gould had written "Little Superman, What Now?" in *Harper's Magazine,* September 1946, to report upon the first postwar science-fiction fan convention in Newark, New Jersey, March 6, 1946. He included damning feint praise for the genre, noting that "the current crisis in science fiction will almost certainly lead to better-written, better-characterized, more convincing yarns." He condemned Ray Palmer's *Amazing Stories* to "the very bottom of the list" of science fiction pulp magazines, and quoted Fred Crisman's first letter to it as an example of the extremism of the magazine's audience. In addition to his follow-up to Crisman's second letter, Ray Palmer responded to Baring-Gold in the November 1946 issue of *Harper's:*
"Letters: Dream World," *Harper's Magazine*
November 1946

To the Editors:

...Quoting Baring-Gould ["Little Superman, What Now?" September 1946]: "Palmer seems anxious to give the impression that he himself is firmly convinced of the existence of Shaver's deros." Baring-Gould does not understand the "Shaver Mystery." From his article, it is apparent at once that he has not read the stories concerned with the "mystery." I am not "anxious to give [an] impression." I believe in the "Mystery" for what it is. Every word uttered editorially in Amazing Stories is my firm conviction, not any attempt at a hoax. ...If he wanted to present my "beliefs" why didn't he ask me what they were? Raymond A. Palmer, Ziff-Davis Publishing Co., New York, NY

To the Editors:
...I have read not only the Shaver stories but all Mr. Palmer's editorial comments thereon, and I am delighted to learn he is convinced of the truth of the Shaver Mystery and is in no way trying to perpetuate a hoax on his readers. This is very reassuring... William S. Baring-Gould, New York

Venture Press, Evanston, Illinois
July 22 1947
Mr. Kenneth Arnold Box 387 Boise, Idaho
Dear Mr. Arnold:
Quite obviously you have been ribbed so much you'd like to forget the flying saucers—but I'd sure like to have your personal story, your photo, pic of your plane, etc, as I asked before. And you won't be made to look silly, because there is more to this then the newspapers and the "experts" have made of it. Besides the article, I have another proposition. You seem to get around quite a bit, and if you can make a trip to Tacoma, Washington at all feasible, I'd be willing to pay expenses plus a nice amount to make it worth your while.
I'd want you to see Fred Lee Crisman, [address redacted] Fern Hill Station, Tacoma, and Harold Dahl, owner of the fishing vessel North Queen. Crisman, Dahl and two other seamen, on a patrol near Maury Island, off Tacoma, saw six discs, one in trouble, witnessed an explosion, saw falling stuff which smashed their wheelhouse and searchlight and landed on the beach. They sent me samples which Chicago U has failed to analyze. I want a picture of the beach and the stuff that landed there (about twenty tons, they said). And I want somebody who'll get the truth to find out if these boys are on the up and up. You could do that. I hope you will. If agreeable, please write and perhaps we can talk business. I think

you'd like to prove this thing too. Anyway, I still want that article.
Sincerely yours, Raymond A. Palmer

Fred Crisman wrote the following in response to a November 1949 article in *Fate* that reported upon Harold Dahl's wife urging that her husband declare the Maury Island incident a hoax.

Fate, January 1950
It is with deepest regret that I note the remarks in your article concerning the so-called "Report On the Flying Saucers" that I am an alleged publicity seeker and a hoaxer who attempted to swindle a Chicago editor out of payment for an unwritten adventure story on the strength of some "rock formations" from Maury Island in Puget Sound. The facts in your alleged "report" are so garbled and twisted as to bear almost no resemblance to what actually happened. If you will bother to contact editor R. A. Palmer of *Amazing Stories* and ask him to recall the telephone conversation I had with him, perhaps he will recall that I refused to write the story. He made the offer to me, I did not ask him to advance money in any manner. I also refused payment from other publications for "true" story of the incident. You state that Crisman and Dahl broke under questioning and admitted the fragments they had secured were really rock formations from Maury Island. This is a bald-faced lie. There are still many questions unanswered, that lend further proof that you have never been given all the facts in this incident, or else you have deliberately (for no reason that I can think of) lied, or else the facts that were presented to you for your article were twisted.
1. What became of the fragments that were aboard the B-25 that crashed?
2. What became of the analytical reports on the fragments that Palmer received, and why did our west coast check differ from that of the University of Chicago, if they were the same?
3. Why did the Air Force refuse to allow pictures of the crash to be made any time?

4. Ken Arnold and I were in the hotel room talking, and the phone rang and the "Voice" made reference to our conversation that was going on at the time he called. There was no known way he could have gotten the information we were discussing.

5. Why, if we were such blackguards as you state we were and deliberately caused the deaths of two Air Force pilots and the loss of a $150,000 airplane, did not the government or some agency there attempt to seek justice through the courts of the state or federal government?

6. I was at the time active in reservist affairs of the Air Force. Why did not the Air Force call me to account for my dastardly actions? You know as well as I do that they would not take such shenanigans from a junior officer of the reserve without some form of punishment.

7. Last and not least, what has become of Hal Dahl? Why would a man who was doing okay and building a new home just up and leave it all? No reason given, just left? In all my life I cannot recall having been so absolutely furious over any matter whatsoever. I want to assure you that if my name ever appears in your cheap publication again, I shall institute legal action. Fred L. Crisman

Note: Ray Palmer edited *Fate* under the pseudonym Robert N. Webster.

Parapsychology Research
Post Office Box 722
Tacoma, Washington 98401
1/4/68
Dear Mr. Farish:

As I pointed out to you in my last letter - I am no longer in office - but have been asked to stay on and help out with mail and communication that has piled up over the Xmas holidays. I must admit that I have been rather shocked at the demands for information that our one advertisement in the *Fate* magazine brought. I did not know that so many of the average citizens in this nation were as aware of the overall field of parapsychology and as frantic for teaching in that area.

Perhaps we have allowed ourselves to be a bit smug and introverted in our decision that only WE were able to make the proper inquiry into a phenomena of some type. Surely where people have this much interest then there must be a great demand for that information. I am at a loss as to what reasons - colleges and universities can advance for a denial of this area of study and investigation.

In relation to being PR director for Arkansas - I will send along a letter of appointment and a series of booklet type information sheets as soon as they come from the printers. The powers that be feel that the old mimeo is not professional enough and all must be printed hereafter.

SO...all new certificates have been designed and the word "INSTITUTE" has been added to the PR name   that will cause some open rebellion in the ranks at the Fe. meeting. There will be screams about "progress" not being progress and demands to "...throw the rascals out..." and after it is all over the new methods will prevail and we will be a new and different organization. (I am not as much against it now as I was several months ago.)

One thing is better now, and that is the shift of the records and headquarters of the American Association of Parapsychologists from Omaha to Seattle. There was more in the way of proper space (at an available rate) and also more money to work with out here. We seem to have a more affluent look at parapsychology than they do on the east coast. They have the members and we have the money available out here...so the natural move was to where the best support could be found.

There are new certificates of membership being printed and a new type of wallet card...as soon as they are finished I will see if I can ship you your credentials and appointment as a state representative.

I am unaware of the amount of interest in your area, but most states have enough people that have a sincere interest in parapsychology to make it worth while to organize a state chapter.

Please forgive the short note, however, I am pressed for time and I will get more of your questions answered next time. Regards, F. Lee

Parapsychology Research, December 5, 1967
Dear Mr. Farish:
I am afraid that you have placed the Parapsychology organization on a basis with many of the small units of a variety of memberships. The members of the Parapsychology Research are a rather backward group and they are seldom in sight at the so-called "conventions" and other gatherings of the followers of the usual UFO and "message from outer space" people. I use the word backward in the social sense, of course.

Several years ago we formed an association with a new graduate school - The American Academy of Professional Arts of Omaha, Nebraska and asked members of their staff to assist us in writing a training and teaching schedule (curricula) for our members. We felt that the field of parapsychology was one that was being by-passed by serious students of a group of related disciplines. This has been finished and most of our new members are asked to take these courses. We felt that qualifications for membership were enough.

In all organizations there are changes of leadership, and our current officers feel that we should open our records and our general training courses to any person that has the interest to enable him to study the material. While I strongly disagree, I bow to the majority and carry out the wishes of the Board of Directors. For the first time we are turning to professional artists for covers for our bulletin and we are to rename it. We will have a set of offices and a completely revamped and redesigned letterhead.

This, of course, appeals to the general public, and that is where we will re-organize our membership to allow many members on a very wide national scale to enter the PR ranks. I have strongly protested as I feel that we have accomplished much more than we will with a large and very unwieldy membership.

Perhaps you noted our advertisement in *Fate* magazine offering our brochure on parapsychology? I do not feel that this is the way to advance the profession. I voted for the formation of the American Association of Parapsychologists, and I feel that it can be a very fine organization, however, I feel that it is still too early to open our ranks to the general public.

I have attended the meetings, as an observer, and noted that many people that seek to enrich themselves from wild tales of UFO and Fortean "happenings." I have also noted that the quality of their research and their general attitude to the field of parapsychology is that of idiots. Parapsychology must be guarded against the inroads of those that would make a silly "ghost-hunters" club of it or attempt to convert it into a forum for the launching of new religions. *Parapsychology Research* has a responsibility to the basic study of these areas that lend themselves to a new-frontier of serious study for all mankind. I fear that we shall soon be eaten alive by the American Association of Para. And we shall become but a hall of records for a series of "happenings" that do not meet our present standards.

Parapsychology Research, as a group, has in the past made careful efforts to actually evaluate certain phenomena on a basis of guidelines worked out over many years of scientific research, and freely borrowed research methods from the procedure guides of large concerns. We have not made most of our research information generally known, although it has been available to those that have requested certain information.

We have devoted much time to making a careful study of certain of the UFO incidents and attempted to reach those involved that could be useful in contributing to the direct knowledge of that incident. We have the most complete file on the famous "Maury Island incident" on record.

You may be familiar with this early UFO incident we spent a great deal of time on it due to its proximity to our headquarters here in the state of Washington. We were even successful in having established contact with the elusive Fred Crisman - getting him to speak to our group. This is something that the proverbial price of "money, marbles and chalk" is very seldom able to do. Strangely enough, this incident - branded by the Air Force Project Bluebook as a hoax, is one of the few that we believe to be the most solidly authentic.

You state an interest in the UFO phenomena - perhaps you have an interest in our methods of evaluation. If so, let me know, and I will send you a report to the *Parapsychology Research* prepared by Mr. David Strong of the Strong Paper Corporation concerning the Maury Island incident. It covers a twenty year period of investigation, interviews and a follow up of the lives of all that were concerned. It represents about $13,000 in expenses and contains two interviews with Fred Crisman and Harold Dahl - and THAT is a real accomplishment. Mr. Crisman, is probably the most informed man in the United States on UFO's and also one of the hardest to find - as the FBI has learned several times.

An interesting fact - one of our members sent a copy of one of the current TV series, "The Aliens" [sic]. It was my understanding that Mr. Crisman was not disturbed or angry, as first reported, as few things seem to disturb him.

However, UFO's are not my personal forte, and I seldom follow the reports on them to any great extent. My own interests lie in other fields of parapsychology. I include the above because you stated that you have an interest in the UFO phenomena. If you have an interest in becoming a member - send along a short resume or your background and we will proceed from there. I hope that this letter has been of interest to you. Yours truly, F. Lee

Parapsychology Research
P.O.Box 722
Tacoma, Washington 98401
November 26, 1967
 Mr. Lucius Farish Plumerville, Arkansas
 Dear Mr. Farish:
 I am not acquainted with the publication that you say referred to an extract from our Bulletin. I do not know of the *Searchlight*. The *Parapsychology Research Bulletin* is a small monthly news letter that is sent to members of our organization. Of course, anyone is free to quote from our pages and we do not care. We do like to be quoted accurately. The men and women that make up the membership of *Parapsychology Research* use the newsletter to place their views and theories on many subjects, before the other members.

 In the past year and a half we have published several articles on, so-called, monsters. The exact article that you refer to is unknown to me. We published an article by Wallace Jones on the Northern California "wasatch" monsters. There was a short piece by Avery Connought comparing the "wasatch" with the Finnish "schstikpi" and marking the similar areas of description.

In an area of more general knowledge, we published rather a long study by Dr. Albert C. Doyle, wherein he traced the history of the Loch Ness monster and went back to the early legend of Douglas McAlistire - wherein he describes quite accurately his view of a UFO hovering over the Loch and depositing living creatures in it in 1215 A.D. There was also a short piece that concerned itself with the theory that many of the pictured and recorded versions of the modern UFO that used some type of gravity disturbance and "pushed" against the ground...had some effect on certain areas of the Earth and in the twenty years or so that UFOs have been remarked upon...that the sightings and reports of many types of "monsters" have multiplied greatly. His articles (I refer to Dr. Doyle) were well-researched and well-presented.

Unfortunately the news letter is restricted to a limited list of members only and is not available for general or a wide circulation. I hope what little I have been able to refer to is a help. Yours truly, F. Lee, Secretary

[undated brochure]
Alas! The old bulletin is no more! The new brochure. The winds of change are upon us - and I am afraid that the old days will never come again! FL

[brochure copy]
Opus a Symphony of Commentary
602 Elliott West, Seattle, Wash. 98119
Are YOU Qualified...?

Opus is a magazine dedicated to the principle that professional executives seldom have the opportunity to express themselves without fear of censorship or editorial cuts.

Opus guarantees its contributors that it will not censor or edit in any manner the accepted material.

Opus does request...actually require...that all contributions adhere to accepted standards of good taste. the contributions and advertisements must remain couched in that area of semantics that is acceptable upon any level of society.

Opus offers advertising rates in direct ratio to the primary prose content of the magazine. Each issue is very carefully designed to appeal to the elite...the professional in his field. Opus offers subscriptions on a closed basis; a recommendation is requested and subscription issued upon approval of the Subscription Department.

Opus is on the verge of making its first elite edition available. It is proud of the list of first issue contributors. The list is available upon request.

Opus has explained its position. If you disagree...then it welcomes your critique!

I have retained Box 722 as a personal box and to wind some of the personal interests I have had. You may write me there.

[brochure copy]
Opus is qualified!

Parapsychology Research
Lucius Farish
Route One, Plumerville, Ark.

Dear Mr. Farish:

It was unfortunate that the applications for the study courses were mailed to you. I placed your name on the mailing list and from there. I assume one of the girls simply mailed you a copy of the mimeoed material. Most of this material is being withdrawn and new printed material substituted.

With your background, I don't feel that there would be any problem in just going ahead and granting your certificate and assign you as the *PR* representative in your state. That is, of course, if you should wish to have such a post.

Along with this letter I am mailing you a copy of the Bulletin and though it is Copy #1 as far as the new open and general public policy is concerned it is the last of the old mimeo productions. I hope you enjoy it, though I feel that it certainly is not up to past standards.

My own term as director will be finished Dec 31, and a Mr. Robert L. Lavender, Ph. D. of Seattle will be taking over in that capacity. I have great respect for Dr. Lavender and he has made some excellent contributions to the *PR* field. He has for the past 2 years been doing research on the San

Juan Lights in the San Juan Isle group in Northern Puget Sound. One of the most interesting phenomena that we have out here. I am not surprised to learn that you were unaware of *PR*. I seriously doubt that more than 1,000 people in the world over are aware that it exists. We have never at any time had any open contact with the general public or allowed our members to make news or capital...in any manner from their relationship with *PR*. Our dues were only $10.00 a year, and that was a surprise to potential members.

Prior to Sept, 1 '67, the only means of membership was to be recommended by a member and then you were only an associate for two years. We asked no dues from Associates. We did require work on the part of an Associate and that he submit one written (later typed) Report for the Bulletin, and we asked that it be in thesis form and it had to be original research and drawn to a conclusion. However, this is changed now and while the courses are still available and a thesis is required. The American Association of Parapsychologists handles all the course material and passes judgement on the written material. They appoint the proctors concerned, and it leaves *PR* with little to do but the spade work and the processing of the Reports.

We are aware of several Fortean Societies and we have a mailing list with over 200 organizations (current and defunct) on it. However, we have little direct contact with them. We have never sought elaborate exchanges of material - probably because we felt that other organizations were not on the ethical level we imposed upon our areas of research. This is not meant to read as "snob" effect, but even if we sought contact with those that were doing worthy work, we were then faced with the winnowing of the grain from the chaff among them, and we felt that it was a time-wasting activity.

We were also faced with the existing fact of our own sloppy production methods. Our whole library of reports and Bulletins have been mimeoed, and they have not always been of the highest grade. Many times our Special Bulletins were sent out to members with only a prospective guide that explained a special project that some member or group of members wished to undertake, and they wanted funds from other members to support the project. These appeals for funds were well understood by our membership, but would have looked "strange" to society in general. An appeal for $6,000.00 to spend the summer on the slopes of Mt. Shasta would have shocked a large and general public membership and it would bring some harsh answers, I feel. Many of us have argued that by the opening up of the membership, we will actually cut down on the moneys we get for projects due to the general lack of interest on the part of the membership at large.

Many people will join simply to get the wall plaque and the professional wallet card that will open many doors for them and their contribution to *PR* in research of financial support will not be forthcoming.

The Maury Island incident, strangely enough, is not finished and we have a series of pictures that were taken this past August of the area where the material was picked up and .. since 1947 there has been no vegetative growth on the section of Maury Island. I might add that the area has been fenced for many years and has U.S. Army signs posted that forbid any trespassing and that is current today.

Mr. Crisman stated that the U.S. IQ. officers took the pictures and the negatives of the "saucers" and that were in Project's Skywatch and Blue Book. The Air Force has denied that they ever existed...and what was not known until the summer of 1966 is that before Dahl and Crisman gave the pictures to the Army officers they has an extra set of negatives made and I have seen the prints from this set of negs.

What we have considered extremely interesting about the Maury Island incident - is not so much as what happened as - the odd conduct on the part of the principals and the U. S. govt. after it happened. Conduct that is still considered off the normal pattern of affairs after twenty years has passed.

For instance: Crisman was called back to active duty as a Captain (fighter- pilot) in 1947 - when the rest of us were under the impression that this could not be done to a veteran. He was sent to Alaska - then to Panama - then to Greenland. The perfect old pattern when the Armed Forces has it in for an officer - sort of a USA Siberian treatment. Evidently - they were never able to shake his story and he was allowed to return to civil life in 1949...they waited only until 1951 and he was re-called again and this time sent to Korea and was flying high-altitude recon missions over China for two years.

He has never followed the pattern that they stated at the time of the Incident...that he and Dahl were after money and notoriety. For one thing, Crisman will not speak to any group that he does not approve of, and if he does decide to speak, he will accept no money. He and Dahl have not tried to sell their pictures, and they only re-printed them so we could have a copy for safekeeping. Crisman has several times told both the Congress and FBI...where they could go and what they could do with their questions. He travels and he has certain areas that he returns to and he has some source of income and no one seems to know what it is...I know that he sometimes shows up (strangely enough) at one of the "space meetings" and that he flies a surplus F-51 at times.

I have had the experience of writing to Hal Dahl - in my original efforts to help find Crisman - and having the answer come back from Crisman postmarked in England or in some part of the U.S. Any letter sent to Hal Dahl is usually answered by Crisman - if he bothers to answer at all.

Project Bluebook has stated in their records that the Maury Island incident was a hoax and that these two men were after cheap publicity and trying to sell some story to Ray Palmer - editor of the old *Amazing Stories* magazine. Crisman has not only denied this but has called Capt. Edward J. Ruppelt a cad and a liar and further made an accusation that Ruppelt was himself a serious participant in a grand hoax conducted by the U.S. Air Force. He did this in public and time after time from the lecture platform. He wrote to Sen. Jackson and asked that Ruppelt be made to prove his charges and that he was willing to meet him in open forum. No authority of the U.S. ever took up the challenge. All this was, I believe, in 1956 upon the release of Ruppelt's book *UFO's* wherein he makes great hay of the Maury Island thing. We have it on good authority that the Air Force was willing to meet the challenge, but they were tipped in some manner to the fact that Crisman and Dahl were well supplied with evidence to prove what a foolish story Ruppelt had printed...so they ignored it as a tempest in a teapot.

We would have loved to see this happen - because as we know now - they still had the original negative copies, and they also (we are quite certain) have some of the material of the UFO. It was not all aboard the B-25 that night when it crashed. The B-25 was recovered in it's every piece and is still under wraps at Edwards Air Force base in California. The plane was perforated in a 1,000 (?) places by what is now the same type of holes that a laser beam makes in metal. That was 20 years ago, and no one knew a thing about laser beams then. I have read the Thurston County Sheriff's report of the crash that state that the pilots were still strapped in their seats and burned completely...in a plane that didn't burn.

Hope this is of some interest to you - we feel that most serious researchers feel strangely about the Maury Island thing. It has too many loose ends and those ends are still flapping about and it is certainly not the last of the story.
Yours truly, F. Lee

Gary Lesley, Director
U.A.P.R.O.
737 "A" Street Northeast Auburn, Wn. 98002
23 July 1967
   Mr. Harold Dahl
   c/o Columbia Industries
   P.O. Box #38 Tenino, Washington
   Dear Mr. Dahl:
   At the annual N. W. UFO convention in Seattle on July 22nd, I met and talked with Dr. Lee Crisman. Dr. Crisman informed me of this address for the reason that I would be able to obtain copies of the Maury Island photographs (UFOs) from you. He gave a very good lecture on the implications of the Maury Island incident, explaining that the accounts of it were generally false that were to be found in UFO books and magazines. I agree with this, that the past and present Maury Island stories are muddied in facts. It is because of this that our organization is interested in clearing up publicly the true affairs that transpired. It was a shock to the UFO researchers present there (excluding the persons that claimed contact with beings and traveling to other planets in flying saucers that were so prevalent there), including myself, that the photographs taken were in possession of the person who took them. A great shock that came to us was when we learned that the photographs are the first UFO photographs taken. Already, from a few new facts, many old beliefs of researchers have been shattered. We also greatly realize the tremen-

dous value the photos have in supporting the story. We also have learned that the slag-like material is not smelter substance, but something quite unusual. Other news facts were presented that further backed my determination to bring out the full truth of the incident. After knowing what actually happened, I felt that the public should know.

I understand why and how the newspaper reporters and radio reporters jumbled and messed up the factual data to a point that has never been resolved to this day. The difference this time is that, if I can obtain the full story, I will report it as I will write it: in its entirety and factuality. All I need is your kind assistance and patience and also that of Dr. Crisman's.

First of all, I would like to make a proposal concerning the photos. If you send the prints, we will have copies made immediately and return the prints as soon as we are finished (within 4-5 days). No damage will result to the prints you send. Secondly, I would like to have your written testimony of the account as you remember it entirely. Or, if this is too much trouble, I would appreciate only a write-down of the essential facts—mainly the facts that have been jumbled in the many magazines and book accounts of the case. Your written statement that the facts that you have cited are true to the best of your knowledge, would be most appreciated and useful. And lastly, it would be very helpful if you would contact Dr. Crisman (he has not given me his address or telephone number, as he states that he does not like the publicity—I do not really blame him) and please tell him that a brief written testimony to the effect of all that he knows that actually transpired would be of great value to proving the validity of the Maury Island case. It would be in the form of your written statements, including your final written statement. Any addresses of other witnesses, persons somehow connected with this incident, etc., would be of great help also to our research report. It should be emphasized that any names and/or addresses that the person(s) do not wish to be given, will not be given by our organization and will be filed confidentially. It is urged by our group, that names not be withheld in simple light of the veracity that this material adds to the incident.

I would also like to ask you two questions. (1) The boat that served as the "target" for the slag-like material from the

UFO's: Is it still intact? (2) If so, are there dents or other damage visible on the boat as of this date? Dr. Crisman emphasized to the audience at the Convention the importance of the seriousness of the UFO problem, that it should not be a thing of space-songs, space jokes, etc. (as was, unfortunately, in evidence at the Convention). We fully agree. It is with this seriousness in mind, that we have contacted you for assistance in helping clear up one facet of why the UFO remains a mystery—ignorance. We trust that you will answer this letter and that our efforts to research this mystery has not been in vain. We hope to hear from you soon.

Yours sincerely, Gary Lesley, Director: U.A.P.R.O. Auburn Scientific Staff International

P.S.: I have enclosed some information about the U.A.P.R.O., grl, Enclosure

Mr. Gary Lesley Auburn, Washington Director
UAPRO
August 22, 1967
Dear Mr. Lesley:
Please forgive the fact that there has been a delay in answering your letter, however it is due to out "rules of the game" in that we felt many years ago that any speaking on the subject should be with the full knowledge of the other man.

Mr. Crisman has been in the deep South for some time and I have also had occasion to travel and we did not have the chance to meet until several days ago here in Texas.

I will be quite frank with you Mr. Lesley - it has been our policy for some years not to answer any letters of any individual or organization that wanted to discuss the Maury Island incident. I am sure that you can understand the way our story was received by the public and the press when it first appeared in 1947! No person would like to go through that treatment a second time. I refer in particular to Mr. Crisman - he was the one that tried to show a very unbelieving world what was happening and for his trouble...was subjected to some very harsh charges and treatment. I decided in the favor of simply a long and studied silence...until lately, I felt that the matter had passed into history. However, for some large and unknown reason here..in..1967..twenty years later...I find that interest has been inspired all over again and also that people are not quite so ready laugh and call me (us) insane.

I have left the matter up to Mr. Crisman as to what and to whom we would discuss this matter with and where...after all, he is the one that suffered the most from the publicity (all bad) at the time. He returned to the Air Force to fly in Korea and finish his schooling after that as a psychologist.

I simply changed my business and retired to an out of the way place to allow the world to forget I existed. There is a TV series running now that I swear is based in the main on the life of F. Lee Crisman. I know him better than any living man and I know of some of the incredible adventures he has passed through in the last twenty years. I do not mean that his life has been that of this TV hero on the "Invaders" show...but, there are parts of it that I swear were told to me years ago by Mr. Crisman...and I know of several that are too wild to be believed...even by the enlightened attitude of 1967.

However, he is a serious investigator...and he has never sought any publicity and I know certainly does not at the present time. He has never used his knowledge of the Saucer thing for personal gain and has only contempt for those that do so...I agree with him.

I do not know what his reason was for speaking to the group in Seattle...I do know it was not for the knowledge of those that attended for mere curiosity. It is not his policy to do any public act that will bring attention to himself...on this matter. I questioned him (day-before-yesterday) about his being there...and he simply stated that it was better that I did not know all of the facts.

I know he was invited to appear in Omaha Nebraska - at a large Midwest convention of some type with a Dr. Stranges...and they even printed his name on their posters...but, he did not show up there or in New York...still he did speak to a rather small group in East Texas...I feel that there are certain people that he wishes to see or that he wishes to warn at these places...for he will not stay around but does leave within 10 or 15 minutes of the finish of his speech. I know he is an accomplished speaker...still says he is not...is very well trained on the lecture platform...but, will not admit it.

From my conversations with him over the years - I know that he is probably the most learned individual in this country in the general knowledge of UFOs. He is one of the few men that have studied the files of Project Blue Book and has not hesitated to call a spade a spade, concerning the material there.

For all my years of contact with him, I cannot say that I know him better than I did in 1947. I know him better than any living person...but, that is not saying a great deal. He comes and goes...and I will say this...he never was the same man I knew after the Maury Island thing. Something changed for Lee and I have seen him less and less through the years.

[redacted paragraph]

I think that with this background material you can grant me some leeway if I hesitate to answer all your questions. I will, as well as I can, but, I will not make any statements on matters that Lee Crisman has not wanted me to discuss. I will not discuss any contacts with other persons of any nature at all until he says it is O.K.

In answer to your questions:

No. 1. I can allow copies of the photos...not send...them or give them into your keeping. I can allow you to have copies.

No. 2. I can give you my written account of the incident as it happened but, only after Lee Crisman has read it and approved.

No. 3. I have already sent along your name and address to Lee's New Orleans address, but if you receive an answer it will be a very big change in his usual attitude.

No. 4. My son is living in this area and I can get you his statement as to what happened that day...but, again, only after Lee has read and approved.

No. 5. The boat is still intact...but sold many years ago, however. I know the man that has it now and I have been friends with him for many years...I have not seen the boat for several years. As for damage...much of it was repaired at the time...but we still have pictures of it as it was at that time.

You state that Lee specified that the UFO situation was a serious thing and not one for jokes...he is right...I doubt very much that many men know what the real facts are...I certainly do not 'nor do I pretend to know. Lee Crisman does, and he is sought after by many areas of research. I do know that he has become a world traveler and that certain government areas are very interested in his movements at all times. He sometimes drops out of sight for months on end and returns just as quietly. I do not know how he supports his manner of living, but he never lacks for money.

I served under him both in the service and in the Harbor Patrol and obedience is a way of life while one is with him. One simply does not pry into his business and he is quietly obeyed by most people.

I discussed the whole thing with him, and I feel that he is willing to once again put the whole thing into proper perspective. Due I feel to the change in popular attitude and the fact that one is not always classified as some kind of nut...in the UFO...field today.

I can give you a Tacoma address that will allow a letter to reach him - but his telephone is unlisted...the number you find in the book is actually another residence where messages are left for him. Should you have an answer from him...(and it is quite unlikely) then you may ask him directly for his comments on the Maury Island incident.

I can give you one suggestion that will be of value to your research...ask the Tacoma Public Library for permission to look at their August, 1947 file of the *Tacoma Times*...a newspaper that no longer exists today. There you will find much of the story as it was reported in the press at the time. It is not accurate but it is the beginning of the news releases...and it does back up much of what was done and said at the time,...in many ways it is what one reads between the lines that the reporters were afraid to print that impresses one. I do not mean a fear from some "outside" force...but, a fear of local ridicule.

I hope that I have answered some of your questions...

Yours truly, Harold Dahl [redacted PS]

Gary Lesley, Director
UAPRC International
717 "A" Street Northeast Auburn, Washington 98002
26 August 1967
    Mr. Harold Dahl
    c/o Columbia Industries P.O. Box #38
    Tenino, Washington
    Dear Mr. Dahl:
    Thank you very much for your reply of 22 August 1967. I very much appreciate your cooperation in this matter.

    You stated in your letter that you could give us testimonies only after this material was cleared by Mr. Lee Crisman. I assume that you have sent him you and your son's testimonies and he is checking them. I would certainly appreciate the material as soon as possible because if I can gather the data and compile it properly and write it before October 15th, I stand a good chance of getting the story and photos to *Saga* magazine for their December, 1967 issue.

    Concerning the photographs, since you are unable to send them to us and have us copy them, then I would also very much appreciate the photographs of the boat as they would add much value to the story when it is printed. Please let me know the costs of copying all of the pictures, and I will send you the amount including the coverage of postage cost.

    I thank you very much for the suggestion of finding the *Tacoma Times* article, but I have already obtained that article as well as all others on the subject from both the *Tacoma News Tribune* (then the *Tacoma Times*) and the *Seattle Times* newspapers. I am trying to be as thorough as possible in my research on this matter, and I do not want to overlook any possibly important facts. I have read every account of the Maury Island Incident including the official Air Force verdict. All I can say (and I echo your feelings) is that great misjustice has been done to all those concerned in the incident and the facts must now be laid on the line, so to speak, and the public should know what it is really up against.

    I trust to hear from you soon.
Yours sincerely,   Gary Lesley, Director

September 1, 1967
Mr. Gary Leslie
717 A Street N.E. Auburn, Wash.
Dear Sir,
    I have read the correspondence that has been exchanged between you and Hal Dahl. I do not approve of it. He has broken a long standing agreement of ours, and I have spoken of the matter to him. He will not correspond with you again. I do not want the matter in public print!
    I do not want public opinion - be it favorable or adverse opinion. The photos are not available to you at this time! I do not want any speculation as to my reasons for travel or my interests in the UFO appearing in print or in any correspondence that I can control! I can assure you that I have little interest in UFOs and that what I do have is far removed from being of interest to any organized group or those people that read *Saga* magazine.
    Hal Dahl has little information that would interest you - your letter to him stated that you had researched the news files...you have the story...I do not pretend to be able to alter the newspapers of this nation.
    You must realize that the larger share of those people that are interested in the UFO thing fall into two major divisions - with a very tiny third. The first group are those - that have no other purpose but to attract attention to themselves - bizarre adventures and messages from "spacemen." They are fools! The second group see the UFO as an opportunity to make money...some do! Most are not interested in UFOs - only the money. The tiny third group have a serious and scientific interest...admirable, but, mostly a hobby group...and mostly fools!
    We have no interest in any group—serious or not—we have no need for any association with any unit. I say we for I can assure you that Hal Dahl does join me in this opinion.
    It may appear to you that I am being rather abrupt about your interest in a matter that should be of public concern...I am, as far as I can research or investigate, the public laughed away it's right to be informed many years ago.
    You people that have your organizations - UAPRO, etc. etc. have everything you need to do your own research and

most of you play games and make a silly hobby out of a matter that should scare you to death. I have little patience with most of your organizations.

I will tell you this much, the Maury Island incident was no hoax. The FBI and the Air Force know it was no hoax. the pieces of the UFO that are still in our possession have proven that it was no hoax.

I assure you of this because I can anticipate your question of our basic reasons for retaining our personal lives to ourselves...and it is that alone...we simply do not want any more publicity of any type. The very idea of your publishing a magazine article gives me right to say no. I do not want to be on public display for any purpose.

Each time I find it necessary to speak to a group, I must follow up with a series of denials of my (our) time and effort to help some group or person to write of the Maury Island incident. Despite Mr. Dahl's ideas...this is the only reason that I so seldom consent to speak to any group.

Please excuse my abrupt answer to your letters to Hal Dahl, but I hope that this will end the matter. We have no information for you!
Yours truly, F. Lee Crisman

Gary R. Lesley
International Headquarters
717 "A" Street Northeast Auburn, Washington 98002

16 Sept. 1967
    Mr. Hal Dahl
    c/o Columbia Industries, P.O. Box 38
    Tenino, Washington
    Dear Mr. Dahl:
    I have received a letter from Mr. Crisman in answer to a letter that I sent to you. I don't understand why Mr. Crisman is handling your mail, but I would like him not to interfere with correspondence if at all possible. I think this is rude and completely uncalled for. I simply wish to research this case to release the true information to a somewhat confused public. The reason why they are confused lies in people like Mr. Crisman. I don't know what his effort to conceal UFO information is for, but I assure you, that I don't approve of his

attitude. You warned me in your letter that his attitude would be quite reversed. You were right! Now, you probably believe that I am aiming this letter with an attack at your friend; you are correct. When I am attacked, I see no alternative but to counter-attack. But attacking isn't going to solve this problem. We must cooperate. You may ask me what the problem is. Perhaps the problem, you believe, is me. Perhaps I am sticking my nose into taboo things. Why then, if this is correct at all, did Mr. Crisman give me your address???? Why, if he hates persons prying into this case, did he give me your address??? I realize that this letter most likely will never be answered, but I correctly would appreciate whole-heartedly an answer to this question!

How in God's name, Mr. Dahl or Mr. Crisman, or whoever is reading this letter, can mysteries be solved when the mystery is compounded by ignorance, or the suppressment of information that is pertinent?

Mr. Crisman stated that the public "laughed away its right to be informed many years ago." That was, in the truth of this statement, many years ago. Not now. It is time that this be corrected! I have not spent over two months researching this case to come out with material in print that will make them laugh again. I do not want this. Maybe *Saga* isn't a very good magazine, but that does not mean that the people that read it are all high school drop-outs, etc. I don't have any choices other than *Saga*. The last place I would ever think of putting such a story would be in a UFO magazine. This type of magazine is the type to be looked down on. I have my own group publication, yet I will not print such a story in it. I know that this would be the worst place to publish the Maury Island incident.

But, I should not talk about publishing the Maury Island truth because I most likely will never be given the chance to clear up the mystery surrounding it once and for all time. So, I guess it is up to you and Mr. Crisman. Since both of you persist now in being silent, I can only conclude that there is no hope for the story to be printed.

I cannot understand, Mr. Dahl, why Mr. Crisman speaks to only the little more "deep end" groups at their conventions. Why not air his statements to the Congress of Scientific UFOlogists? They are not scientific, but at least they are not fanatics raving about trips to Venus in saucers.

I imagine this letter boils down into a plea to reconsider the decisions that you and Mr. Crisman have made. I suppose it will do nothing, but I am not one to give up without trying. I feel a bit sorry that you have not granted me permission to handle this story. You may not realize it, but I am the tiny third that Mr. Crisman mentioned in his letter. I am open-minded to the UFO mystery and I am very concerned about the way it is handled by researchers. This is not a hobby group as Mr. Crisman believes it to be. It is not a hobby, but an almost full-time commitment. I work on solving UFO sightings for as many as 3 to 4 hours per day, trying to dispel the unfortunate veil of mysticism that has enveloped it for many years. Others working in this group are not enthusiasts, but dedicated, serious, scientific persons. We are probably fools like Mr. Crisman said in his letter. Yes, we are fools because we do not attempt to gain publicity and money like many groups are doing now. We are fools, also, because we believe that persons in this field, who appear as though they want something solved, are willing to cooperate with us to solve it or lend light on it at least.

Yours sincerely, Gary Lesley, Director, grl

September 16, 1967.
Mr. Gary Leslie
Auburn, Wash.

Dear Mr. Leslie:

I have at times been contacted by some of the very prominent speakers and investigators in the UFO picture. Most I pay but small attention to, but I do respect the work of Dr. Frank E. Stranges of Van Nuys, California. I have recently been contacted by him with reference to organizing one or more 3-4 day conferences in Washington or Oregon. This is to take place in December.

I would like to do so very much, because, I feel that he has something to offer. He has an 80 minute full color movie that is well worth the time and money to see. I do not feel that I have the contacts and the ability to make a thing like this into what it should be...and I also feel that there should be some organization to sponsor this, for it is good. I would like to know if your organization is interested in sponsoring a thing like this. I was thinking of the hall in Seattle where Maj. Aho held his meeting last summer. I feel that with a good organization sponsoring and with a good publicity start it would be something to offer that would be worthwhile. I am sure that we could gather other speakers to assist...but, you would know more about that than I.

Please let me know. Dr. Stranges has all the needed printing and posters. Hal Dahl, Rt. 2, Twin Gates Centralia, Wash.

Gary R. Lesley, Director
UAPRO International Headquarters
717 "A" Street Northeast
Auburn, Washington 98002
30 September 1967
Mr. Hal Dahl
Rt. 2 Twin Gates
Centralia, Washington
Dear Mr. Dahl:
Thank you for your letter dated 16 September 1967.

Re: the Dr. Stranges film, our organization will sponsor this film and we will be glad to arrange publicity (etc.) for its showing. However, because our full efforts are now concentrated on our 2nd Annual UFO Assembly next June and our money is also being funneled into this next assembly, I have to state that we are not in the position to go "all out" for the showing of the film. This is our proposal and our only one: We can arrange to have the film shown for, perhaps, two days in the large assembly room of our library in Auburn. Since this will be in the library, it would not be permitted for Dr. Stranges to charge admission fees. But he may be able to clear up some kind of freewill offering thing. I think that the library will approve of this. The assembly room can accommodate about 80 persons. It has a full size movie screen, and all we would need is the projector. Our group will be glad to arrange the necessary publicity. We have good contacts with the *Seattle Times* and *Tacoma News Tribune,* as well as all local papers and radio stations. This is our only offer. If it is suitable to him, then please have him send all printing and posters as soon as possible. We would like to get started right away.

The sooner, the better for us as we may be able to arrange a lot more publicity if we have more time to work with. Before I forget, Dr. Stranges will have to give us a definite date in December as soon as possible for we can notify the library. The Auburn Library, if not notified some time ahead, is often all backed up with meetings, etc. Major Aho's hall in Seattle, according to our Seattle director, is all booked up for most of December. And, besides, the hall is very expensive. I think it is about $160 per day, that is a "day" consisting of about 6 hours—and it is $10 for each additional hour or something very close to that. Please let me know within a few days what the verdict is.

I received yesterday a letter from Mr. Crisman, and I feel that I must apologize somewhat as I did get a little "hot under the collar." I now understand Mr. Crisman's feeling, but, in his first letter, it was all very hazy to me and seemed as though he was deliberately hiding information.

At your earliest convenience and that of your son's, I would like written testimonies as I requested in my first letter. Also, I would like copies of the photographs, and I will be glad to pay all expenses to have you make copies of them. If you have any photographs of the boat and its damage, I would certainly appreciate it. And, as I said, I will be glad to pay all expenses to have the photographs copied by you.

Dr. Crisman told me in his latest letter that there were a number of unusual things going on in the area where the UFO substance fell on to Maury Island. Do you know this?

I am arranging to have the *Seattle Times* print the true facts of the Maury Island case. I know Mr. Ted Duncan very well, and he says it will be most probable that the paper will publish the facts, perhaps under his column, *Driftwood Diary*. I know Mr. Duncan as a reliable columnist who takes the UFO situation seriously and has written numerous articles about it for several years.

I am also arranging with other national magazines who have a serious interest in the UFO mystery, to print the story. I have had some luck with *Look* and *Fate*. It seems *Life* and *Post* aren't a bit interested in setting the facts straight. *Fate,* with a reputation that has often been questionable, is now a much better magazine and much more reliable and scientific. Mary Fuller, the publisher, is very interested in printing the story again—this time with the facts as they should be. May I emphasize, Mr. Dahl, that the only thing I want out of all this is to see the record set straight. I have no publicity or big money thing in mind at all. I do not think that the UFO mystery should be a commercial racket, as it is, unfortunately, at the present. I don't especially like publicity, and for that I seldom appear on radio, t.v., or in newspaper articles. I have been asked by some of the big radio stations in Seattle (KIRO, KING, etc.) to be on their phone-in programs. I have turned them all down flatly. I do not wish a lot of publicity, although I feel some is necessary in order to promote this organization to some degree.

I am not a reporter. I am a freelance writer and, perhaps, a bit frustrated journalist at heart. I have a serious interest in the UFO...a point I must emphasize. All I can say is trust me. You may be suspicious, as I must be taken constantly in life, and this is no exception. I am sure you understand what I am saying.

I trust to hear from you soon.

Yours sincerely, Gary Lesley, Director

Tenino, Washington
9/27/67
Dear Mr. Leslie:

I am very sorry to have to again step into the correspondence between you and Hal Dahl. He turned your letter over to me, and I have read it with interest...but I do have some puzzlement. I felt that I had a command of English that would allow me to present our side of the matter to you and still not really hurt your feelings.

I feel the problem stems from several sources - one, of course, is that we do not like bringing attention to ourselves, and like it or not...I am irrevocably tied to Hal in any of the questions that arise on the Maury Island incident. Any and all attention that he is given is also given to me.

Mr. Leslie, I am an industrial psychologist - I deal with a very large group of hard-headed businessmen. I do not like to be always explaining why my name has popped up in some author's book or article that refers to UFO's. I was under the impression that all that was past...and here we have a whole series of new and reprinted books on the market...all of whom seem to refer to the old Maury Island matter.

I have never been any man of "mystery" as so many of these old books and the newer authors attempt to describe. I simply had to make a living and in doing so, the groupings of people that I had business relations with were those that reacted in a most avid manner to UFO reports.

Secondly, I gave away Hal's name and address on the basis that if he wished to make any statements concerning Maury Island, he certainly could. You must be made aware of the fact that certain areas, and some people have openly accused me of "private censorship" of facts and knowledge that I had no right to censor. Some of those people were in attendance at that meeting. I did not (and do not know you) know what your interests were aside from an idle and passing interest in UFOs.

I am at a loss to understand...why people insist on making me the focal point of interest in a matter that happened twenty years ago. I have repeated over and over...it is a simple matter of $$$ that such public attention is not good for my business relations. No matter how loud I say this...I am answered...with the same old tired arguments... "You are suppressing certain facts..." I have no secret facts, beyond the truths that were suppressed in Project Blue Book.

There are and always have been certain small groups in the business and academic worlds that have extra and advanced interest, and to them and for them I have told what I know...this has led to a reputation of speaking to only selected few and special groups. While this may have basic truth in it...there has always been a reason. Most of the time these people were of that calibre that knew and understood what I was talking about. I have out of my own interest kept close track of certain types and trends in the mystery of the UFOs. I have files of materials and I have run into incidents that are very odd. However, I travel widely and this allows me to be in areas that do have certain of the "extra" attentions of the UFOs. It has always been a type of precise "high-wire" balance act to keep up an investigative and recording interest...and at the same time deal with the areas of a business world that has no interest in such matters.

Hal has talked to me extensively in the last week and he feels that it is time to let up and cooperate with certain people...why you, I don't know...but, he seems to feel that you were treated a bit unfairly. I don't quite see it that way...but, I will not object to what he wishes to do about the matter.

As far as I am concerned it is his "baby," and I will not make any interference...as long as it is handled in the manner that you describe...and not with tongue in cheek...and making Hal and I look like fools. You must understand that we have been approached afore and with all the promises in the world to handle the matter with a serious approach...only to find out that the reporter lied and in his article made us look...not only as fools...but, as careless pranksters that cared not a whit that men died in the prank.

This is not easy to take...and it is easy to make a rule that no one talks to anyone on the Maury Island affair. However, if you and Hal wish to go ahead...I will say no more.

One thing that stemmed from the correspondence with you was a trip back to Maury Island to see the place again. We found some startling things going on. For one thing...the area where the material fell...had no plant growth. For a second thing...the place was posted and a federal project was going on to remove and level the whole area. We ignored the signs (it was Sunday) and explored until a watchman came and removed us. The question is...after all these years...why? A bit of inquiry revealed that government men of some agency have returned over the years...many times for soil samples and pictures. We also took pictures. You may have an interest there.

Yours truly, F. Lee Crisman, Box 722, Tacoma

Easy Papers Correspondence:
[undated]
stamped: FABRICATION
Dear Mrs. Banfield:

After you have read the enclosed material, perhaps you will not feel so smug and self-satisfied. This man, Crisman, is a man that is dangerous to the future of America.

We do not know how many agents that the U.S. has in this category, but it must be plain to you, that if you do love this nation we cannot have CIA people such as him interfering with local government.

A very large amount of time and effort has been taken to trace his record and his work. Some people have risked their jobs, future and even their lives to obtain the information in his file.

We had hoped to obtain more documents and copies of proper documents, but our source of information has been cut off by the introduction of new security measures. We do ask you to be fair and be aware that Crisman is a federal agent of the worst possible stripe. A Disruptive Agent is not a friend to our form of government. He represents no one but a section of the C.I.A. [released to researcher Thomas A. Adams 6/8/81]

9/13/69

Dear [redacted]:

Enclosed you will find the information you requested. I was not able to do as complete a job as you asked, due to the difficult time we had getting to the files. To ask for a report from the file of a CIA is asking for a lot of attention and asking for a report of a 4250ece agent is almost an impossible task. It took over six months to get the information contained herein. We do feel that 4250ece agents are dangerous to the democratic way of life and they should be halted. These men bear no love for the USA. They serve the CIA and what is more they serve only a part of the CIA for they would kill a fellow agent as fast as they would arrange your death. The 4250ece Section is a part of a long range planning commission of some type and it does not reveal in any part what their master plan may be, but it is certain that they operate within a very dangerous pattern. I have felt for a long time that it should be made public and the CIA agents should be made to reveal under oath what they mean by their Internal Security Section and Disruption Agents such as Fred Crisman should be retired from government service. I would urge you to send copies of this report to friends on the Coast and allow them to make Crisman's role as an agent public. No one believed Jim Garrison when he stated that Crisman was a CIA agent.

It might do no good to make any statements out there. After all (sic) he is liable to seek out how this information was acquired. God help us here if it is ever linked to our section. You realize that we never heard of you! Hold this report until after Sept 30 and then we do not care what you do with it but once you use it you will never get another. Good luck!

UNITED STATES GOVERNMENT MEMORANDUM
TO: Deputy Director, DCS SEA-88-70 FROM: Chief, Seattle Office DATE: 3 April 1970
SUBJECT: Fred Lee CRISMAN
REF: (redacted) telecon 2 April 1970

1. The attached papers were given to me by an agent of the Naval Investigative Services Office (NISO), 13th Naval District, Seattle. NISO obtained these papers from [19 space redaction] whom they did not identify but apparently works in the [redacted]. Crisman conducts some type of talk show on the station and is reasonably well known in the Tacoma, Washington, area as a result of his activities. It is my understanding that these papers have been rather widely distributed to individuals unknown to me in the Tacoma area. As you will see, these papers are an attempt to attack Crisman viciously and in so doing put the agency in a bad light. I entertained the thought of trying to run down the author of this material and went so far as to call [3 line redaction] that she did not know the author of the papers which were forwarded to her but indicated that Mr. Crisman thought he knew who the person might be.

2. I thought of calling Mr. Crisman but before doing so made a quick check of some local sources in Seattle and determined that Mr. Crisman has a reputation that is questionable. [5 line redaction]

3. I also checked with the United States General Accounting Office (GAO) in Seattle to determine if they had ever had any contact with Crisman. A Mr. Kenneth Edmonson came to the office because he was interested in looking at the letter which was written on their stationery. Mr. Edmonson advised that Mr. Crisman complained to a member of Congress that the Boeing Company had been misusing U.S. government property by removing the U.S. government identifi-

cation on certain tools and other property and converting it to their own use. The GAO made a thorough investigation of Mr. Crisman's charges and found no irregularities. The letter addressed to Mr. Crisman on the GAO's stationery is a complete fabrication. The regional office of GAO has not used this particular letterhead since 1967. Further, they do not have an Ivan C. Delcoe employed locally or anyplace else in the United States for that matter. Also they do not have a Field Office #4, and the United States government does not issue drafts. He indicated they would make an investigation to determine whether or not someone in their office might possibly be involved, and he said that if I turned up anything that would be of interest to him it would be appreciated if I passed the information along.

4. [Redacted] advises that Mr. Crisman is not now an employee of the Agency and has never been. There is apparently some record in the Agency of Mr. Crisman in connection with the Garrison case. She added that Mr. Crisman is also known as Dr. Jon Gold. This name was mentioned also by [redacted] and it is apparently a name that Crisman uses in connection with his television show.

5. [5 lines redacted]

6. I am reporting this for the record and do not anticipate doing anything further unless advised by you to do so.

[Signature redacted]

UNITED STATES GOVERNMENT MEMORANDUM
TO: [redacted] DATE: 10 April 1970 FROM: Director, Domestic Contact Service
(Chief, Services Division)
SUBJECT: CRISMAN, Fred Lee — Alleged CIA Agent/ Alleged Former OSS Employee Known to District Attorney, James Garrison, New Orleans, Louisiana — SEA-88-70
REF:[redacted] Telephone conversation of 2 April 1970

1. Enclosed for your records and any action deemed appropriate is a copy of a self-explanatory memorandum and attachments from our Seattle Field Office, concerning an attempt to attack subject viciously and, as a consequence, put the Agency in a bad light.

2. Please note the reference in paragraph 3 of the enclosure to our field representative's contact with Mr. Kenneth

EDMONSON, United States General Accounting Office (GAO) in Seattle, in an effort to determine if the GAO had had any contact with subject. The letter, purported to be on GAO's stationary, apparently is a complete fabrication.

3. After checking with your office, we informed our field representative that the subject is not now nor has he ever been an employee of this Agency.

4. Any questions pertaining to this memorandum should be directed to [Four lines and signature redacted] DCD-171/78. 16 February 1978

MEMORANDUM FOR: DDO [redacted]
FROM: [redacted]
DCD [redacted]
SUBJECT: Request on House Select Committee on Assassinations, 19 January 1978

DCD records have been searched on the nine individuals listed in the subject memoranda. All were negative with the exceptions of F. Lee CRISMAN and [redacted]. Copies of DCD material on these two individuals are attached for your retention. Signatures Redacted

Appendix 6

An Interview with Ron Halbritter, May 27, 1997

Q: How did your interest in Maury Island develop?

A: I lived there. I was a small boy in that area. I didn't actually live on Maury Island, but we lived in that Seattle/Tacoma area in 1947. So then all of this excitement, the Kenneth Arnold sighting and the Maury Island thing...

Q: When it happened, was the excitement in the papers? It was like the buzz of the town?

A: Kenneth Arnold was in the paper. Maury Island wasn't at the time. However, the following summer was when *Fate* magazine came out, Volume One, Number One, Summer, 1948. It came out and it had the Maury Island story in it. So that's when I first read the Maury Island story.

Q: But there were newspaper accounts when it happened, right? Or not the actual sighting, the newspaper accounts would have happened after the crash.

A: After Davidson and Brown were killed.

Q: Had you read about it in the papers then?

A: Not really. I was really a small boy at that time. I wasn't really paying too much attention at that time.

Q: How old were you?

A: Eight years old. My dad, who was an avid reader, and my uncle Jack, they would talk about Kenneth Arnold and those things. And I was an avid reader, I just didn't read newspapers. I read *Amazing Stories* and those other things, but then in the summer of '48 *Fate* magazine came out. I saw it on the magazine stand at Girard's Corner Grocery, and I went to Girard and asked if there was any work I could do that I could work and pay for it. It was a quarter! He said no, but what he'd do was he could set it on the back of the shelf and save it for me until I got a quarter. We'd pick strawberries, raspberries, all kinds of things. I picked berries to earn the quarter to go pay for the magazine.

Q: You bartered your labor for it.
A: Yeah! And I still have it!

Q: You still have your original copy?
A: I have every single issue of *Fate* magazine, to present.

Q: You still get it?
A: I still subscribe to *Fate* magazine. I write for *Fate* every now and then.

Q: Let me check a memory of yours. I was just reading this book *Alien Agenda* by Jim Marrs. He wrote *Crossfire,* which is one of the books that Oliver Stone based his *JFK* movie on. There's a small section in *Alien Agenda* on Maury Island, and one of the things that he mentions is that in that first year, before that first issue of *Fate* came out, people knew Kenneth Arnold's story but they thought it was all some kind of secret Soviet or maybe U.S. aircraft that he had seen. He didn't really call it a UFO or anything strange like that for a whole year. Is that your impression, too?
A: No. In my family at least, we really think these were alien spaceships.

Q: Right from the get-go.
A: Right from the beginning. In the summertime we used to lay out in the frontyard. We didn't have air-conditioned houses then, and we'd all lay on our backs in the yard, watching the sky, trying to see something. We knew what airplanes looked like. They didn't have too many jets then. We were close enough to Boeing field that the P38s would go over us. And we thought that a P38 was the most spectacular, strong, powerful, wonderful airplane the world would ever have. But there were no jets then. It was along time before we saw jets—'52, '53 or so before we saw jets.

Q: Was there talk of flying saucers then?

A; We talked of flying saucers, called them flying saucers, flying saucers were a thing.

Q: I imagine you went to the site where it all supposedly happened.

A: You know what? I never went to Maury Island until many decades later.

Q: You were right there in the area and never went?

A: We were farm folks and had to work hard on the farm. You have to go to the ferry and take the ferry across. And nobody ever told you where that site was. When people start telling me how much they know about Maury Island and how we know this is a hoax and a fake and all that, a couple of the questions I ask are, "What was the name of the boat?" And where is the location of Maury Island. When they don't know the name of Dahl's boat and they can't take a map of the island and put an "x" where the spot was, then they obviously haven't looked into this.

Q: When did you start looking into it?

A: When I was a high school sophomore, I had to do a term paper in English, and I wrote an English term paper on flying saucers.

Q: What year?

A: Probably '52, '51. So I did this term paper on flying saucers. I like to think I'm a pretty good writer; although I have bad handwriting, I can put pretty intelligent words on paper. The teacher gave me a "D" and said "NOTHING HERE" in big letters across the front of my page. So obviously, he did not believe in flying saucers. So I thought I'd set out then as a goal to prove to people that I really did know what I was talking about, that I really was a bright young man. From then on I actively worked to collect flying saucer information and books. I have a major library, all of the magazines...

Q: All of it specifically focused on Maury Island?
A: No, UFOs in general. Flying saucers in general.

Q: I imagine that you belonged then to some of the area groups.
A: I didn't join because they all charge too much money. NICAP and APRO and all of them, a dollar a year, two dollars a year, that was money that I didn't spend on books! I'm a book collector and magazine collector. I never joined any of the actual organizations.

Q: So you were kind of a loner in this interest?
A: Pretty much. I read all of the magazines and the books.

Q: When did you start focusing on Maury Island?
A: I don't know if you could say there was a theme when I suddenly started to really focus on Maury Island, but through the years people like Jerry Clark in particular would toss off this, "Well, Maury Island was a hoax" business when I knew that they hadn't done their research. Very few people have ever done their research.

Q: You knew this from everything that you'd read.
A: Everything I had read. People just copied each other. Nobody had done any original research. After 1959, I went to work in the shipyards. Worked in shipyards, and I know that among other things ships are like airplanes and cars. They're all registered. They're all recorded. You can go to the library and pull out the Coast Guard records from 1948, and you can find the boat that Harold Dahl owned. So from like 1965, I knew the name of the boat that Harold Dahl owned, and yet people who would nonchalantly toss off this flippant "that was all a hoax, we know it was hoax because Ruppelt said so" didn't know the name of the boat. Ruppelt, who wrote *The Report on Unidentified Flying Objects,* didn't even know what date this thing occurred.

Q: He's got the date wrong?
A: He didn't put the date in! He said early in June, in the spring, or something like that. But he didn't put a date in there. And the ridiculous thing was that Maury Island took place in 1947, and Ruppelt took over in '52, he wrote his book in '56, and he didn't have those Project Blue Book files. Maury Island didn't even have a Project Blue Book file number. I've gotten the Project Blue Book microfilms, and there's like 18 pages in there on Maury Island and virtually all of them are Kenneth Arnold's story. The story that Kenneth Arnold wrote and gave to the Air Force.

Q: That was the extent of what they had?
A: That was the extent of what they had. And Ruppelt was saying that this was one of the biggest hoaxes and more expensive hoaxes. I had read Ray Palmer. I read his *Flying Saucers* magazine, before I read Ruppelt's book. Ray Palmer was criticizing him, saying that he hadn't done his research.

Q: Were you familiar with Crisman's Shaver mystery stories?
A: We didn't connect Crisman's letters to Maury Island until the 60s. Then I went back, I hunted bookstores until I found copies of those original *Amazing Stories* that Crisman had written in. So I do have the original magazine and original letters.

Q: When did you look up the name of the boat?
A: It was when I was working in shipyards, and I realized we had the ability to look at these Coast Guard books. When you work in the ship repair business and a ship comes in for repairs, the first thing you do is look up the real live owner. Just because there's somebody on this boat saying "I want to have this work done"—at first, we find out who owns this boat, and the second thing is we contact them directly and say, "are you going to authorize these repairs? Are you going to pay for this work?" So when I became aware that there was such a book like this, then I just went to the library and asked to look at

1947 and 1948 and sure enough, here it lists Harold Dahl as owning the boat. And it says that this boat was a World War II mine-sweeper.

Q: But it was a privately owned boat, right?
A: Correct, but it was Navy surplus.

Q: And when we say that Harold Dahl—by the way, I notice in some of your research notes you call him "Haldor."
A: That's the way it actually is printed in the Coast Guard records.

Q: The Coast Guard records call him "Haldor"?
A: Whether that was a typo or that was really is this name...Harold was just a common usage.

Q: I did a Lexis/Nexus search on Harold Dahl and discovered an obituary for a "Harold Dahl" who owned a fishing boat—but he was in Maine. When they say that Harold Dahl was part of the harbor patrol, what is that?
A: It wasn't harbor patrol at all. These guys scavenged logs, they do that to this second. What do fishermen do when they are not fishing? The fishing season, the salmon season and the fishing season, is only like three months, four months out of the year. The rest of the year you still have to eat, you still have to pay payments on your boat. What the fishermen do is they scavenge the logs. They salvage logs. You know about how lumberjacks chop down trees way up in the mountains, and they throw them into the river and the river takes them down to the bay. At the bay, they collect them and they send them to the saw mills. And they brand them. Each log has a brand put on it. They brand their thing into the log, and they go down into the bay. Once in a while, logs break loose. Once in a while logs get away. They float around in the harbor, where two things happen: One is they are definite menace to navigation because logs don't have lights on them or anything, and boats can crash into them. And second thing, they actually have a cash value of $20 to $30 a log. So these scavengers go around; even now, there are guys out there scavenging. They go around and hunt for a log.

They find a log that has a brand on it, they hook on to it and take it to the saw mill and say, "Hey, look we found this log, it's got these people's brand on it, pay us for it." And they collect money. Harold Dahl said he had a boom (a line of collected floating timbers) of $3,000 worth of logs that he lost.

Q: This was at the time of the incident.

A: Right after the incident, he was talking to Kenneth Arnold, and he said that his life just had so many misfortunes, and one of them was that he had lost a boom of $3,000 of logs. You could have bought a new Buick for $800. Whether that was actually because of the UFO incident or whether that was related—a day or two before or after, but it was right in that same time frame. So they were log scavengers. So when the story came out, they said they were patrolling the harbor. So this guy over in England, Wilson, a British bloke who doesn't talk English very well, or American style English (Wilkins, Harold T., *Flying Saucers on the Attack,* New York: Ace Books, 1954), comes to the conclusion that not only that they were harbor patrolman, but that they were in the Coast Guard. In the *Coming of the Saucers*, Ray Palmer has a dedication to Harold Wilkins, "who is a great researcher" or something like that. I often wondered if that was satire or sarcasm or what he really meant there. So Wilkins wrote a letter to the U.S. Coast Guard, addressed to Harold Dahl care of the U. S. Coast Guard. Well, the Coast Guard sent the letter back saying that they never heard of him. So then Wilkins said, "See, these guys were imposters, they were impersonating Coast Guardsmen."

Q: Now, the main experience happened to Harold Dahl, who reported it to his "superior" who was Crisman. The way you describe it, it doesn't sound like "superior" is the right word.

A: I don't know the relationship between Dahl and Crisman.

Q: Isn't that one of the big mysteries?

A: We know that Crisman actually was into black leather, S&M, gay lifestyle in Seattle sometimes. So it could well be that going on between these two. We don't really know.

Q: When you talk about Crisman's S&M gay life, I know we've got the *Murder of the City* to rely on...

A: And what happened in the *Murder of the City?* His friend, who was a printer over in Seattle, and somebody stabbed him so many times? Who did that stabbing? I've always suspected Crisman did.

   And there's more in Mike Sylwester's interview with Crisman's son [looks through research notes]—not to get sidetracked, but here's an interesting thing. When Fred Crisman Sr. was reading Budd Hopkins' book about alien abductions at home, he passed out. He had kidney failure. This was just before he died.[1]

Q: Crisman was reading Hopkins right before he died?

A: Yeah. It was even more bizarre. He was reading this book, and he passed out. When he woke up, he was in the hospital, hooked up to lots of hospital equipment, surrounded by people who were in masks and gowns, and he thought he was being abducted. He thought they'd got him.[2]

Q: What did you find out about Charles Dahl's medical report?

A: Never could. I wrote to the FBI under the Freedom of Information Act and asked for a copy of it. The FBI wrote back saying it would not release that information without Charles Dahl's death certificate. Charles Dahl is probably still alive. I know where he's living but I didn't want to invade his privacy. Harold Dahl's widow is still alive. [Getting back to Crisman's alleged homosexuality] I'm reading here: "Sylwester then showed interviewee, Fred Lee, Jr., a copy of the report that Lavender had made to Garrison's investigators about Crisman and Beckham. Interviewee, Fred Lee, Jr., had known nothing about this report previously and was dismayed to read it. In particular, interviewee was confounded by statements in report where Lavender accused subject of being a homosexual and a sado-maschist. Interviewee was not able to give any further explanation to Lavender's role in the incident." So in the Bob Lavender report to Garrison, the official statement for the investigation, Lavender says that Beckham and Crisman were into the S&M scene.

I've always had the impression that Crisman was strictly an opportunist. That Harold Dahl actually did see something. This is my personal opinion. Harold Dahl did see something. Harold Dahl obtained samples of not only the slag but the white metal. The white metal is important because it keeps coming back to the white metal, at Roswell and in Maury Island. So Harold Dahl actually got hold of the white metal. Harold Dahl had some of the slag. He went back and told Crisman about it in some fashion. I doubt that he reported to his superior, because Harold Dahl owned the boat. But they had some sort of relationship. And he told Crisman about it. Then Crisman said, "Oh, the next day I went out and found the very same UFO," which simply doesn't make sense.

I think that Crisman conned Dahl out of the white metal. I think that once Crisman had the white metal in his possession, that put him in a position of power. How does it happen that three weeks later he gets interviewed at the Atomic Energy Commission, not the one at Hanford where you'd expect, which is right next door, but the Atomic Energy Commission at Los Alamos. Why did they process him there? Not only that, but when they processed him, he didn't even put any social security number. He wasn't blacked out, he really didn't know it. Yet they're going to process this guy as an applicant? I think he had some power. I think he was able to do that because he had possession of the white metal. And I think that's when he got himself into the spook community.

Q: What do you know about Brown and Davidson?
A: One of the strangest things is that nobody got excited when they got killed. This mystery just went away then. That always seemed very, very bizarre to me. These were government agents on official business, and yet they got killed and people like Ruppelt said, "Yeah, there was a mistake, so we'll just ignore this." We know that Davidson

and Brown had traveled earlier to Boise, Idaho, where they met with Captain Emil Smith. Captain Emil Smith is still alive. He lives in Florida but doesn't talk about it.

Q: Their basic job was to interview people about this UFO stuff. It wasn't like they were just called out to investigate this particular incident because Kenneth Arnold had Air Force friends. But they were assigned to interview people, and they reported it all back to Nathan Twining, right?

A: Yes. They went to Boise, Idaho. They met Captain Smith, they met the guy who was the editor of the Boise newspaper, Johnson, and they met with Kenneth Arnold. All three of them sat together and discussed UFOs and their respective sightings. This guy Johnson had also seen a UFO. Kenneth Arnold came to Boise and said, "Boy, you won't believe what I saw." And the editor of the paper said to Johnson, "You belong to the National Guard, you can get one of them airplanes and fly around and look." So he spent three days flying around, and sure enough he saw one too. Then Davidson and Brown came to Boise, and they met with all three of them, and they all sat together and Davidson and Brown gave Kenneth Arnold and Captain Smith and Johnson their business cards and said, "If you hear anything further, let us know." Two weeks later, Kenneth Arnold flies to Tacoma to investigate the Maury Island incident. One of the curious things that happened was that Johnson then sent a telegram to Davidson and Brown saying, "There's something wrong here. Why is Kenneth Arnold investigating this?" I also think that Kenneth Arnold was being a retainer and collecting some money from the Boise newspaper to write about it. When Kenneth Arnold gets to Tacoma and he calls Davidson and Brown. Now they had given him their business card and said "Call us if you have any information." He called them and what did they do? They said, "We can't talk to you on this phone, we have to go off base and call you back from a pay phone." This was an official government agency. I've worked for government agencies. To say that they can't accept a phone call? These are investigators, investigating a case, and then they can't accept a phone call? That is so bizarre.

They called him back and said they would come look at it. They flew to Tacoma. They crashed and burned. And then what happened is that the Air Force said, "Never mind, it was a mistake." These are investigators investigating a case and they were killed in the process. And no one cared? That just doesn't seem real, under any circumstances.

Q: They were specifically assigned to investigate UFO stuff in the overall. It wasn't just this one particular investigation that there happened to be an accident at, but two of the top investigators of all UFO reports that were happening, people who were responsible for reporting back to Nathan Twining of all people—somebody who recurs in the other little things that keep popping up in UFO history, like the Cutler-Twining memo...

A: And after they were killed, what happened to their investigations on everything? They just went away.

Q: Precisely. Have you done Freedom of Information Act searches on those two guys?

A: I have asked for Freedom of Information files and haven't received anything to date.

Brown's wife was waiting at the airbase in San Francisco, waiting on the runway, waiting for her husband to come home. She was supposed to pick him up at two in the morning, and she waited and waited and waited and waited. She finally went in the building, and they said, "Didn't anybody tell you? He got killed on the way. He's going to be late."

Just as an aside, I am good friends and I am in touch with Kim Arnold, daughter of Kenneth Arnold. I tracked her down because I wanted the film. Particularly the film of the boat. Remember, Kenneth Arnold took motion pictures of the boat. That would show that this was a 70-foot-long mine-sweeper, not a hunk of junk as Ruppelt said. Ruppelt said it was junk that was hardly seaworthy.

Q: Did you get to see the film of the boat?
A: It doesn't exist. Got stolen somewhere about '72 or '73. All of his film got stolen.

Q: Are there any photos of the boat at all?
A: No. Nor of Dahl and Crisman from then. There is some leftover film that she has possession of, and she's gone over it several times with friends and they've all agreed that they are only family movies. There's no strangers there, nobody they don't recognize.

Q: But the photos that supposedly were taken of the event itself have long disappeared.
A: Long gone.

Q: Was there one particular break-in where all this disappeared?
A: It was in Arnold's aircraft hangar. The film was kept in his aircraft hangar, and the break - in was there and they stole the film and left the camera, left a projector, and only stole film, which is curious because most burglars would take everything.

Q: What about the slag?
A: Kenneth Arnold did not have any of the slag. When I went to Maury Island with the *Sightings* television show in February of this year, they filmed me standing there on the beach at the spot. And Reverend Bob LeRoy was there also. We stood on the beach and found some rocks that was slag. It was slag leftover from the Tacoma Smelter. The Tacoma Smelter Works had these piles of slag, and people would use them to put on the beach for break water. You could see that this was obviously terrestrial slag. There was no doubt about it. In fact, in one of the scenes that they film but never showed on TV, I picked up a piece and held it in my hand and said, "Look at this. You can see that this is slag and you can see that this is terrestrial, there's no question about it. There's no way anyone would be fooled." And yet the material that

Dahl had was curious enough that it did manage to fool people, that did manage to catch their attention and say this is unusual.

Q: Let's talk about the Reverend Bob Leroy, who claims his brother was also a Maury Island witness. There have recently been some other witnesses as well, is that right?
A: Yes, but they passed away.

Q: And what about LeRoy's brother?
A: He was a witness. That was a mistake that I had made and didn't know it until we met on Maury Island and were talking. Remember, because Dahl had two crew members on the boat with him. There was Harold Dahl, his sixteen-year-old son, and two crew members. So one of the questions I keep asking is "what were the names of the other two crew members?" How could very clever people like the FBI not write down the names of those other two crew members somewhere? The FBI investigated, the Air Force investigated, Tacoma police—everybody investigated. How could they not have written down the names of those crew members? So then when I found out—and the statement of Emil Smith on the first page, on the bottom paragraph, which has been blacked out by the Air Force, he says there was Dahl, his son, and "Mr. Bernard." This was Barney LeRoy. His name was Bernard LeRoy. I made the assumption that Captain Smith, who has never been introduced to him properly, and so he heard somebody named Bernard and he assumed it was a last name and not a first name. So I jumped to the conclusion that Barney LeRoy was one of the people on the boat. Then in February, when I was actually on the site with Reverend Bob LeRoy, he said, "Oh no, Barney was on his boat. It was over here. That's where Barney's boat was. Dahl's boat was over at this location."

Q: So when Smith refers to "Bernard"...
A: It wasn't Barney LeRoy, or he may have misunderstood some other thing. When you hold the microfilm up to the light, and it's been marked over with a highlighter, but if

you hold it up to the light, you can read through. And it
seems to me that it's saying "Bernard," but maybe I'm
not right. Maybe it's "Gerard" or something else that
I'm not reading correctly. We know that there were two
other people on the boat. There was Dahl, his son, and
two other people. It's a 73 foot boat. It takes one person
to drive the boat, one person to snag the logs and one
person to tie them up. So it takes a couple of people to do
this. The other two now-deceased witnesses lived at
Salmon Beach. Salmon Beach in 1947 probably had a
population of fifty. Maybe a population of a hundred. And
in *The Coming of the Saucers* it says there that the fire
chief of Salmon Beach initially told the Seattle reporter
the story. So we know that the people in Salmon Beach
were talking about this incident. So when we say that
these witnesses in Salmon Beach—when I get a chance
one of the first things I'm going to do is see if I can find
somewhere where there's a record of who was the fire
chief in Salmon Beach in 1947. I'm sure we're going to
find that it was one or the other of these witnesses.

Q: Did Bob LeRoy know those two guys?
A: Yes. But they've been dead for a while.

Q: Do you know if Barney LeRoy was connected to the Minutemen group?
A: I'm sure he was not.

Q: It's curious that both Bob LeRoy and Crisman have in
   their background this connection to the Kennedy assassination. Have you explored that at all with LeRoy?
A: No. The idea that got the *Sightings* TV people excited
   was that I said that the Maury Island episode, the Kenneth Arnold episode, the captain Emil Smith episode, and
   the Roswell crash were all the same incident. They were
   all connected. That of all of the UFOs that are going to
   crash at Roswell on the second of July, the one that had
   mechanical trouble on the 21st of June seemed to be most
   likely the one that would crash. On the 21st of June, Dahl
   saw a UFO with mechanical trouble, and the UFO

dropped metallic slag, white metal and something he described as fishline. We might have call that fiber optic cable maybe. On the 24th of June, Kenneth Arnold saw a search and rescue team of nine UFO hunting for the broken one, or one their way to fix it or to take care of it or whatever. On the night of the fourth of July, over Boise, Idaho, Captain Emil Smith saw two sets of UFOs, headed south, towards Roswell. Two hours later at Roswell, one crashed. That was the same rescue team, or same mechanics, that were involved in all of them. That was my theory.

Notes:
1. Researcher Mike Sylwester's interview with Fred Lee Crisman, Jr. on August 4, 1993 at the Glenwood Restaurant at the University of Oregon yielded other clues about Crisman's life. Crisman Jr. Described his father as gregarious and egocentric with a genius level IQ. He also revealed that his father was addicted to barbiturates due to his military service, explaining the anxiety he experienced in Korea. Although he tried to pursue a conventional career in radio, Crisman Sr. also regularly developed get-rich-quick schemes according to his son, including buying large numbers of records by Mark Evans/Tom Beckham to help them perform better on the pop charts, and then reselling the records. Crisman Jr. also reported that his father "somehow obtained a wide variety of forms and would use it for various pranks and schemes."

   Of the Maury Island incident, Crisman Jr. said that his father never confessed to a hoax and insisted that he and Dahl "had really seen some kind of unusual phenomenon." Dahl and Crisman Jr. were involved in a dispute over the ownership of some antique guns Crisman left behind when he died. Crisman Jr. also seemed to be aware of the Minutemen group, but characterized it as "so far right they made normal conservatives look like Communists." His father, by contrast was a "Goldwater Republican," a registered Democrat who wrote speeches for George Wallace and strongly supported the Vietnam War. "Even though [he] lived in Washington state, he was quite well known among a circle of southern politicians." His father's explanation of the Garrison subpoena was that Garrison primarily wanted to grill him "about some Louisiana politicians and also about other associated Southern politicians," using the Kennedy assassination as a pretext. Crisman Jr. could not rule out the possibility that his father worked for the CIA, although he felt that such a career would have given him more money than he ever seemed to have. His father believed in a conspiracy between the CIA and the Mafia to kill JFK and once remarked that Dealey Plaza had been landscaped in preparation for the assassination. The interview also discussed family background, that the family name came from Germany under a name "something like" Krimsen. Family members included "traveling medicine men" but no Gypsies. Crisman Jr. reviewed details of his father's military, post-war and teaching careers, mentioning that his 1958 arrest for reckless driving had to do with barbiturate abuse and lost him his job as superintendent of schools in Huntington, Oregon. "There were strict social expectations of teachers in that time and place and that, for example, teachers would even drive to another town if they wanted to buy a beer." His father "aggravated this situation by making strange remarks, such as that he had a metal plate in his head." From 1961 to 1962 his father's job at Boeing Aircraft in Seattle involved dark-to-dark, 12-hour shifts.

Crisman Jr. met and knew Tom Beckham and Bob Lavender, but did not know of a relationship between the two. He was "confounded by statements in [Lavender's interview with Garrison's investigator] where Lavender accused [Crisman] of being a homosexual and sado-masochist."

When Crisman Jr.'s mother died, her last husband presumably sold the house that held Crisman's personal papers and photographs, although the chance existed that the papers were given to Crisman's widow.

2. According to Greg Bishop, publisher of the ufological/paranormalist zine the *Excluded Middle,* Crisman could not have been reading Budd Hopkins, since Hopkins' first book, *Missing Time,* was published in 1981. Bishop notes that two other widely distributed books on "abductions" (or at least encounters with beings) before that: *The Humanoids* by Charles Bowen, published in 1974; and perhaps more notably, *Abducted!: Confrontations with Beings from Outer Space,* authored by Coral and Jim Lorenzen from APRO. That book was published in 1977, a pretty neat fit with Crisman's death in 1978. The Lorenzens also released two other "occupant" books: *Flying Saucer Occupants* in 1967 and *Encounters with UFO Occupants* in 1976. The abduction experience of Betty and Barney Hill was documented in the 1967 book *Interrupted Journey,* but the incident had occurred in 1961. If Crisman was current in the UFO literature, MUFON published occasional articles on what it was already calling "abductions" in 1977 as well.

Appendix 7

An Interview with Michael Riconosciuto
by Kenn Thomas, 2/10/96

Q: Do you remember Fred Crisman, or Jon Gold? What can
you tell me about him? Are you familiar with his memoir, *Murder in the City*?
A: *Murder in the City* really wasn't a memoir for Fred
Crisman. *Murder in the City* was about a political episode in Tacoma that Fred Crisman played a role in.

Q: But it is written by him, right?
A: He's the author of it, yes. He had a talk show there, and
there was a big, heated political battle in Tacoma. My
father was on one side, and Dave Rowlands was on the
other side. These are two guys that grew up together and
were rivals.

Q: This is what's mapped out in Jon Gold's, aka Fred
Crisman's, book.
A: Yes. I had known Fred ever since I was a small boy,
probably about eight years old. And I traveled all over
the world with him. I probably made twenty trips abroad
with him.

Q: One of the gray areas with Crisman for me is what role
he played in the Maury Island UFO thing.
A: The Maury Island UFO was an event that he created.

Q: He created it out of whole cloth?
A: I have about almost 1,600 pages of handwritten notes by
Fred Crisman.

Q: Oh yeah?
A: Uh huh.

Q: An unpublished manuscript?
A: Yes.

Q: That's a new one.
A: Fred was working with Mary C. Johnson at Boeing.

Q: What is the name again?
A: Mary C. Johnson. Mary Catrina Johnson. In securities at Boeing. And they had done some tests or something and...

Q: This is late 1940s?
A: Yes. And there was a public outcry over it. Too much public scrutiny into what was going on. So Fred came up with this cover story.

Q: The cover story was intended to cover up what was happening at Boeing?
A: Yes.

Q: Which was what?
A: Some sort of test.

Q: Test?
A: Some sort of aircraft.

Q: Aircraft tests at Boeing?
A: Yes. And what happened was that something had gone wrong and some debris had fallen over Maury Island, and they had to get the stuff back. Fred did, in fact, got the stuff back.

Q: That is my understanding just from reading the books on the thing, that he held onto it. There is no indication that he turned over everything he had to those two investigators that died.
A: Now the two investigators that died were basically in on it. They were out to investigate the security screw-ups at Boeing and the procedures for running their test program.

Q: I see. So you're saying this was a test on an advanced but conventional aircraft that went awry? This is what fell on Harold Dahl and Crisman wasn't actually part of the actual incident, right? He comes in later?

A: He comes in later, yes. But the problem is that a dog that belonged to Harold Dahl died of radiation sickness.

Q: Oh, really?
A: Yes. And there was something...

Q: Dahl's son was also injured.
A: Yes. There was something radioactive on board. It was a big scandal, a big problem. When these Air Force guys died, Fred was absolutely bent out of shape, and he related that to me.

Q: All of this is in this manuscript that you talked about, right?
A: Yes, and personally, he told me what went on behind it.

Q: Do you know anything more about that slag that fell on them? Do you know what it was?
A: No. Other than there was a reactor of some sort on board this aircraft. It was an advanced radar platform of some sort. And Mary C. Johnson has corroborated the story many years later, like in 1982 and 1983 and '84. I spent a lot of time with Mary C. Johnson.

Q: Does she still work for Boeing?
A: Oh, no. She's deceased. She was up there in years.

Q: When you say she corroborated it, you mean corroborated it to you. She didn't talk to the press or anything like that.
A: Oh no. She wouldn't have any reason to. She was a career type person and she was a kind of mentor to our little group up in Seattle. She and Arlen Bell's widow were on the board of directors of one of our companies. I had bought her home out in Lake Bay, Washington. She used to come out and visit us all of the time. I spent a lot of time with her.

Q: OK. So, at the time, Crisman was working for what, military intelligence or something of that sort?

A: He was a point man on cleaning up a mess. And it was just a fluke that those Air Force guys died in that plane crash.

Q: So as far as you understand Kenneth Arnold's role, for instance, and Ray Palmer's role in this, is that Crisman helps to inject into the media that this was some kind of UFO event and Palmer kind of glommed onto that. He has no direct role in the cover-up, right?

A: Crisman was a master at emotional contagion. An absolute master at it. In the OSS, over-occupied territories in Europe where they were doing nuclear research, Crisman had a deal with some guys out in the Army Air Corps, and they were dropping these do nothing, sophisticated gizwidgets that were in bombs. The Germans couldn't ignore them. They looked like high-tech surveillance devices, you know?

Q: How large were they?

A: Oh, probably 12 to 15 pounds each. And there were would be several of them in a good-size aerial bomb. The German High Command's attitude was that they were sophisticated somethings and they were being dropped in their most sensitive areas. The German scientists kept telling them, "No, no, no, nothing." And it was one of the...the story's been documented in a book but I can't think of the name of it. It was a great brain-drain on their nuclear program. Fred gave me some astronomical figure on how many man-years it took away from the scientific effort of their nuclear program at a critical time. And Fred got these scientists from Princeton and the University of Chicago, and he got some real eggheads to come up with this scam that he ran on them. Fred was a master of this kind of thing.

Q: We're still talking about late 40s here, right?

A: Right. In Indochina, Fred had a history of doing that stuff.

Q: These widgets that you're talking about were just totally fake little things that they attached to bomb drops?

A: Well, they actually did have some substance. Enough so that they couldn't be ignored.

Q: I have a news article from July 11, 1947 talking about Guy Banister, then working as a SAC (Special Agent in Charge) for the FBI in Butte, recovering what is reported as a flying disc that's 30-1/2 inches in diameter. I wonder if there's a connection there.

A: In post World War II they had a development phase with these radioactive discs to cloud the film of aerial surveillance platforms. They used different schemes, and they had a lot of trouble recovering them. They had a lot of screw ups.

Q: So these things had a function then?

A: Yes. And extreme radiation will destroy most films, especially in sensitive aerial photography. Now Fred was very, very close to George Wackenhut.

Q: I don't know if that's been established before.

A: Oh, yeah. Absolutely. I've known of it since 1963, maybe the first time I ever saw them together. Do you know who Chuck Emmert is?

Q: I haven't heard the name yet, no.

A: OK. His mother was a wealthy Florida socialite who financed George Wackenhut when he originally stared Wackenhut.

Q: Is that a name that I could do a Lexis/Nexus search on?

A: I doubt it, He managed to stay pretty buried, although his mother—I can't remember her first name—but she was big in southern Florida, with anybody in social circles down there would be able to steer you to her.

Q: Did Crisman ever talk about the Kennedy assassination with you?

A: Yeah, he did.

Q: What about this idea that some people have that he was one of the three hoboes in the railroad yard behind Dealey plaza?

A: Well, I don't know about that. He gave me his version of what happened.

Q: He did give it to you.

A: Oh, yeah. A mutual friend of ours was a former Treasury Department agent who, during the Warren Commission, was one of the investigators for the committee.

Q: Do you want to name him?

A: His name is Bob. I don't know where he is now. I lost track of him about ten years ago.

Q: Do you not want to give a last name?

A: I really don't. I think he just wants...he was very, very ill at the time I last saw him. He was working for us. I was with both him and Fred when Fred found out that he had turned over information to Garrison.

Q: Fred had turned over information?

A: No, this guy Bob.

Q: Bob turned information over to Garrison?

A: Right. What I found astounding was that when Bob was working on the Warren Commission. What the hell was that? Why didn't he turn that over to the Warren Commission. And one day I asked him, and he said he did. They knew everything.

Q: Now when you say that stuff, what exactly are you referring to here? Crisman's story of his role in the assassination?

A: Right. What had gone on.

Q: Is it possible for you to summarize that briefly, or is that in the 1,600-page manuscript you were talking about?

A: Here's something that happens: everybody says, "hey, how come you know about everything?" Every conspiracy that's ever gone down the pike. It kinda seems that. If something happens, hey, Riconosciuto's got something to say about it. Well, I can't help it that I was raised around Fred Crisman. I mean, I can't help that cosmic act of fate in my life.

Q: I understand what you're saying, and things really are connected. People have trouble accepting that fact at all, that there are connections to be made.

A: I get treated like I'm delusional. So I find that around certain things, the less I say, the better off I am because most people are not going to take the time to go check it out. Very few people even know who Fred Crisman is or what kind of a player he was. I tried to tell some reporters from the *Village Voice,* "I knew Fred Crisman." They refused to believe me. "There was a thing written about it.." "Yeah, yeah, sure, show us the book..." How can I show a book when I'm in a jail cell? I have a friend who was a SAC the day that happened.

Q: The day of the Kennedy assassination?

A: Yeah. I'll tell you what, I got it more than just from Fred.

Q: I'm still curious about exactly what Fred Crisman told you. Is it possible to summarize it?

A: I really don't want to go into that. Calls are taped here. Fred left a momentous...

Q: What about that manuscript?

A: He had it squirreled away, and as far as I know, it's safe. The party that has it is very reliable. At this point in time, it is irrelevant to me getting out of prison. The things that concern me are the things connected to this case [the Inslaw case]. I was just fascinated by the fact that Crisman came up. It seems that *Contact* magazine found out that Crisman knew my father and then they found out that he actually knew me and they just went wild. They made a big deal out of it.

Q: Which magazine?

A: *Contact.* And *UFO Magazine*...This Colin Brown was hanging around Ted Gunderson...

Q: Brown was the guy who worked for *Technical Consultant* magazine.
A: I think so.

Q: And you did an interview with him.
A: Not really. I talked to him on the phone a couple of times, and I wanted some help on my case. I didn't want to talk about weirdness. I was research director at Wackenhut, and at the time I was there we took over Area 51 in Nevada, and we also had the Nevada test site, and he was pumping me for all kinds of stuff out of there and I just told him, "Hey, I don't want to get into that. I've got enough problems right now. I'm facing life in prison on drug charges, and it all stems from the Cabazon/ Wackenhut joint venture and I just don't need to get into this stuff."

Q: Did Danny Casolaro pump you for information about that?
A: Yeah. Danny found out a lot of stuff. In fact, Danny had a lot of information on that, and I'm surprised you didn't get it.

Q: The papers that were collected after he died originally went to ABC's *Nightline*. By the time they got to me, they had been picked over pretty cleanly. But there are notes in there about Area 51. Some, not a lot.
A: That whole subject matter with Wackenhut is one that I would want to steer clear of. Again, there's an aura of being delusional, and I'm concerned about credibility here and the fact of the matter is that Wackenhut is the only company that has ever had the security contract for any of these places, even though they are supposed to go up for open bid. And this is the way it's been since the early 50s, when these various agencies in these various places were set up. Wackenhut was steered right in, and I happened to have been born into a situation by virtue of my father's contacts—my maternal grandfather's contacts, I was just around.

Q: You appear in that book, *Murder of a City,* as wiring your father's office.

A: Well, no. We ran a cable TV company.

Q: I'm currently trying to track this article that has a photograph of you, and it talks about a child prodigy, a child genius working with various kinds of sound equipment. It's really this glowing piece about what a genius you are working with sound.

A: I was doing commercial sound as a teenager. I made a lot of money as a teenager doing commercial sound. I was involved with various rock'n'roll groups during what is known as the instrumental sound era. Most of these groups hit the charts. The Viceroys. The Ventures. The Wailers. Paul Revere and the Raiders. I don't know if you're familiar with any of those groups.

Q: Sure. Who wouldn't be familiar with the Ventures? The guitar groups are what you're talking about.

A: Yeah, the instrumental sound.

Q: And you worked with them?

A: You bet.

Q: Like producing albums and so forth?

A: Kearney Barton and myself.

Q: You did the sound at the gigs, or you produced albums?

A: The whole bit. Back then we had Ampex three track recorders. That was the state of the art at that time. I was doing special effects and things like that. I was pretty involved, and I made a lot of money.

Q: So as a teenager you were working as an entrepreneur?

A: Right. I was building sound systems, building these new huge 300-watt tube amplifiers, transmitting tubes, sound reinforcement systems—you know, PA systems.

Q: And this was at the time that your father was involved with Crisman?

A: He knew Crisman ever since he was in high school.

Q: He has his own business going on.

A: Advertising, public relations. My father worked on Kennedy's campaign staff when he got elected and he got Governor Al Rosellini elected up in the state of Washington. He was the point man for former Senator Warren Magnuson, Scoop Jackson. He was one of Scoop's top advisers. So this thing with Fred Crisman is kind of an aside here.

Steamshovel Press is a newsstand magazine that examines conspiracy topics in the tradition of such great conspiracy researchers as Mae Brussell, Jim Garrison and Ace Hayes. It explores strange dimensions of current events and parapolitics with dependable and complete documentation. A single issue costs $6, and a four issue subscription costs $23, from POB 23715, St. Louis, MO 63121. The *Steamshovel* web site acquaints new readers with *Steamshovel* and offers a glimpse of the back issues and affiliated books. It includes new articles and reviews not available in the newstand version. It is located at www.umsl.edu/ ~ skthoma.